T0339520

# AN EXCHANGE RATE HISTORY OF THE UNITED KINGDOM

How did the Bank of England manage sterling crises? This book steps into the shoes of the Bank's foreign exchange dealers to show how foreign exchange intervention worked in practice. The author reviews the history of sterling over half a century, using new archives, data and unseen photographs. This book traces the sterling crises from the end of the War to Black Wednesday in 1992. The resulting analysis shows that a secondary reserve currency such as sterling plays an important role in the stability of the international system. The author goes on to explore the lessons the Bretton Woods system on managed exchange rates has for contemporary policy makers in the context of Brexit. This is a crucial reference for scholars in economics and history examining past and current prospects for the international financial system.

Alain Naef is a research economist at the Banque de France working on the international monetary system.

# STUDIES IN MACROECONOMIC HISTORY

Series Editor: Michael D. Bordo, *Rutgers University*

## EDITORS:

Owen F. Humpage, *Federal Reserve Bank of Cleveland*
Christopher M. Meissner, *University of California, Davis*
Kris James Mitchener, *Santa Clara University*
David C. Wheelock, *Federal Reserve Bank of St. Louis*

The titles in this series investigate themes of interest to economists and economic historians in the rapidly developing field of macroeconomic history. The four areas covered include the application of monetary and finance theory, international economics, and quantitative methods to historical problems; the historical application of growth and development theory and theories of business fluctuations; the history of domestic and international monetary, financial, and other macroeconomic institutions; and the history of international monetary and financial systems. The series amalgamates the former Cambridge University Press series Studies in Monetary and Financial History and Studies in Quantitative Economic History.

*Other Books in the Series:*

Barrie A. Wigmore, *The Financial Crisis of 2008: A History of US Financial Markets 2000–2012* (2021)

Max Harris, *Monetary War and Peace: London, Washington, Paris, and the Tripartite Agreement of 1936* (2021)

Kenneth D. Garbade, *After the Accord: A History of Federal Reserve Open Market Operations, the US Government Securities Market, and Treasury Debt Management from 1951 to 1979* (2020)

Harold James, *Making a Modern Central Bank: The Bank of England 1979–2003* (2020)

Claudio Borio, Stijn Claessens, Piet Clement, Robert N. McCauley, and Hyun Song Shin, Editors, *Promoting Global Monetary and Financial Stability: The Bank for International Settlements after Bretton Woods, 1973–2020* (2020)

Patrick Honohan, *Currency, Credit and Crisis: Central Banking in Ireland and Europe* (2019)

William A. Allen, *The Bank of England and the Government Debt: Operations in the Gilt-Edged Market, 1928–1972* (2019)

Eric Monnet, *Controlling Credit: Central Banking and the Planned Economy in Postwar France, 1948–1973* (2018)

Laurence M. Ball, *The Fed and Lehman Brothers: Setting the Record Straight on a Financial Disaster* (2018)

Rodney Edvinsson, Tor Jacobson, and Daniel Waldenström, Editors, *Sveriges Riksbank and the History of Central Banking* (2018)

Peter L. Rousseau and Paul Wachtel, Editors, *Financial Systems and Economic Growth: Credit, Crises, and the Regulation from the 19$^{th}$ Century to the Present* (2017)

Ernst Baltensperger and Peter Kugler, *Swiss Monetary History since the Early 19th Century* (2017)

Øyvind Eitrheim, Jan Tore Klovland, and Lars Fredrik Øksendal, *A Monetary History of Norway, 1816–2016* (2016)

Jan Fredrik Qvigstad, *On Central Banking* (2016)

Michael D. Bordo, Øyvind Eitrheim, Marc Flandreau, and Jan F. Qvigstad, Editors, *Central Banks at a Crossroads: What Can We Learn from History?* (2016)

Michael D. Bordo and Mark A. Wynne, Editors, *The Federal Reserve's Role in the Global Economy: A Historical Perspective* (2016)

Owen F. Humpage, Editor, *Current Federal Reserve Policy Under the Lens of Economic History: Essays to Commemorate the Federal Reserve System's Centennial* (2015)

Michael D. Bordo and William Roberds, Editors, *The Origins, History, and Future of the Federal Reserve: A Return to Jekyll Island* (2013)

Michael D. Bordo and Ronald MacDonald, Editors, *Credibility and the International Monetary Regime: A Historical Perspective* (2012)

Robert L. Hetzel, *The Great Recession: Market Failure or Policy Failure?* (2012)

Tobias Straumann, *Fixed Ideas of Money: Small States and Exchange Rate Regimes in Twentieth-Century Europe* (2010)

Forrest Capie, *The Bank of England: 1950s to 1979* (2010)

Aldo Musacchio, *Experiments in Financial Democracy: Corporate Governance and Financial Development in Brazil, 1882–1950* (2009)

Claudio Borio, Gianni Toniolo, and Piet Clement, Editors, *The Past and Future of Central Bank Cooperation* (2008)

Robert L. Hetzel, *The Monetary Policy of the Federal Reserve: A History* (2008)

Caroline Fohlin, *Finance Capitalism and Germany's Rise to Industrial Power* (2007)

John H. Wood, *A History of Central Banking in Great Britain and the United States* (2005)

Gianni Toniolo (with the assistance of Piet Clement), *Central Bank Cooperation at the Bank for International Settlements, 1930–1973* (2005)

Richard Burdekin and Pierre Siklos, Editors, *Deflation: Current and Historical Perspectives* (2004)

Pierre Siklos, *The Changing Face of Central Banking: Evolutionary Trends since World War II* (2002)

Michael D. Bordo and Roberto Cortés-Conde, Editors, *Transferring Wealth and Power from the Old to the New World: Monetary and Fiscal Institutions in the 17th through the 19th Centuries* (2001)

Howard Bodenhorn, *A History of Banking in Antebellum America: Financial Markets and Economic Development in an Era of Nation-Building* (2000)

Mark Harrison, Editor, *The Economics of World War II: Six Great Powers in International Comparison* (2000)

Angela Redish, *Bimetallism: An Economic and Historical Analysis* (2000)

Elmus Wicker, *Banking Panics of the Gilded Age* (2000)

Michael D. Bordo, *The Gold Standard and Related Regimes: Collected Essays* (1999)

Michele Fratianni and Franco Spinelli, *A Monetary History of Italy* (1997)

Mark Toma, *Competition and Monopoly in the Federal Reserve System, 1914–1951* (1997)

Barry Eichengreen, Editor, *Europe's Postwar Recovery* (1996)

Lawrence H. Officer, *Between the Dollar-Sterling Gold Points: Exchange Rates, Parity and Market Behavior* (1996)

Elmus Wicker, *The Banking Panics of the Great Depression* (1996)

Norio Tamaki, *Japanese Banking: A History, 1859–1959* (1995)

Barry Eichengreen, *Elusive Stability: Essays in the History of International Finance, 1919–1939* (1993)

Michael D. Bordo and Forrest Capie, Editors, *Monetary Regimes in Transition* (1993)

Larry Neal, *The Rise of Financial Capitalism: International Capital Markets in the Age of Reason* (1993)

S. N. Broadberry and N. F. R. Crafts, Editors, *Britain in the International Economy, 1870–1939* (1992)

Aurel Schubert, *The Credit-Anstalt Crisis of 1931* (1992)

Trevor J. O. Dick and John E. Floyd, *Canada and the Gold Standard: Balance of Payments Adjustment under Fixed Exchange Rates, 1871–1913* (1992)

Kenneth Mouré, *Managing the Franc Poincaré: Economic Understanding and Political Constraint in French Monetary Policy, 1928–1936* (1991)

David C. Wheelock, *The Strategy and Consistency of Federal Reserve Monetary Policy, 1924–1933* (1991)

# An Exchange Rate History of the United Kingdom, 1945–1992

**ALAIN NAEF**

Banque de France

CAMBRIDGE
UNIVERSITY PRESS

# CAMBRIDGE
## UNIVERSITY PRESS

Shaftesbury Road, Cambridge CB2 8EA, United Kingdom

One Liberty Plaza, 20th Floor, New York, NY 10006, USA

477 Williamstown Road, Port Melbourne, VIC 3207, Australia

314–321, 3rd Floor, Plot 3, Splendor Forum, Jasola District Centre, New Delhi – 110025, India

103 Penang Road, #05–06/07, Visioncrest Commercial, Singapore 238467

Cambridge University Press is part of Cambridge University Press & Assessment, a department of the University of Cambridge.

We share the University's mission to contribute to society through the pursuit of education, learning and research at the highest international levels of excellence.

www.cambridge.org
Information on this title: www.cambridge.org/9781108813938

DOI: 10.1017/9781108878333

First published 2022
First paperback edition 2023

*A catalogue record for this publication is available from the British Library*

ISBN    978-1-108-83999-0    Hardback
ISBN    978-1-108-81393-8    Paperback

# Contents

# Figures

# Tables

# Acknowledgements

This book is the result of discussions, exchanges and debates with many people over the last eight years, and it is difficult to mention them all here. Walter Jansson has read many drafts of this book and provided insightful comments. Eric Monnet was a continuous source of motivation and support. Mike Bordo has always fed my intellectual curiosity and helped me move forward at various steps of the way. William Allen was kind enough to read the whole manuscript over the years and sense-check it using his experience of working at the Bank. The support of Susan Howson was extremely helpful, and her insightful comments have much improved this book. Yasmin Shearmur read various drafts and made it much better. Barry Eichengreen has also been kind enough to welcome me in Berkeley, and part of the work here is derived from joint efforts. This book is an extension of my PhD dissertation, and the support of David Chambers and Duncan Needham needs to be acknowledged in getting me through the hurdles of the dissertation and making it more incisive and relevant. Duncan also helped me navigate the complexities of the 1976 IMF crisis and sense-checked the chapter on the crisis.

A historian is useless without access to archives. Sara Brimble, Piet Clement, Mike Anson, Rachael Muir, Margherita Orlando, Ben White, Holly Waughman, Julie Sager and Patrick Halbeisen all helped at various stages, and I am extremely grateful to them.

I am indebted to people who have encouraged me to embark on my initial PhD journey by reading my first proposal and providing guidance, mainly Olivier Accominotti, Lars Borner, Rui Esteves, Patrick Halbeisen, Benoit Lecat, Andrea Papadia and Tobias Straumann. Many colleagues have read all or part of this book or have helped to shape my ideas. I am especially grateful to Marc Adams, Simon Amrein, Maylis Avaro, Kathleen Burk, Jason Cen, Devika Dutt, Sam Foxall, Max Harris, Simon Hinrichsen,

Ryuichiro Izumi, Craig McMahon, Chris Meissner, Duncan Needham and Tinashe Nyamunda. I also thank Muriel Demottais for excellent research assistance and Dayna Plummer for proofreading the manuscript at various stages. Part of this research was supported by the Economic and Social Research Council (grant number ESRC KFW/10324121/0) as well as the Swiss National Science Foundation (grant number P2SKP1_181320), and I appreciate that support.

# Introduction

Some government policies are costly. Others are unsuccessful. Rarely are they as unsuccessful and costly as they were for the Bank of England on Black Wednesday. On that day, in an attempt to defend the pound, the Bank spent in a few hours as much as the annual GDP of Bulgaria and Croatia combined. But it was all in vain. The United Kingdom abandoned the peg, along with the idea that it could one day join the euro.

In this book, I explore the various crises the pound went through over the last half century, from the end of the war to 1992, when Britain left the European Monetary Union. After the war, the pound was still the second most important currency in the world. Today, it is the fourth most important if we take the pound's use as a reserve currency. I explore the exchange rate crises that accompanied this loss of importance for the British currency in the international monetary system.

From after the war to 1992, the pound was almost always pegged to another currency. The dollar from 1945 and the Deutschmark after 1987. The various pegs meant that the foreign exchange rate dealers at the Bank were busy managing the exchange rate. This book tells their story. I ask one question: How did the Bank of England manage the currency?

The main argument in this book is that the Bank of England progressively lost control of sterling. In 1952, the Bank was still the largest player on the market. It could sway sterling in one direction or another. But as the 1967 crisis unfolded, the operations were more difficult. During the 1976 International Monetary Fund (IMF) crisis, the Bank showed that it could not devalue the pound discreetly without generating a large-scale currency crisis. In 1992, losses were so heavy and abrupt that the United Kingdom abandoned exchange rate management altogether. After this upsetting event, the United Kingdom decided to let the market, rather than the state, set the currency's value.

During the Bretton Woods period, American policymakers thought that a crash in sterling would drag the dollar down with it (as I show in the first chapters). By the end of the period, this was no longer the case. The pound had lost its relevance. The United Kingdom was left to its own devices. Managing the pound became more difficult. This became apparent in 1976 when international support from the IMF came at a high political cost. The United Kingdom appeared to be begging for support. By 1992, the pound was no longer important enough for German policymakers to want to keep the United Kingdom in the exchange rate mechanism (ERM). Britain was pushed out of the future euro project without receiving German support to stay (as I show in Chapter 14).

Exchange rate management matters. Still today, most countries are on fixed exchange rate regimes. This forces them to intervene frequently on foreign exchange market. Many emerging economies and some advanced economies such as Denmark and Switzerland intervene on foreign exchange markets. Here I analyse the challenges raised by foreign exchange interventions. Taking a historical approach makes it possible to enter into a world that is mostly secret. Still today, central bankers rarely communicate about interventions. By looking at history, I show what happened behind closed doors.

Many monographs delve into sterling's management, analysing decisions by the government. This is not one of them. The focus here is in the interaction between the Bank of England and currency markets, not the government. The Bank of England, the main character in our story, never decided the value of the pound. The government took that decision. Remember that the Bank only became independent in 1997. And even today, setting the exchange rate management is the responsibility of the government, not the Bank. Here I look at the operational side of exchange rate policy, focusing on the executors, not the deciders. The Bank still had agency in its exchange rate management. It is this agency that we will analyse.

In this book, you will meet the very people who tried to manage (or possibly manipulate) the pound. These men (as they essentially were all men) are depicted in the middle part of the book. Despite the haircuts, which changed with passing fashions, these were very much operational people. While today's central banks are populated by economists with PhDs using (often overly) complicated models, these dealers were experts in day-to-day transactions and market animal instincts. They were essentially currency traders, but instead of generating profit, they aimed to stabilise the pound at the level the government wanted it to be. We will get to know them quite closely, reading their letters and memos. We will even eavesdrop on their phone conversations. Part of this book relies on transcripts of telephone conversations between the New York Fed and the Bank. They give concrete flavour to abstract international negotiations.

One of these dealers, Roy Bridge, was a bank official for over forty years. A colourful character, Bridge was at the very centre of British exchange rate management. In the first chapters, we will try to better understand him and his thought processes. As the years progressed, the field professionalised and people like Bridge became rare. Management at the Bank now mostly had a formal training in economics. One of these economists, William Allen, was working in the dealing room. Today, Allen is an economic historian. He was kind enough to read through parts of this manuscript to distil his knowledge, and correct some of my shortcuts and flawed explanations. He also provided a minute-by-minute description of Black Wednesday.

Beyond the Bank, this book also has its fair share of heroes and villains. Civil servants who at times helped or hindered international cooperation. Charles Coombs was a key force in the golden age of central bank cooperation during the Bretton Woods period. He increased communication and cooperation between the Bank of England and the Federal Reserve. He was a firefighter, preventing the international monetary system from collapsing. Bundesbank President Schlesinger is also important in our story. We will get to know him better when delving into the 1992 ERM crisis. He was a force against monetary cooperation. He sealed the fate of the pound, ending almost two centuries of fixed exchange rates.

Several other monographs cover related topics. My work is in dialogue with the official history of the Bank of England by Harold James, but with a narrower focus on exchange rates and further quantitative analysis.[1] This story is also in conversation with Catherine Schenk's work on the decline of sterling, but again here the focus is more quantitative and less on the sterling area which Schenk analyses.[2] My analysis also complements and updates the 1983 history of sterling crises by Alec Cairncross and Barry

---

[1] Harold James, *Making a Modern Central Bank: The Bank of England 1979–2003*, Studies in Macroeconomic History (Cambridge: Cambridge University Press, 2020), https://doi .org/10.1017/9781108875189.

[2] Catherine Schenk, *The Decline of Sterling: Managing the Retreat of an International Currency, 1945–1992* (Cambridge: Cambridge University Press, 2010).

Eichengreen, adding the missing history from 1967 to 1992, and updating their analysis with new archives, data and literature.[3]

But first, let us look at the pound after the war. Sterling was still the second most important currency in the world as the story begins. The Bank was instrumental in setting the exchange rate.

---

[3] Alec Cairncross and Barry Eichengreen, *Sterling in Decline* (Oxford: Wiley-Blackwell, 1983).

# 1

# Sterling's Post-War Role and Lessons
# from the 1947 Convertibility Crisis

After the Second World War, Britain was still a heavily regulated economy. In 1939, the country introduced exchange controls that were not lifted after the war.[1] Imports were limited by quotas and licences. The state oversaw all foreign exchange transactions. For example, when travelling abroad, the amount individuals could take was limited to £100.[2] In 1947, the Exchange Control Act formalised capital controls and divided the world into four sterling regions.

The state played a major role in everything from imports to production.[3] This applied to finance, where capital flows were controlled by the government. The Bank of England oversaw the exchange rate, and only authorised banks were allowed to deal in foreign currencies, within narrow official bands. The United States hoped that removing these controls would be a swift process, and American officials were keen to see markets in Europe develop. The process took much longer than policymakers anticipated.

Between 1948 and 1952, Europe was flooded with $13 billion in grants and loans from the United States.[4] Britain was the biggest recipient under the Marshall Plan (or European Reconstruction Plan, ERP). A key

---

[1] For readers interested in questions of exchange rate management before 1939, see the excellent monograph by Max Harris, *Monetary War and Peace* (Cambridge: Cambridge University Press, 2021).

[2] Bank of England, 'The U.K. Exchange Control: A Short History', *Bank of England Quarterly Bulletin*, September 1967, 252.

[3] For a fresh view on the role of the state during the Bretton Woods period, see Eric Monnet, *Controlling Credit: Central Banking and the Planned Economy in Postwar France, 1948–1973*, Studies in Macroeconomic History (Cambridge: Cambridge University Press, 2018), https://doi.org/10.1017/9781108227322.

[4] Michael D. Bordo, 'The Bretton Woods International Monetary System: A Historical Overview', in *A Retrospective on the Bretton Woods System: Lessons for International*

objective was to encourage convertibility and facilitate trade within Europe and with the United States. In that regard, the policy would boost demand for US products. After the war, as most countries had capital controls in place, trade was complicated.[5]

In 1947, the United States forced the restoration of convertibility on Britain. This led to a currency crisis. The United Kingdom was not yet ready to open up to global markets, and its government was unprepared. Convertibility lasted as long as the government was able to use the Anglo-American loan to defend the pound. It ended as soon as the Bank exhausted the loan proceeds. As the Bank started to use its own gold reserves once the loan ran out, the United Kingdom chose to cease convertibility.

Convertibility meant 'the freedom for individuals to engage in current account transactions without being subject to exchange controls'.[6] People could trade freely, transfer remittances and repatriate returns from existing investments. These operations are also known as current account transactions. Capital account convertibility was not included. This would have allowed foreign investment in securities or property, for example.

Britain attempted to restore current account convertibility at the insistence of the United States, but the government abandoned the policy after a mere thirty-seven days. Policymakers, markets and the press drew two conclusions from this: first, sterling was no longer the pre-eminent currency it had been before the war; second, re-establishing an international monetary system with free capital flows would take longer than anticipated a few years earlier at the Bretton Woods conference.

Chapters 2–6 trace the slow unfolding of a new international monetary system from 1947 to the introduction of convertibility in 1958 (current *and* capital account convertibility this time). The international monetary system was characterised by fixed exchange rates, limited capital mobility and relatively uncoordinated domestic monetary policies. Sterling

---

*Monetary Reform*, ed. Michael D. Bordo and Barry Eichengreen (Chicago, IL: University of Chicago Press, 1993), 42.

[5] Ibid., 38.

[6] Other periods had different definitions of convertibility: 'Under the classical gold standard, *convertibility* referred to the ability of a private individual freely to convert a unit of any national currency into gold at the official fixed price. A suspension of convertibility meant that the exchange rate between gold and a national currency became flexible, but the individual could still freely transact in either asset (Triffin, 1960, 22). On the eve of World War II, *convertibility* referred to the ability of a private individual freely to make and receive payments in international transaction in terms of the currency of another country' (ibid., 38–9).

convertibility was difficult because of the sterling overhang problem, as it was known at the time.

## THE STERLING BALANCES PROBLEM

Contemporary debates on the question of sterling focused on the issue of the sterling balances.[7] These balances were in Britain but held by foreigners living in former colonies and overseas territories. They could not be converted into dollars due to British regulations.[8] If all the sterling holders abroad converted these balances into dollars, there would be a run on sterling. In 1947, the Bank for International Settlements (BIS) warned, 'The balances and other short-term sterling assets which accumulated in London on overseas account during the war constitute a major factor in the United Kingdom's external payments problem.'[9]

Catherine Schenk has written extensively on these balances.[10] She argues that 'Britain's accumulation of enormous sterling liabilities to the Commonwealth and colonies profoundly affected the post-war configuration of the sterling area system.'[11] Sterling balances were a major issue. If the government liberalised capital flows, Britain's creditors could request to convert their sterling balances into dollars at the Bank of England. Without US loans, this would deplete the Bank's reserves and force the country into devaluation. Post-war sterling history is a story of progressively phasing out these foreign balances.

The amount of sterling in circulation tripled between 1938 and 1947, whereas gross national product (GNP) only doubled.[12] At the same time, private and public holdings of gold and dollars in the United Kingdom halved. Barry Eichengreen argues that, in these circumstances, restoring convertibility 'was the height of recklessness'.[13] Paul Einzig, a currency expert and prolific author at the time, also claims that forcing Britain 'to restore the convertibility of sterling involved grave risks' as it would trigger

---

[7] They are sometimes also called sterling overhang by contemporaries or more simply sterling liabilities.

[8] Catherine Schenk, *Britain and the Sterling Area: From Devaluation to Convertibility in the 1950s* (London: Routledge, 1994), 20–7.

[9] BIS, Annual Report, 1947 (1 April 1946–31 March 1947), 16 June 1947 (Basel: BIS, 1947).

[10] Schenk, *Britain and the Sterling Area*; Schenk, *The Decline of Sterling*.

[11] Schenk, *Britain and the Sterling Area*, 17.

[12] Barry Eichengreen, *Globalizing Capital: A History of the International Monetary System*, 2nd ed. (Princeton, NJ: Princeton University Press, 2008), 100.

[13] Ibid., 100–1.

a run on the pound as long as Britain maintained a large trade deficit.[14] Freeing capital flows would lead to an outflow of capital from Britain, especially if sterling creditors were to convert their reserves into dollars. Echoing Eichengreen, Schenk wrote, '[T]he amount of national currency in overseas foreign exchange reserves led to doubts about the ability of the issuing country to sustain their external position and seemed to threaten the stability of the international monetary system.'[15]

The sterling balances were posing a systemic risk to the Bretton Woods system and participants in this new regime needed to unite if the international monetary system was to survive. The British exposure partly explains the lenient American attitude towards Britain and the numerous lines of credit opened to the Bank of England.

## DIFFERENT STERLING AREAS

The Emergency Powers (Defence) Act 1939 introduced the legal basis for wartime exchange controls. At the end of the war, the 1947 Exchange Control Act extended the policy of controls. Sterling was too weak to be exposed to international capital markets. The United Kingdom had also amassed an onerous war debt. The responsibility for exchange control was held by the Treasury, which delegated its management to the Bank of England. In turn, the Bank entrusted commercial banks with some of the day-to-day management of controls. For UK residents, the Exchange Control Act stipulated that 'no person, other than an authorised dealer' was allowed to 'buy or borrow' or 'sell or lend any gold or foreign currency'.[16] Authorised dealers were UK banks. They were allowed to deal only with customers holding a licence to import or export. British banks could also give limited amounts of foreign currency to people travelling abroad.[17]

The controls classified sterling into four main categories, reflecting four geographic areas: the sterling area, the dollar area, the transferable-account

---

[14] Paul Einzig, 'The Case against Convertibility', *Commercial & Financial Chronicle*, 2 October 1947, 158.

[15] Barry Eichengreen, 'Sterling's Past, Dollar's Future: Historical Perspectives on Reserve Currency Competition', working paper (National Bureau of Economic Research, May 2005); Schenk, *The Decline of Sterling*, 12.

[16] Exchange Control Act 1947 (London: HMSO, 1947), 1.

[17] In November 1945, an allowance for travel of £100 a year was introduced. It was withdrawn from October 1947 to May 1948, then reintroduced in 1952, when the limit was set at £25.

countries and the bilateral countries.[18] All other countries were referred to as unclassified-account countries. More categories would emerge over time, but these four categories would remain in place until the introduction of convertibility in December 1958. Each category had its own set of rules. The goal was 'to restrict convertibility of sterling into dollars in the context of the post-war dollar shortage and generally to conserve foreign exchange'.[19] These different types were a means to manage capital controls. The dollar area was centred on the United States. The USSR and other countries benefited from transferable sterling status. Finally, most of Europe and the European colonies benefited from bilateral status.

Sterling area members all pegged their exchange rates to the pound, 'maintained a common exchange control against the rest of the world while enjoying free current and capital transactions with the UK' and kept their central bank reserves in sterling.[20] Dollar area sterling was held by 'residents of the United States, Canada, the Philippines, Liberia, and thirteen Latin American countries'.[21] These sterling reserves had the advantage of being 'convertible into dollars, with no strings attached'.[22]

The transferable-account sterling countries observed the following rules: 'Payments of sterling from one transferable sterling account to another were allowed freely, as were payments between transferable accounts and sterling area accounts. Transfers were not permitted from transferable accounts to bilateral or American accounts.'[23] The Radcliffe Report noted that transferable sterling 'transactions took place in unofficial markets at a discount on the official rate'.[24] The report continues by arguing that the price of transferable sterling 'indicated and affected the state of overseas confidence in sterling'. It played the part of a confidence barometer.

Bilateral countries, the most restricted group of countries with regard to capital controls, could transfer sterling to the sterling area only. These countries had to ask the Bank of England for 'administrative transferability' to move capital from one bilateral country to another. However, with the introduction of the European Payment Union (EPU) in 1950,

---

[18] See Alain Naef, 'Sterling and the Stability of the International Monetary System, 1944–1971', PhD dissertation (University of Cambridge, 2019), 65, https://doi.org/10.17863/CAM.32540, for a map with current borders giving an idea of the different types of sterling.

[19] Schenk, *Britain and the Sterling Area*, 8.  [20] Ibid., 8.

[21] Charles Coombs, 'Consolidation of Nonresident Sterling', internal memorandum, 18 November 1953, New York, Archives of the Federal Reserve, box 110278.

[22] Ibid.  [23] Schenk, *Britain and the Sterling Area*, 9.

[24] *Radcliffe Report*, Cmnd 827 (London: HMSO, 1959), para. 327.

'administrative transferability for bilateral OEEC [Organisation for European Economic Co-operation, former OECD] countries became virtually automatic'.[25]

Unclassified account countries were 'small and relatively unimportant countries', according to Coombs.[26] Sterling balances in these countries were generally not transferable to zones or countries.

Beyond these five main classifications, other types of sterling existed, among them security sterling and 'cheap' or 'free' sterling. Security sterling was created in 1940 when the British monetary authorities witnessed capital outflows from foreign-owned funds mainly to New York. Security sterling holders had the right to transfer these between residents of the same monetary area, and this type of sterling was traded at a discount.[27]

Figure 1.1 presents the variety of exchange rates for different types of sterling. The data come from an internal memorandum at the Federal Reserve Bank of New York and show the complexity of the system over a few days. Figure 1.1 presents boxplots of eighteen transferable sterling rates and ten bilateral rates for different locations. Both parts of Figure 1.1 have the same scale on the left-hand side (from $2.4 to $2.9 per £1 sterling). Bilateral rates occupy most of the space on the panel, but the difference between the eighteen transferable rates is limited. The standard deviation for the bilateral countries sample is almost five times greater than for the transferable sample (0.10 for the bilateral countries; 0.02 for the transferable countries). This means that sterling markets in transferable sterling countries were much more integrated than in bilateral sterling countries.

## THE CONVERTIBILITY CRISIS OF 1947

Sterling convertibility was a condition of the Anglo-American Financial Agreement of December 1945 (Anglo-American loan, in short). This explains why the United Kingdom had to implement it despite the risks posed by the sterling balances. As the provider of the Anglo-American loan, the United States wanted to rebuild Europe as a trading partner as quickly as possible. Convertibility was a key step for US policymakers. Not only was it on the agenda of the Bretton Woods agreement, but it later became a condition of the Marshall Plan.

---

[25] Schenk, *Britain and the Sterling Area*, 9.
[26] Coombs, 'Consolidation of Nonresident Sterling'.
[27] John Atkin, *The Foreign Exchange Market of London: Development Since 1900* (London: Routledge, 2004), 108.

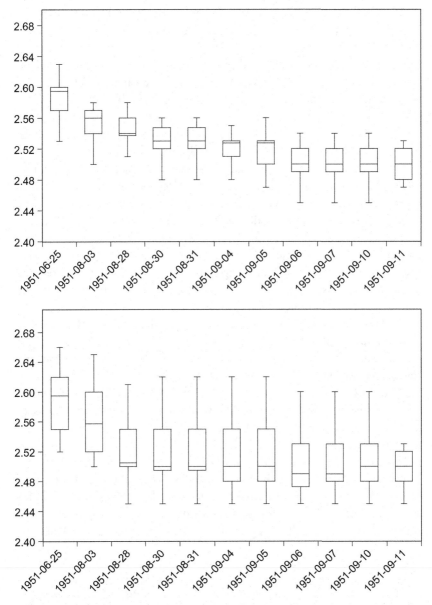

Figure 1.1. Sterling exchange rates for ten bilateral countries (top panel) vs eighteen transferable sterling rates (bottom panel)

*Source*: Cheap Sterling Quotations, internal memoranda, June–September 1951, New York, Archives of the Federal Reserve, box 110278.

Bradford De Long and Barry Eichengreen attribute the success of European post-war economic growth to the conditionality of the Marshall Plan. It 'pushed European political economy in a direction that left its post-World War II "mixed economies" with more "market" and less "controls" in the mix'.[28] Marshall Aid forced European nations to liberalise their economies. Forrest Capie noted that convertibility took place 'at a time when only the United States had the productive capacity to supply the goods that were needed to rebuild the war-ravaged economies of Western Europe'.[29] For the United States, convertibility was self-serving.

The Anglo-American Financial Agreement was settled in December 1945. The agreement stipulated that current account convertibility had to be introduced one year after the effective date of the agreement, on 15 July 1946. A year later, convertibility of the pound was put in place. Within a month, the Bank of England had lost $1 billion.[30] Schenk found that between 10 and 15 August, $175 million in reserves were lost. This led the Cabinet to consider withdrawing from convertibility while still keeping the United States on their side, as not all the money promised in the Anglo-American loan had been disbursed.[31]

On Sunday, 17 August, the Cabinet met to debate convertibility. The debate quickly moved 'to when and how to inform the Americans' about the British intention to halt convertibility.[32] On 19 August 1947, convertibility was suspended. It was not sustainable. The 1947 experience was well anchored in the minds of British and US policymakers. This event, along with the sterling devaluation in 1949, weakened sterling's credibility as an international currency, though it was still the second most important reserve currency.[33]

New data presented highlight daily movements on the Exchange Equalisation Account's (EEA's) gold and dollar accounts (see Figure 1.2). During the crisis there were three significant dollar inflows: on 15 July for $150 million; on 26 July for $300 million; and on 12 August for $150 million. These $600 million represented drawings on the Anglo-American

[28] Barry Eichengreen and Bradford De Long, 'The Marshall Plan: History's Most Successful Structural Adjustment Program', in *Postwar Economic Reconstruction and Lessons for the East Today*, ed. Rudiger Dornbusch, Wilhelm Nolling and Richard Layard (Cambridge, MA: MIT, 1993), 189–231, cover page.

[29] Forrest Capie, *The Bank of England: 1950s to 1979* (Cambridge: Cambridge University Press, 2010), 143.

[30] Bordo, 'Bretton Woods', 44.     [31] Schenk, *The Decline of Sterling*, 63.     [32] Ibid., 63.

[33] Michael D. Bordo, 'The Operation and Demise of the Bretton Woods System: 1958 to 1971', working paper (National Bureau of Economic Research, February 2017), 10.

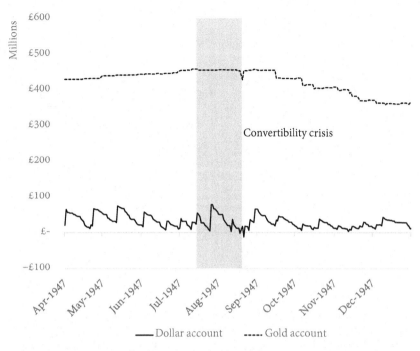

Figure 1.2. EEA gold and dollar holdings, April–December 1947
*Source*: 'Ledgers of the Exchange Equalisation Account', 1947–70, London, Archive of the Bank of England, 2A141/1–17.
*Note*: The dollar holdings have been converted to sterling at the $4.03 per sterling parity.

loan, which were all lost during the thirty-seven days of the crisis. Gold reserves remained relatively unaffected until 18 August, dropping by only $18 million. On both 19 and 20 August, the Bank bought $50 million with gold to deal with losses arising from the crisis. Convertibility was stopped when the Bank started losing its own gold reserves. The Americans no longer funded dollar losses.

Figure 1.2 highlights how the 1947 crisis did not trigger large gold losses for the EEA. Apart from a $100 million gold loss during the final days of convertibility, the crisis left gold reserves untouched. Unlike the 1949 devaluation, which drained gold reserves, as we will see, the 1947 crisis did not affect British reserves. The Anglo-American loan funded the currency crisis. This loan, unlike reserves, was no immediate concern for British policymakers. The United Kingdom's dollar holdings persistently fluctuate (bottom line in Figure 1.2). These fluctuations are market losses followed by inflows from US loans or grants.

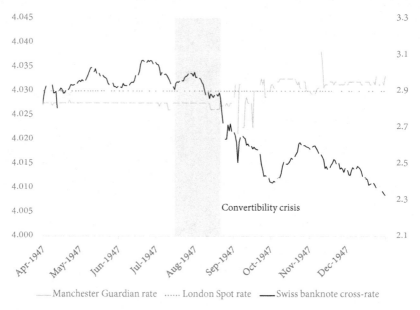

Figure 1.3. Offshore, *Manchester Guardian* and official daily dollar/sterling exchange rates
*Source*: Global Financial Data for the *Manchester Guardian* rate, Accominotti et al. (*The Financial Times*) for the official London spot rate and Swiss National Bank for the banknote cross-rate.

But what was the impact of the crisis on sterling's exchange rate? Looking at different rates gives different answers. The *Manchester Guardian* rate reported in Figure 1.3 shows little sign of the crisis' lasting negative impact. It looks as if the crisis only briefly increased the volatility of the currency, and the exchange rate then settled at a higher dollar rate, around the official parity of $4.03/£. The Bank of England controlled the official London spot rate, and it shows no variation. The picture is different when we look at the sterling–dollar cross-rate based on the Swiss franc–dollar and Swiss franc–sterling rates (scale on the right-hand side in Figure 1.3). Here I present new data on offshore rates from Switzerland collected from the archives of the Swiss National Bank. Using the free Swiss banknote cross-rate gives a more accurate picture of the crisis.[34] The offshore rate dropped by 1.5 per cent during the day of the crisis and fell further after the actual crisis. At the end of 1947 the offshore rate reached a

---

[34] The cross-rate is obtained by dividing the dollar/Swiss franc rate by the sterling/Swiss franc rate. It is therefore not a direct market rate but a good indicator for an offshore dollar/sterling rate.

low point of \$2.30/£, representing a drop of almost 21 per cent in less than six months. Convertibility put pressure on the pound, even if this was not directly reflected in the controlled official exchange rates.

## CONSEQUENCES OF THE CRISIS

What were the longer-term consequences of the convertibility crisis? Official exchange rates do not answer this question. They were tightly controlled until the opening of the foreign exchange market and so offer no information on the pressure on the exchange rate.

I use an Exchange Market Pressure (EMP) index to measure the pressure on the pound. I will use these indices on several occasions in this book, with variations that I will explain. In short, the higher the index, the more pressure on the pound. EMPs were used in the macroeconomic literature to determine stress on a currency with fixed exchange rates.[35] The belief is that if the price of the currency does not reflect market pressure, other indicators do.

Traditionally, the indices use the exchange rate, the central bank interest rate and central bank reserves. The Bank of England did not change the Bank Rate during the period in question, making the interest rate an uninteresting variable. Equally, using the official spot rate alone is misleading. It was highly controlled and displayed little volatility, as Figure 1.3 illustrates. I have computed a daily EMP index using offshore Swiss banknote cross-rates, EEA gold and dollar reserves and the official exchange rate. This latter rate is stable, but tends to move during crises. All three indicators are divided by their standard deviation to weight them equally.

The 1947 crisis shook the foundations of sterling. Exchange rate pressure started to increase immediately after. The British currency had lost its international currency status, and this was now public knowledge. The consequences were long-lived, as shown in Figure 1.4.

After the 1947 crisis, the index follows an upward trend. The trend continues until the 1949 devaluation, when the chart stops. The aftermath

---

[35] Barry Eichengreen, Andrew K. Rose and Charles Wyplosz, 'Speculative Attacks on Pegged Exchange Rates: An Empirical Exploration with Special Reference to the European Monetary System', in *The New Transatlantic Economy*, ed. Matthew Canzoneri, Paul Mason and Vittorio Grilli (Cambridge: Cambridge University Press, 1995); Barry Eichengreen and Poonam Gupta, 'Tapering Talk: The Impact of Expectations of Reduced Federal Reserve Security Purchases on Emerging Markets', *Emerging Markets Review* 25 (December 2015), 1–15.

Figure 1.4. Sterling EMP index, 1947–49

*Source*: Computed using the official exchange rate (Global Financial Data), offshore exchange rates (archives of the Swiss National Bank) and EEA gold and dollar reserves (archives of the Bank of England).

*Note*: Data are indexed at March 1947 = 100. The shaded area highlights the convertibility crisis. The pressure is cumulative in this index.

of convertibility marked a continuous period of decline in reserves and lower exchange rates. This meant more pressure on the pound. Note that the sudden drop in the index in January 1948 was due to a Marshall Aid inflow. The United States disbursed $100 million, and this affected the reserve position and hence the EMP index.

The global financial community knew that the Bank of England did not have the firepower to defend a convertible sterling. Sterling declined from being an international currency with positive externalities for the United Kingdom to a concern for the international community to manage.[36] Now there was no longer a bipolar sterling–dollar paradigm; instead, sterling

---

[36] For more on the decline of sterling, see Schenk, *The Decline of Sterling*; Maylis Avaro, 'Zombie International Currency: The Pound Sterling 1945–1973', IHEID Working Paper (Economics Section, Graduate Institute of International Studies, 3 March 2020), http://repec.graduateinstitute.ch/pdfs/Working_papers/HEIDWP03-2020.pdf; Maylis Avaro, 'Essays in Monetary History', IHEID PhD dissertation (Graduate Institute of International Studies, 3 March 2020).

was a problematic international currency. The 1947 episode brought the United States and United Kingdom together to manage an orderly retreat for sterling. In the following pages I explore how the British currency was managed by the United States, the United Kingdom and the international community. All stakeholders hoped to avoid contagion from sterling to the dollar. If it was clear that sterling was only a shadow of its former self, contemporaries still *believed* that sterling was an important currency. And this mattered.

2

# The 1949 Devaluation

*Readjusting the Post-War Parities*

After the failed convertibility attempt of 1947, the 1949 devaluation demonstrated that sterling still played an important role when it came to Europe. Governments across the continent, aware that their currencies were overvalued against the dollar, waited for sterling to devalue before they followed. More than nineteen countries followed sterling. The devaluations reshuffled the whole currency equilibrium not only in Europe but across the world. The devaluation also laid the ground for negotiations that would lead to the European Payments Union (EPU).

What is not clear is whether the devaluation was triggered by external international pressures or if the decision was based on domestic policy. The timing of the devaluation suggests that British policymakers took the decision to devalue only once reserves were exhausted. Using new archival materials, I demonstrate that the key issue was a worsening of the balance of payments. From May to August 1949, imports from the United States saw an up to six-fold increase. These spikes were mainly due to two factors: worsening economic conditions in the United States, and speculation through leads and lags.[1] I establish a precise timeline for the run on the pound by using daily data, which was unavailable in previous research.

Claudio Borio and Gianni Toniolo argue that the 1949 devaluation and the realignment of currencies were planned in a 'coordinated fashion, reflecting the new postwar cooperative mood, and moved exchange rates closer to the purchasing power parity of European currencies'.[2] Despite

---

[1] Leads and lags occur when importers and exporters adjust terms of payment when foreseeing a devaluation. This is explained in more detail later.

[2] Claudio Borio and Gianni Toniolo, 'One Hundred and Thirty Years of Central Bank Cooperation: A BIS Perspective', in *One Hundred and Thirty Years of Central Bank Cooperation*, ed. Claudio Borio, Gianni Toniolo and Piet Clement (Cambridge: Cambridge University Press, 2008), 41.

more coordination among central banks, the timing of the devaluation was very much an internal decision made by the British government. While Borio and Toniolo are right to emphasise that there was more cooperation during that period, Britain's decision to devalue was made without regard to the international situation.[3] US policymakers did use the threat of withdrawal of funding through the Marshall Plan or other means as a way to force Britain to comply. But at the end of the war, Britain still believed it played a major role in the world and was not keen to compromise.

This chapter also explores the impact of the 1949 sterling devaluation on US policies and monetary gold reserves. The 1949 devaluation marked a shift in US gold accumulation. Monetary gold reserves had been increasing since the war but the 1949 devaluation would reverse this trend. And during this period, there was an increase in demand for gold relative to the dollar, a phenomenon referred to as the dollar gap.[4]

## THE POLITICS OF THE DEVALUATION

The British government and Bank of England were for the most part against devaluation. On the other side of the Atlantic, the IMF and US government were in favour of it. In late 1948, the British Board of Trade suggested devaluing sterling. But Harold Wilson, who presided over the Board at the time, was opposed to the idea.[5]

In March 1949, a recession in the United States began to have an impact on Britain. At this point, Sir Robert Hall, director of the Economic Section of the Cabinet Office, 'initiated a campaign to change minds in the Treasury and Foreign Office in favour of devaluation'.[6] The Chancellor of the Exchequer, Sir Stafford Cripps, was the principal opponent.[7] In July, however, Cripps went to Switzerland for medical treatment as he was suffering from abdominal cancer. His absence resulted in mounting

---

[3] Similar debates can be found today with regard to the impact of US monetary policy on international currency flows and exchange rate crises. See the debates on taper tantrum or, for example, Olivier Blanchard, Gustavo Adler and Irineu de Carvalho Filho, 'Can Foreign Exchange Intervention Stem Exchange Rate Pressures from Global Capital Flow Shocks?', working paper (National Bureau of Economic Research, July 2015).

[4] Charles P. Kindleberger, *Europe and the Dollar* (London: MIT Press, 1968).

[5] Cairncross and Eichengreen, *Sterling in Decline*, 116.

[6] Schenk, *The Decline of Sterling*, 72.

[7] John Bew, *Clement Attlee: The Man Who Made Modern Britain* (New York: Oxford University Press, 2017), 474; Cairncross and Eichengreen, *Sterling in Decline*, 116; Schenk, *The Decline of Sterling*, 72.

pressure on the Cabinet to devalue.[8] Hugh Gaitskell, Minister of Fuel and Power and a figure of increasing importance in the Cabinet, believed that 'devaluation might buy the government a brief "lull" in economic conditions'.[9] This would allow Labour to call a general election 'before it had to put further controls on consumption and imports', a decision that would prove electorally unpopular.[10] Morgan Phillips, general secretary of the Labour Party, wanted to call an election *well after* the devaluation. He opposed Gaitskell's strategy. Philips did not prevail and the election was held in February 1950, just a few months after the devaluation.

According to Cairncross and Eichengreen, most of the officials at the Bank of England were against devaluation.[11] Still, the Bank was preparing for it and, as early as February 1948, was working on a devaluation communication plan. The goal was to assess how much notice to give to other sterling area countries, the United States and international institutions.[12] The main questions were who to communicate with and when. The Bank of England revised this communication plan frequently and several drafts have been kept in its archive. The first drafts mention partner countries and institutions to contact, but next to 'U.S.A.' there are two question marks. The Bank was not sure when to involve the United States in the process. In later drafts, the authors of the memo listed the United States as a country to be consulted between two and six days before the devaluation. This was still relatively short notice for an important partner such as the United States. The risk was that the information would leak. A leak would create a run on sterling before the official devaluation.

As the US government was pushing the United Kingdom to devalue, it expected more transparency. During a meeting in June, William McChesney Martin, who at the time worked for the US Treasury Department, stressed 'the importance of consultation prior to action' and that the IMF would have a role to play in a devaluation.[13] Willard Thorp, of the US State Department, also stressed 'the need for close cooperation',

---

[8] Bew, *Clement Attlee*, 474.     [9] Ibid., 475.     [10] Ibid., 475.

[11] Cairncross and Eichengreen, *Sterling in Decline*, 116.

[12] The various drafts of the communication plan can be found in the 'Gold and Foreign Exchange Office File Relating to Exchange Control: Devaluation of Sterling, 1949', 2 February 1948 to 31 August 1949, London, Archive of the Bank of England, C43/18.

[13] Draft Memorandum of Conversation 9 June 1949, in Ralph Goodwin et al., eds., *Foreign Relations of the United States 1949*, vol. IV, Western Europe (Washington, DC: United States Government Printing Office, 1975).

noting that 'we had passed out of the honeymoon phase of the ERP program'.[14] The US government was informed in June 1949 of 'the possibility that the UK may be confronted this summer with a major financial crisis not unlike that which developed in 1947'.[15] In early September, the US position became clear. The United Kingdom had to inform US officials not of 'the precise rate to which they propose to devalue or the precise day on which they would expect to make their approach to the International Monetary Fund', but they should 'have a rough idea'.[16] The constant demands for information-sharing show that in this period, British policymakers did not see the United States as a partner in its domestic decision-making. US policymakers in turn thought that devaluation was a decision the United Kingdom should make 'in its own interest, if it has a realistic view of its own situation'.[17]

The IMF was in favour of devaluation and made this public.[18] Harold James argues that the IMF thought a devaluation was necessary to 'clear the way for general European adjustment'.[19] An IMF report of May 1949 notes that 'U.K. export prospects in the U.S. and Canada would be improved by a parallel devaluation of currencies other than the U.S. and Canadian dollars'.[20] Schenk describes how the IMF consulted European nations in May and June 1949 and concluded that 'any general change of rates would have to be led by a devaluation of sterling'.[21] The fact that the IMF was consulted, Schenk argues, is proof that the devaluation was implemented with the IMF's blessing.

The 1949 devaluation took place with pressure from the United States to stabilise the European situation. The United States was emerging as a world leader and in response began imposing its views on Europe. Still, the ultimate decision to devalue, and the process that led to it, remained very much within Britain's domain.

---

[14] Ibid.

[15] Telegram from the Ambassador in the United Kingdom (Douglas) to the Acting Secretary of State, London, 16 June 1949, in Goodwin et al., *Foreign Relations of the United States 1949*.

[16] Position paper for the discussions with the British and Canadians on pound–dollar problems, prepared by the Policy Planning Staff, 3 September 1949, in ibid.

[17] Ibid.    [18] Cairncross and Eichengreen, *Sterling in Decline*, 117.

[19] Harold James, *International Monetary Cooperation since Bretton Woods* (Washington, DC: Oxford University Press, 1996), 92.

[20] 'Sterling since the Convertibility Crisis', report prepared by Brian Rose and approved by Roger V. Anderson, 12 May 1949, Washington, DC, Archive of the IMF, 5.

[21] Schenk, *The Decline of Sterling*, 72.

## CAUSES OF THE DEVALUATION

Explanations for the 1949 sterling devaluation have emphasised the role of a structural trade deficit with the dollar area. Another cause was a minor recession in the United States in the second quarter of 1949, followed by speculation against the pound. And finally, political pressure from the United States played a role.

The literature is unanimous in the belief that the devaluation was predictable. Cairncross and Eichengreen highlight the 'growing conviction in financial circles that the current exchange rate would eventually have to be devalued'. Howson writes that it 'was always likely that Britain would have to devalue the pound'. Schenk argues that a 'gradual build-up of evidence and opinion' led to devaluation. Capie and Wood refer to 'outside opinion' waiting for devaluation.[22]

Contemporary observers were aware that devaluation was imminent and the *Economist* in April reads:

There is a steadily mounting volume of discussion throughout the world of what is somewhat euphemistically referred to as an adjustment of currencies but what it would be more honest to call the devaluation of all the world's soft currencies. All over Europe it is a general topic of speculation in one, if not the other, meaning of the word.[23]

Even Cripps later admitted that it was expected: 'Our action had been discussed, debated, and indeed almost expected, throughout the world.'[24]

The decline in reserves leading to devaluation was largely due to three factors: a recession in the United States; stockpiling; and speculation through leads and lags, which worsened the dollar balance of payments.

Leads and lags occur when importers and exporters speculate by adjusting the terms of payments.[25] For instance, a British importer could stockpile goods bought in dollars, hoping for a devaluation. Later, they would make a profit when the price of the goods from the dollar area increased as a result of the devaluation. British exporters could ease the

---

[22] Ibid., 5; Susan Howson, *British Monetary Policy, 1945–51* (Oxford: Clarendon Press, 1993), 238; Schenk, *The Decline of Sterling*, 71; Geoffrey E. Wood and Forrest Capie, 'Policymakers in Crisis: A Study of Two Devaluations', in *Monetary and Exchange Rate Policy*, ed. Donald R. Hodgman and Geoffrey E. Wood (Basingstoke: Palgrave Macmillan, 1987), 184.

[23] 'Currency Adjustment', *Economist*, 30 April 1949; issue 5514, 778.

[24] Mansion House speech, 4 October 1949, quoted in Cairncross and Eichengreen, *Sterling in Decline*, 141.

[25] Paul Einzig, *Leads and Lags: The Main Cause of Devaluation* (London: Macmillan, 1968).

terms of payment of their US counterpart. They could move the payment terms from, say, thirty to ninety days, to be paid after the devaluation.[26] It would be a bet that the devaluation would occur between thirty to ninety days after delivery of the goods. In his essay 'Leads and Lags: The Main Cause of Devaluation', Paul Einzig argues that the 'main reason why the Government felt impelled to dishonour its pledges and devalue sterling was because of persistent selling pressure caused by leads and lags'.

Contemporaries were aware of leads and lags. On 9 July 1949, *The Financial Times* observed that 'in recent months the growing fear of sterling devaluation has sped up sales to Britain and has slowed purchases and the payment for them'.[27] The British Ambassador to the United States mentioned the issue. He explained: 'withholding of payments by US importers, slower repatriation of dollar receipts by UK and Empire exporters and some postponement of purchasing commitments by US and other countries, all of these traceable to widespread talk about possible sterling devaluation'.[28] The Bank for International Settlements (BIS) reported that 'foreign importers of sterling goods delayed their orders and payments, while sterling-area importers tried to speed up purchases and payments as much as they could'.[29] Leads and lags were putting a strain on British reserves, as Figure 2.1 illustrates.

In 1949, Exchange Equalisation Account (EEA) dollar and gold reserves dropped by more than 40 per cent. They moved from £318.2 million in January to £190.2 million in early September, before the devaluation.[30] The loss represents $517.1 million at the official $4.03/£ parity. The most striking result can be seen in the EEA dollar account, which was almost emptied. The account held only $3.2 million at its lowest point on 7 September 1949, from just under $300 million in April (Figure 2.1). At the beginning of the run on sterling, the losses can be seen only in the dollar account.

---

[26] In this example, the US importer would benefit from the better terms of payments but would still have to pay the same amount in dollars, so it can be presented as a win–win situation.

[27] Reported in *The Financial Times*, 9 July 1949.

[28] Telegram from the Ambassador in the United Kingdom (Douglas) to the Acting Secretary of State, London, 16 June 1949, in Goodwin et al., *Foreign Relations of the United States 1949*.

[29] BIS, Annual Report, 1950 (1 April 1949–31 March 1950), 12 June 1950, (Basel, BIS), 150.

[30] Ledgers of the Exchange Equalisation Account, London, Archive of the Bank of England, 2a1417 EEA.

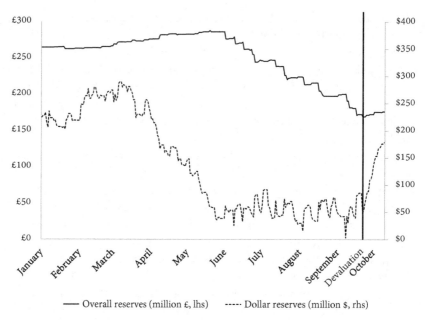

Figure 2.1. EEA dollar and overall reserves

*Source*: 'General Ledger of the EEA', 1947–9 and 1949–52, London, Archives of the Bank of England, 2a141/6 and 7.

*Note*: Overall reserves are on the left scale, EEA dollar reserves (in $ million) are on the right scale. The overall reserves are the sum of the gold and dollar reserves (other currencies were negligible).

The gold reserves fell later than the dollar reserves. Between June and September, the EEA sold over £86 million of gold to buy dollars. Until June, the EEA bought gold from South Africa against sterling, which explains the delay in the drop of overall reserves. The dollar account suffered dramatic losses starting in March 1949.

## THE BALANCE OF PAYMENTS PROBLEM

At the heart of the 1949 crisis lay balance of payments problems. This was not the overall balance of payments, which had been improving since 1947, but the trade deficit with the dollar area.[31] In previous research, data on the trade deficit have been collected by the quarter and usually from statistical

---

[31] Cairncross and Eichengreen, *Sterling in Decline*.

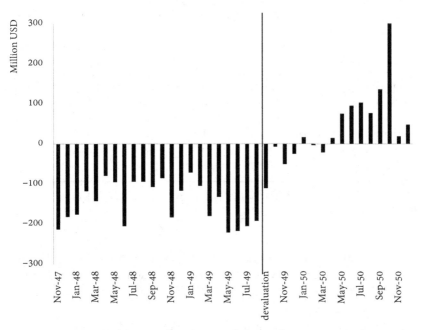

Figure 2.2. Variation of the overall sterling area balance of payments in millions as the sum of all the sterling area deficits with the non-sterling area
*Source*: Monthly Reports on External Finance, London, Archive of the Bank of England, EC5/1.

yearbooks.[32] Here I use the confidential monthly reports on external finance. These reports circulated in numbered copies between the Bank of England, the Treasury and the Cabinet. These are the data policymakers used to decide on the future of sterling. I use these data to show evidence of the channels through which leads and lags went. Previous literature mentions leads and lags but does not provide data to substantiate their existence.[33]

Figure 2.2 presents the dollar deficit. The worst trade deficits for the sterling area since 1947 (the year of the convertibility crisis) occurred during May to August 1949. Deficits for these four months are 57–81 per cent higher than the average of the preceding twelve months. The losses in these months provide an explanatory factor for the drop in EEA reserves. Marshall Plan aid was insufficient to mitigate the losses suffered. Despite these losses, officials were wary of publicly increasing drawings from the

---

[32] For example, Schenk, *The Decline of Sterling*; Alec Cairncross, *Years of Recovery: British Economic Policy 1945–51* (London: Methuen, 1985).

[33] For example, Einzig, *Leads and Lags*.

Table 2.1. *Percentage increase/decrease of British exports, imports and trade deficit with the United States*

| UK imports | May-49 | Jun-49 | Jul-49 | Aug-49 |
|---|---|---|---|---|
| Food and drink | 700% | 918% | 736% | 155% |
| Raw materials | 180% | 180% | 57% | 57% |
| Oil | 13% | −29% | −8% | 27% |
| Machinery and other manufactures | 51% | 87% | 44% | 8% |
| Total UK imports | 77% | 86% | 45% | 53% |
| **UK exports and re-exports** | −35% | −39% | −15% | −31% |

*Source*: Monthly reports on external finance, London, Archive of the Bank of England, EC5/1 (author's calculations).

Marshall Plan as this would cause the market to react negatively. During this same period, the EEA's combined gold and dollar reserves fell below £300 million for the first time. The 1949 crisis draws its roots from losses during these few months.

In the monthly reports, British imports are divided into six categories: food and drink, tobacco, raw materials, oil, machinery and other manufactures, and others.[34] The reports organise exports into three categories: exports and re-exports, diamonds and others.

Do these import and export figures for May to August 1949 stand out when compared with the averages for these months in other years? This would indicate speculation against the pound. It is unlikely that anything else would suddenly increase the country's need for, say, food and drink, assuming that the population size remains constant.

Seasonality concerns require a comparison with similar months. To mitigate this, I compare the trade figures for May–August 1949 with the average for May–August 1948 and 1950 together. For example, in summer there would probably be more imported beverages consumed. But this would not change much from one summer to the next. Table 2.1 presents the results. To check the robustness of my findings, I also compared May–August 1949 to the twelve months before the devaluation. The results are broadly similar, but I do not show them here.

---

[34] The categories change slightly. For certain years there is a category called films, which is merged with the 'others' category. The name for the oil category changes slightly over the years as well, but otherwise the content of each category is constant.

In absolute terms, the UK trade deficit with the United States for May–August was $307 million, 1.36 times the EEA dollar reserve at the beginning of 1949. Without Marshall Aid, the government would have been forced to devalue earlier. The figures in Table 2.1 are only imports and exports with the dollar area. The dollar area is where the United Kingdom was spending dollars needed by the Bank of England to defend the pound. In June 1949, food and drink imports were more than ten times higher than in the previous and following years. This stands out, and shows that it was most likely due to speculation. Equally, exports for these four months were down by approximately a third. Here also speculation is the likely culprit, and not a change in economic activity.

Why did imports rise tenfold and exports drop by a third for this period? Leads and lags offer the most convincing explanation. As seen earlier, contemporary economists and analysts reported the practice. To find evidence in the data, a closer look is needed. When analysing import and export data just before and after the devaluation there seems to be evidence of the practice. The rise in imports and fall in exports presented in Table 2.1 is the first explanation. But leads and lags also played a role after September 1949. Following a devaluation, at least in the short term, economists at the time agreed that exports were expected to rise and imports fall, as demand for domestic products increased, substituting for more expensive products.[35] Therefore, the expected short-term effect would be to see imports decrease and exports rise.

When looking at the data on exports to the United States in Figures 2.3 and 2.4, the effect is different. First, before the devaluation exports dropped drastically. This is due to exporters waiting for a devaluation before requiring payment from their counter-parties. After the devaluation there was a sharp increase in exports, but this lasted only two months. The peak in exports shows exporters being paid after the devaluation. On the import side, a similar occurrence can be seen. Importers were heavily stockpiling before the devaluation. Then, they used their stocks for the months following the devaluation when imports paid for in sterling were more expensive. These figures, presented here for the first time, offer further evidence of leads and lags.

---

[35] For example, in 1952 Alexander argued that with 'reduced prices, foreign demand for the country's exports will be increased' and that 'the initial effect of the devaluation is to raise the domestic price of imports, presumably leading to some reduction in the country's demand for imports'. Sidney S. Alexander, 'Effects of a Devaluation on a Trade Balance', Staff Papers (International Monetary Fund), 2, 2 (1952), 263–78.

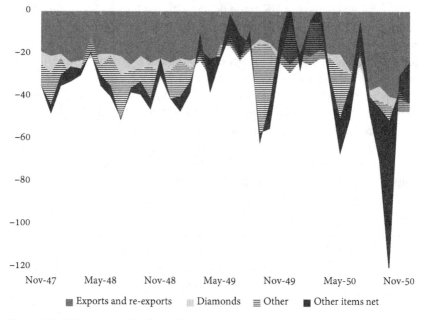

Figure 2.3. UK exports with the dollar area
*Source*: Monthly reports on external finance, London, Archive of the Bank of England, EC5/1.

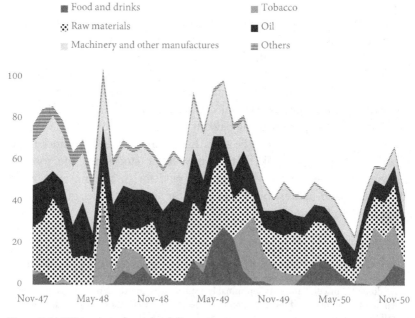

Figure 2.4. UK imports from the dollar area
*Source*: Monthly Reports on External Finance, London, Archive of the Bank of England, EC5/1.

A few years after these events, the Radcliffe Report summarised the devaluation: 'Devaluation may take place as the only way out of an exchange crisis rather than a deliberate decision of policy.'[36] This is what happened in 1949, as the loss of reserves shows. The report continues, 'but in that event, it is likely to be due to earlier policy decisions or failure to take them in time'. In 1949, the government failed to devalue before devaluation debates became public knowledge. This cost the United Kingdom valuable reserves. The devaluation occurred when Marshall Aid could no longer finance the reduction in reserves. The government decided to devalue not because of political pressure from abroad, but because of a run on sterling. Despite capital controls, the run operated through leads and lags. The deviation of imports and exports figures from previous trends makes this clear, and additional evidence comes from the drop in exports and increase in imports just before the devaluation, which was then reversed. What were the international repercussions of the devaluation?

## INTERNATIONAL REPERCUSSIONS

The IMF and the United States wanted Britain to lead the rest of the world in adjusting the value of the dollar.[37] Nineteen countries followed sterling in the currency adjustment. The BIS noted that since the gold standard was first established, 'there have been only two years in which adjustments of foreign exchange rates have been so sweeping that the expression "wave of devaluations" has been justified'.[38] Table 2.2 summarises this 'wave' using an article in the *Economist* published a few days after the devaluation. It presents a list of all countries that followed the United Kingdom into devaluation. Sterling's importance meant that most countries did so. With the approval of the IMF and the United States, even countries outside the sterling area devalued. This was the case for France, the Netherlands, Portugal and Sweden, among others. Most countries devalued by 30.5 per cent against the dollar. The last group in the table, however, did not change parity with the dollar and consequently also revalued their currency by 30.5 per cent against sterling.

Beyond political coordination, did the 1949 devaluation reduce global economic imbalances? Was this sterling-led move beneficial for the

---

[36] Committee on the Working of the Monetary System, Cmnd 827 (London, 1959).

[37] See Schenk, *The Decline of Sterling*, 72.

[38] BIS, Annual Report, 1950 (1 April 1949–31 March 1950), 12 June 1950, (Basel: BIS), 148.

Table 2.2. *Devaluation against the dollar by country*

| Country | Devaluation |
|---|---|
| Australia, Burma, Ceylon, Denmark, Egypt, Finland, Greece, India, Iraq, Ireland, Israel, Netherlands, New Zealand, South Africa, Sweden, UK | 30.5% |
| France | 22.2% |
| Portugal | 13.3% |
| Belgium | 12.3% |
| Canada | 9.1% |
| Czechoslovakia, Pakistan, Persia, Poland, Switzerland | No devaluation against the dollar |

*Source*: 'The Exchange Adjustments', *Economist*, 24 September 1949, 681.
*Note*: The table is missing Germany which also devalued the Deutschmark by 20.7%.

stability of the international monetary system? Parallel market data show that the devaluation reduced global imbalances. Carmen Reinhart and Kenneth Rogoff provide a data-set of parallel markets for ninety-three countries.[39] The premium is calculated as a percentage of the official rate. The data comes from either free markets or black markets. Reinhart and Rogoff compute the market premia as follows: premium = (parallel − official)/official. A premium of 100 means the parallel market rate is twice the official rate. A premium of 0 means that parallel rates are the same as the official rate, which is the case for most exchange rates in a mobile capital economy. Figure 2.5 presents the average of the premium index for ninety-two countries from the Reinhart and Rogoff sample.[40]

Figure 2.5 shows the rapid decline in parallel market premia, based on Reinhart and Rogoff. The index falls from almost 100 before the devaluation to around 50 six months later. For example, sterling traded around $2.4 on free markets in Switzerland and $4.03 in the official market. As a result of the sterling devaluation, the Reinhart and Rogoff index for the pound declined from a 42.4 per cent discount to a 9.8 per cent discount. After the devaluation, the average black and free market premia for the ninety-two countries from the sample dropped drastically and did not return to pre-devaluation levels until the 1960s. The devaluation played a

[39] Carmen M. Reinhart and Kenneth Rogoff, *This Time Is Different: Eight Centuries of Financial Folly*, reprint ed. (Princeton, NJ: Princeton University Press, 2011).
[40] Bolivia is excluded as it distorts the average significantly and is not central to the argument.

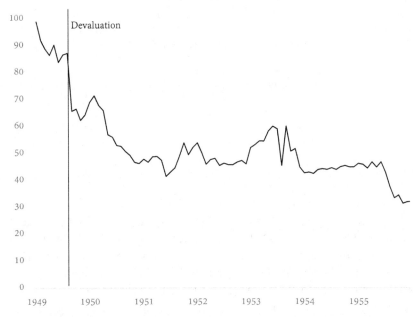

Figure 2.5. Average parallel (black or free) market premium, average of ninety-two countries
*Source*: Reinhart and Rogoff database.

positive role in the reduction of free market premia. This also meant less tension on global capital market and less illegal arbitrage.

The devaluation dealt with global imbalances as it reduced black market premia worldwide. It prepared the ground for the EPU. But what was the effect of the devaluation on the world's leading currency, the dollar? And what effect did it have on the Federal Reserve? The devaluation of nineteen currencies against the dollar is akin to a revaluation of the dollar. The effects were also felt in the short run and the mechanism was as follows: The United Kingdom experienced large capital outflows during the run-up to the devaluation. Investors, importers and exporters all tried to move their assets out of sterling into the most liquid and safe currency, the dollar. After the devaluation, they repatriated their capital to the United Kingdom or the sterling area. This large inflow of dollars ended up in the hands of the Bank of England, which did not want such large dollar holdings and preferred gold. The Bank, as well as many European central banks in possession of dollars, went to the Federal Reserve gold window to convert their dollars into gold. This put some pressure on US gold reserves.

Table 2.3. *Bai–Perron structural break testing specifications and results*

| Sample | Break dates (max. breaks allowed) | Specifications |
|---|---|---|
| 1947–70 | November 1949 (1) March 1958 (3) December 1967 (2) | Significance: 1% Trimming: 10% Max. breaks: 1–5 |
| 1947–59 | November 1949 (1) September 1951 (3) February 1958 (2) | Significance: 1% Trimming: 10% Max. breaks: 1–5 |

*Note:* The figures in parentheses represent the maximum number of breaks.

The sudden run on US gold is confirmed by econometric analysis. A Bai–Perron structural break test shows a break in US monetary gold holdings in November 1949, the month after the devaluation.[41] Bai–Perron break tests are used to identify a sudden structural change in a data series, first on a sample of monthly data from 1947 to 1959 and then on a broader sample from 1947 to 1970, for the whole Bretton Woods period. Table 2.3 summarises the results of various break tests: the model is specified to allow from one to five breaks for each of the two specifications; the figures in parentheses explain when a given break date appears. In the first sample (1947–70), 1949 appears as the significant break when only allowing for one break. When allowing for two breaks, 1949 and 1967 stand out. Finally, when allowing for three breaks, all the dates in Table 2.3 emerge. Adding a fourth or fifth break does not yield significant break dates. This confirms the robustness of November 1949 as a break date, as it appears as the most significant and first break in both samples.

Another notable factor after the devaluation is a fall in the dollar Real Effective Exchange Rate (REER). The REER weighs the value of a currency against a basket of currencies. It is not only trade-weighted (the more a country trades with the United States, the more important it is in the basket of currencies in the REER) but is also adjusted for inflation and approximates the real value of the dollar. When taking a 140-year sample of annual observations of the REER, 1949 stands out as the year when the dollar lost the most value. The dollar gained value in nominal terms as it was then worth more in terms of sterling, French francs and Dutch florins,

---

[41] Jushan Bai and Pierre Perron, 'Estimating and Testing Linear Models with Multiple Structural Changes', *Econometrica* 66, 1 (1998), 47–78; Jushan Bai and Pierre Perron, 'Critical Values for Multiple Structural Change Tests', *Econometrics Journal* 6, 1 (1 June 2003), 72–8.

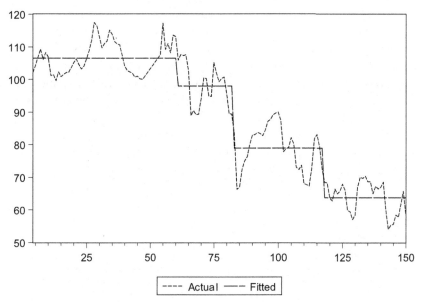

Figure 2.6. US Real Effective Exchange Rate (REER), 1870–2010
*Source*: FRED, REFXRUKA, author's calculation.
*Note*: Bai–Perron break test result. The red line is the US REER and the green line is best-fitted average.

but it lost real value as it marked a period of challenge for the dollar. Figure 2.6 plots the REER and fits it to a constant using a Bai–Perron structural break test. One of three breaks over the 140-year period is 1949 (the other two are 1927 and 1984).[42] This suggests that 1949 represented a fundamental change in the value of the dollar. The devaluation had a negative impact on the value of the dollar, as expressed by the REER. US inflation was also increasing from 1950, especially in 1951 in the wake of the Korean War, and negatively impacted the REER. The break of 1927 is possibly a consequence of the Great Depression in the United States. The break in 1984 accounts for a general trend of weaker dollar in the late 1980s and 1990s.[43]

Another consequence of the devaluation is that it paved the way for more trade integration within Europe. The 1949 devaluation was a necessary condition to open European Payments Union discussions. The

---

[42] This is done using standard parameters of trimming 0.15, max. breaks 5, sig. level 0.05.
[43] On the dollar weakness in that period, see Barry Eichengreen and Alain Naef, 'Imported or Home Grown? The 1992-3 EMS Crisis', *CEPR Working Paper*, no. DP15340 (2020).

*Economist* noted that 'every Western European currency, save the Swiss franc, has now made some response to the sterling devaluation'.[44] Adjusting European currencies against the dollar helped bring trade deficits under control. A year after the devaluation, on 19 September 1950, European nations and the United States put in place the EPU, starting with an initial working capital of $350 million provided by the United States as part of Marshall Aid. The mechanism allowed monthly clearance between European countries, including the sterling area and franc zone. The BIS acted as an agent. The currency of the system was the dollar. Member countries could pay in gold, dollars or EPU credit.[45]

[44] 'The Exchange Adjustments', *Economist*, 24 September 1949, 681.
[45] Bordo, 'Bretton Woods', 43.

# 3

# The Reopening of the London Foreign Exchange Market

## Sterling's Window on the World

On 17 December 1951, the London foreign exchange market reopened. It had been closed since 1939. The reopening allowed sterling to test international waters. After the failed convertibility attempt of 1947, this was a step towards the reintegration of sterling into global finance. Capital controls remained and the Bank of England frequently intervened in the spot market. After the reopening of the market, the influence of the pound would grow. The newly reopened market gave investors a daily barometer reading of the state of the UK currency. Daily sterling quotes became available to any investors in New York who were concerned about the state of the international monetary system. The reopening of the market was smooth and did not trigger a crisis. The consequences were positive for market participants, who could trade currencies at a lower cost in London. It reinforced the position of the City in international foreign exchange markets. But sterling was still divided into different geographical convertibility areas and was far from a fully functioning international currency.

Looking back further in history, London emerged later than other financial centres as an international foreign exchange market. It was late to the game partly because international trade operated in sterling and this did not require London to have access to foreign currencies. Einzig shows that after the Napoleonic Wars, London and Paris were the two leading foreign exchange markets.[1] London lagged behind, in part because it did not offer a forward foreign exchange market. In 1870, London briefly overtook Paris when the franc came under stress, but at the beginning of the twentieth century, London was again lagging behind Paris, as well as

---

[1] Paul Einzig, *The History of Foreign Exchange*, 2nd ed. (London: Palgrave Macmillan, 1970), 182.

Berlin and New York.[2] Since 'the overwhelming majority of foreign trade transactions in Britain were conducted in terms of sterling', most foreign exchange transactions were conducted abroad.[3] After the First World War, the London market rose in prominence.[4] When Britain withdrew from the Gold Standard in 1931, the importance of the Bank on the foreign exchange market increased.[5]

Reopening the market in 1951 was a natural step for the authorities. It restored sterling to the international scene. The *Manchester Guardian* called this 'the first essential step, although only a small step, towards the eventual goal of the restoration of full convertibility'.[6] The stability of sterling would become progressively more important within the Bretton Woods system, especially after convertibility in 1958. Thus the reopening of the market was successful in the early Bretton Woods system. It followed the failure of the 1947 convertibility and the 1949 devaluation. The devaluation did not solve Britain's long-run sterling problems, as we have seen.

## NEGOTIATIONS

The negotiations leading to the reopening of the market were essentially a British matter. The United States was never involved. It was a negotiation between the Bank of England, the Treasury and the government. According to John Fforde, the Labour government was reluctant to reopen the market.[7] The victory in the October 1951 general election of the Conservatives, led by Winston Churchill, helped tip the balance.[8] The new government wanted the reopening to be communicated as a technical measure and not a political move.[9] The United States and the IMF were not consulted. It was a domestic policy decision for the United Kingdom,

[2] Atkin, *The Foreign Exchange Market of London*, 1.

[3] Einzig, *The History of Foreign Exchange*, 182–3.

[4] Olivier Accominotti and David Chambers, 'If You're So Smart: John Maynard Keynes and Currency Speculation in the Interwar Years', *Journal of Economic History* 76, 2 (June 2016), 342–86.

[5] Atkin, *The Foreign Exchange Market of London*, 58.

[6] 'Seen from the City', *Manchester Guardian*, 16 December 1951, 2.

[7] This is described in John Fforde, *The Bank of England and Public Policy, 1941–1958* (Cambridge: Cambridge University Press, 1992), 412–17; and in a more succinct and intelligible way in Atkin, *The Foreign Exchange Market of London*, 102.

[8] Atkin, *The Foreign Exchange Market of London*, 102.

[9] Fforde, *The Bank of England and Public Policy*, 415.

unlike the opening of the gold market. The opening of the gold market prompted an international debate because of its obvious consequences for the stability of the Bretton Woods system as we will see.

The United States welcomed the reopening of the foreign exchange market. A press correspondent noted that it was 'regarded here [in Washington] as the most important move yet made by Mr Churchill's Government', and was 'applauded as a step towards greater economic and financial flexibility'.[10]

Treasury officials 'were sympathetic, but Ministers proved reluctant'.[11] Arguments for and against reopening were technical. While Labour was still in power in 1951, Douglas Jay, Financial Secretary to the Treasury, was concerned about wide forward premia or discounts on the new market. He thought they 'would simply encourage rumours and expectations that the sterling–dollar parity was going to be changed'.[12] The fear was that these markets helped speculation. They made speculative pressures measurable. We will use this measure of pressure in many charts in this book, but the forward market also helped protect companies trading abroad. These contracts could be used to hedge exchange risk. Before the opening of the market, the Bank of England was offering its own 'forward cover for genuine commercial exchange operations'.[13] The cost for these contracts was 1 per cent per annum over the official spot rate. A forward market would also offer a cover, but its price would change depending on expectations of the future price of sterling.

But as Einzig argued, leads and lags were a way to speculate. Leads and lags involved using 'genuine' commercial exchange operations for speculation.[14] And forward contracts funded this speculation. We have seen leads and lags at play during the 1949 devaluation, so the system of official forward rates at the Bank did not curb speculation. Worse, it even gave speculators funds from the Bank in the form of cheap forward contracts (remember they were fixed at 1 per cent). The *Economist* explained the issue: 'When sterling has been under suspicion, the authorities have been called upon to cover foreign exchange requirements on an abnormally large scale; when, conversely, rumours of re-valuation have been in the air, the authorities have had to be one-way buyers of forward dollars and other

[10] 'U.S. and Canadian Satisfaction', *Manchester Guardian*, 16 December 1951, 1.
[11] Fforde, *The Bank of England and Public Policy*, 413.     [12] Ibid., 413.
[13] 'The Foreign Exchange Market', *Economist*, 22 December 1951, 1538.
[14] Einzig, *Leads and Lags*.

foreign currencies.'[15] The Bank of England was funding leads and lags speculators.

The Bank used this speculation argument to justify the opening of a free spot and forward market. By offering forward contracts at an official rate, the Bank was inviting speculation against sterling through leads and lags. The outcome was that the Bank was increasingly exposed to foreign exchange risks. It had high holdings of forward contracts with speculators. Atkin notes that since the war, 'monetary policy had been put into deep freeze with the government relying on fiscal policy and direct controls to manage the economy'.[16] He further argues that 'fixed forward exchange rates and flexible domestic interest rates are inappropriate bedfellows'. The Bank used the potential losses from increased speculation against sterling to make a case for a completely free forward market, and this was eventually successful.[17]

## THE REOPENING

Before the reopening of the market in 1951, the Bank fixed the price of the currency and chose authorised traders, who dealt with the public. These dealers were 'clearing their balances daily' and did not hold any foreign exchange.[18] The *Economist* explained that the reopening meant that dealers no longer traded on behalf of the Bank of England. They had 'become genuine dealers again operating on their own account'.[19] The market moved from the Bank of England as a market-maker to 108 authorised banks and brokers setting their own prices.[20] In the view of the BIS, this was a bold move: 'it is interesting to find that while the strain on the reserves was still at its height the authorities decided that the London foreign exchange market ... should be reopened'.[21] Figure 3.1 shows how the market reopening coincided with reserves in decline.

The increase in reserves in 1950 was a result of the 1949 devaluation, which strengthened the Bank's reserve position. Leland Yeager argues that the 'Korean War boom in the raw-material exports of Sterling-Area

---

[15] 'The Foreign Exchange Market', *Economist*, 22 December 1951, 1538.
[16] Atkin, *The Foreign Exchange Market of London*, 102.
[17] Free here means without official imposed limits and not free from central bank intervention.
[18] 'Control Eased – Slightly', *Manchester Guardian*, 17 December 1951, 5.
[19] 'The Foreign Exchange Market', *Economist*, 22 December 1951, 1538.
[20] BIS, Annual Report 1953 (1 April 1952–31 March 1953), 8 June 1953, (Basel: BIS), 132.
[21] Ibid., 138.

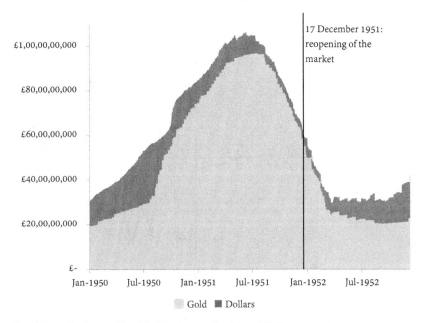

Figure 3.1. Exchange Equalisation Account gold and dollar reserves
*Source*: General Ledger of the EEA for 1949–52, London, Archives of the Bank of England, 2a141/7.

countries benefited the post-devaluation position of sterling'.[22] The position improved 'so much that rumours of its impending upward revaluation ... circulated in the winter and spring of 1950–1951'. Leads and lags speculation had reversed. Yeager argues that 'merchants now tended speculatively to delay receipts and hasten payments due in sterling'. This honeymoon period of capital inflows came to an abrupt halt as the cost of more expensive imports due to the devaluation started to have an impact. Sterling area countries now needed more dollars and gold to pay for imports, which put a drain on the Exchange Equalisation Account (EEA).[23] Over the following two years, notably due to inflation resulting from the Korean War, the reserve position of sterling worsened.[24] Britain's rearmament also had a negative impact on reserves.[25]

---

[22] Leland B. Yeager, *International Monetary Relations: Theory, History and Policy*, 2nd ed. (New York: Joanna Cotler, 1976), 385.

[23] Ibid., 385.     [24] Bordo, 'Bretton Woods', 45.

[25] William Allen, *Monetary Policy and Financial Repression in Britain, 1951–59* (New York: Palgrave Macmillan, 2014), 4–6.

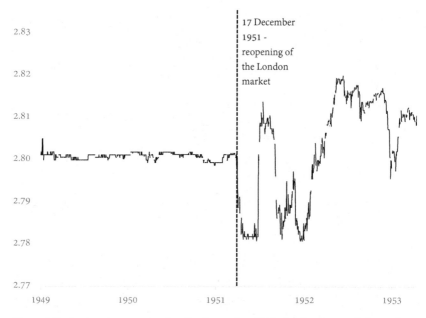

Figure 3.2. Spot exchange rate after the September 1949 devaluation until the end of 1953
*Source*: Global Financial Data.

The reopening of the market did not trigger a major foreign exchange crisis as could have been expected. It had two major consequences: it allowed the rate to float within a larger band; and it lowered bid–ask spreads. Market participants benefited from lower transaction costs. The City saw an opportunity to develop international leadership in the foreign exchange market, which it still retains today.[26]

Figure 3.2 illustrates the broadening of the band on the sterling/dollar market, the most important foreign exchange market in terms of volume. Sterling rates moved from $2.78 7/8–2.80 1/8 per sterling to $2.78–2.82 per sterling for spot rates. The Bank of England allowed the broadening of the trading band from $0.0125 to $0.04, a 220 per cent increase. The new band represents 0.71 per cent on either side of the $2.80/£ official parity. As the BIS noted in its report, 'it is narrower than the swing permitted under the Articles of Agreement of the International Monetary Fund (one per cent

---

[26] Barry Eichengreen, Romain Lafarguette and Arnaud Mehl, 'Cables, Sharks and Servers: Technology and the Geography of the Foreign Exchange Market', working paper (National Bureau of Economic Research, January 2016), 1.

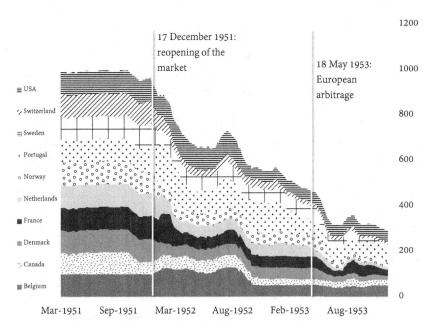

Figure 3.3. Bid-ask spreads, thirty-day moving average data for 1951–53
*Source*: Bid-ask data: Accominotti et al.; computation: the author.
*Note*: The index is based on spreads before the opening of the market (whole year 1950 = 100).

on each side of the official parity)'.[27] This increase allowed the authorised banks to make a market. The role of the Bank of England was reduced to interventions and was no longer market-making. Forward rates, unlike spot rates, benefited from 'full freedom of movement' and were not constrained to a band.[28]

The opening of the market was a success. Fforde quotes Bolton of the Bank of England, who wrote that authorised banks had done 'amazingly well in view of the short notice'.[29] The *Economist* noted approvingly that Canadian and US dollar spreads were 'no more than a quarter of a cent'.[30] Spreads are the difference between the buying and selling price (referred to as bid–ask spreads). Figure 3.3 illustrates for the first time the decline in the spreads of ten major currencies on the London market using data from

[27] BIS, Annual Report, 1952 (1 April 1951–31 March 1952), 9 June 1952, (Basel: BIS), 136.
[28] Ibid.    [29] Fforde, *The Bank of England and Public Policy*, 416.
[30] Ibid., 416.; 'Revival in Foreign Exchanges', *Economist*, 29 December 1951, 1596.

Accominotti et al. at a disaggregated level.[31] The cumulative index for the ten currencies fell from 1,000 in 1951 to just under 300 in 1953, representing an average decrease of more than 70 per cent in two years. Consequently, it became cheaper and more attractive to trade currencies in London. This advantage remained with the City for most of the twentieth century and into the twenty-first.[32]

Using a Bai–Perron break test on the data in Figure 3.3, two dates stand out.[33] As the figure shows, the first is the opening of the market in 1951 and the second arises in May 1953. This second shock is due to the liberalisation of arbitrage among European markets. The liberalisation simplified foreign exchange transactions after the introduction of the EPU.[34] The *Economist* describes the situation before liberalisation: 'A British bank in possession of French francs could sell them in Paris for sterling but not for guilders. A Belgian bank requiring guilders had to obtain them in Amsterdam, even though the cross-rates showed them to be cheaper in London.'[35] Liberalisation meant all European currencies could be traded throughout Europe. Dollars could still be traded only in the home centre of the currency in question (for example, the sterling–dollar pair in London).

This 1953 liberalisation applied to London, Paris, Amsterdam, Brussels, Frankfurt, Copenhagen, Stockholm and Zurich.[36] It led to 'very substantial' business on the first day of liberalisation according to a telephone conversation between the Federal Reserve and the Bank of England.[37] A few days after the liberalisation of arbitrage, Knoke of the New York Fed wrote to Menzies of the Bank of England to summarise the position: '[P]eople generally seem to feel that the new arrangement is not a major change but a step in the right direction.'[38]

---

[31] Olivier Accominotti et al., 'Currency Regimes and the Carry Trade', *Journal of Financial and Quantitative Analysis* 54, 5 (2019), 2233–60. https://doi.org/10.1017/S002210901900019X.

[32] BIS, 'Triennial Central Bank Survey of Foreign Exchange and OTC Derivatives Markets in 2016', BIS Triennial Report, 11 December 2016.

[33] Regressing a constant against both the sum and the mean of the indices presented in Figure 3.3 using a standard Bai–Perron structural break test (trimming 0.15, max. break 5, sig. 0.05) indicates 18 May 1953 (the first day of European arbitrage) as one of four break points. Using the median of the indices with the same specifications indicates 18 December 1951 (the day after the market reopening) as one of four break points.

[34] Bordo, 'Bretton Woods', 43.

[35] 'European Arbitrage Again', *Economist*, 23 May 1953, 531–3.

[36] BIS, Annual Report 1953 (1 April 1952–31 March 1953), 8 June 1953, (Basel: BIS), 132.

[37] Telephone conversation with Mr Roy Bridge of the Bank of England, memorandum, T. J. Roche, 18 May 1953, New York, Archives of the Federal Reserve, box 617031.

[38] Letter from Knoke to Menzies, 29 May 1953, New York, Archives of the Federal Reserve, box 617031.

The opening of the foreign market and the 1953 liberalisation made it easier to trade in currencies without making sterling fully convertible as numerous capital controls remained in place. This is in line with modern financial literature, which argues that foreign exchange market liquidity is largely driven by market-wide shocks; the reopening of the market is one such example.[39] The increase in turnover resonates with findings by Lyons, who argues that liquidity and market efficiency are closely related.[40] The reopening of the market and further liberalisation in 1953 increased the efficiency of the market and so reduced spreads.

## ALTERNATIVE MARKETS

The reopening of the market and later liberalisation increased liquidity. What is unclear is whether it helped strengthen the credibility of sterling. The analysis in the BIS annual report reveals that although the pound started to present signs of weakness, after the March 1952 budget the position improved.[41] Unlike the 1947 convertibility, the reopening of the market did not trigger a serious currency crisis. And this despite it being a step towards greater openness in international markets.

To assess the impact of the reopening, I look at the valuation of sterling in the free offshore markets. The Swiss National Bank reported the situation of banknote markets in Switzerland every day. Figure 3.4 shows cross-rates for banknotes in Switzerland as used previously. Instead of plotting the actual exchange rate, the figures present the difference between the spot rate in London and the Swiss banknote cross-rate. When the premium is close to zero, there is no incentive to transport cash to Zurich for speculation.

During the period after the 1949 devaluation until the reopening of the market (819 days), the average black-market rate was $2.49/£. This rate is a discount of 11 per cent against the official parity. In the same period after the market reopening, the average banknote rate was $2.57/£, an average discount of 8 per cent. Looking at Figure 3.4, after the market reopened, the discount decreased. The data do not offer any statistically significant structural break on the date the market reopened. The market constantly fed on new information and it is unlikely that the reopening came as a

---

[39] Loriano Mancini, Angelo Ranaldo and Jan Wrampelmeyer, 'Liquidity in the Foreign Exchange Market: Measurement, Commonality, and Risk Premiums', *Journal of Finance* 68, 5 (2013), 1806.

[40] Richard K. Lyons, *The Microstructure Approach to Exchange Rates* (Cambridge, MA: MIT, 2006), 77.

[41] BIS, Annual Report,1952 (1 April 1951–31 March 1952), 9 June 1952 (Basel: BIS).

Figure 3.4. Discount on the sterling/dollar banknote cross-rate
*Source*: Swiss National Bank.

surprise. Restoration of convertibility in 1958 finally reduced the discount in this market almost to zero (far right in Figure 3.4). At this point, black, offshore and official markets were integrated.

Despite the relative success of the reopening of the market, officials at the Bank and the Treasury were worried about mounting pressure on reserves early in 1952 (see Figure 3.1). This led to debate about the introduction of floating in the form of the ROBOT scheme. The name of the scheme came from its main advocates: Leslie Rowan and Otto Clarke from the Treasury and George Bolton from the Bank. The scheme has received considerable attention in the literature despite never being adopted.[42] The idea was to float the pound immediately while still blocking some large sterling balances in the United Kingdom and abroad.[43]

[42] Peter Burnham, *Remaking the Postwar World Economy: Robot and British Policy in the 1950s* (London: Palgrave Macmillan, 2003); Cairncross, *Years of Recovery*, chapter 9; Capie, *The Bank of England*, 147–9; Fforde, *The Bank of England and Public Policy*, chapters 6b and 6c; Schenk, *The Decline of Sterling*, 102–15; Schenk, *Britain and the Sterling Area*, 114–19.

[43] Susan Howson, 'Money and Monetary Policy since 1945', in *The Cambridge Economic History of Modern Britain: Volume 2*, ed. Roderick Floud and Paul Johnson, 2nd ed. (New York: Cambridge University Press, 2014), 149.

The float would have been controlled within bands that were kept secret from the public.[44]

The ROBOT plan failed and was not implemented. It was followed by 'the collective approach' to convertibility at the end of 1952.[45] British officials discussed the 'collective approach' during several Commonwealth conferences at the end of 1952 and later with the American administration.[46] The idea was to make major currencies convertible simultaneously with financial support from the United States. Howson notes that the 'only short-term result was to feed rumours which weakened sterling in the foreign exchange markets and obliged successive chancellors to disclaim all intentions of letting sterling float'.[47] After the ROBOT plan and the 'collective approach' both failed, no new attempts to float were made until after the 1967 devaluation.

Floating was never put in place during the Bretton Woods period. Yet the reopening of the market remained an important step towards the liberalisation of sterling. American officials were optimistic about the move; IMF officials were more sceptical about completely freeing the forward market. Unlike previous liberalisation attempts such as 1947, the reopening of the foreign exchange market did not precipitate a crisis. It generally improved the situation for market participants. The international credibility of sterling improved, and for customers in London a freer market meant lower transaction costs.

[44] Capie, *The Bank of England*, 147.   [45] Schenk, *Britain and the Sterling Area*, 119–24.
[46] Howson, 'Money and Monetary Policy since 1945', 149–50.
[47] Ibid., 149–50; and see also Fforde, *The Bank of England and Public Policy*, chapter 7.

4

# The Bank on the Market

With the opening of the London foreign exchange market in late 1951, the Bank of England took an active role in managing the exchange rate. This was Britain's responsibility as a signatory of the Bretton Woods agreement. It had to keep the sterling–dollar exchange rate within a 1 per cent band above and below the official parity. Although this was a national responsibility, as the Bretton Woods system became less stable, maintaining sterling parity started to have international repercussions. The United States became ever more aware that a sterling devaluation could trigger a run on the dollar. This could threaten the whole system. If sterling as a reserve currency failed, so could the dollar, the other reserve currency.[1]

Here I review how the Bank of England managed sterling after the opening of the foreign exchange market in London in 1951. I present a new database on Bank of England intervention and assess the performance of the Bank in defending sterling during the Bretton Woods period. Analysis of the database highlights that the pressure on the Bank to intervene increased following convertibility in 1958. Using a reaction function, I also demonstrate that the Bank of England failed to embrace intervention on the forward market, which the Federal Reserve used as its main intervention tool. Finally, results from an event study show that intervention was more often than not unsuccessful.

Bordo et al. have written on US intervention in the foreign exchange market.[2] They argue that US intervention was an effective short-term remedy during the Bretton Woods period, delaying the collapse of the

---

[1] Charles A. Coombs, *The Arena of International Finance* (New York: Wiley, 1976).

[2] Michael D. Bordo, Owen F. Humpage and Anna J. Schwartz, *Strained Relations: US Foreign-Exchange Operations and Monetary Policy in the Twentieth Century* (Chicago, IL: University of Chicago Press, 2015).

system. British intervention has received no more than sporadic attention in the literature. Bordo et al. wrote the first econometric paper on foreign exchange market intervention for the United Kingdom during the sterling crises between 1964 and 1967.[3] They argue that Britain maintained the peg with the dollar thanks to loans and external help, such as swap contracts and international rescue packages.

The Bank mainly intervened in the dollar/sterling market, with the dealers' reports registering negligible intervention in the Canadian dollar and French franc in the early 1950s and sporadic mention of Deutschmark intervention in 1957.[4]

## FOREIGN EXCHANGE INTERVENTIONS

The Bank of England was active in the market every day, as recorded in the dealers' reports. The goal of intervention was two-fold. The first goal was to keep the exchange rate within the Bretton Woods bands. For example, bands were \$2.78–2.82/£ in 1949–67. The second goal was to avoid 'undue fluctuations in the exchange value of sterling'.[5] This second point derives from the Finance Act of 1932 and is a woolly definition of maintaining 'orderly' markets. It can be understood as foreign exchange market house-keeping. The concept of 'orderly markets' was not based on any metric or model and is unclear. The goal of keeping markets tidy was a recurring theme at the Bank. It can also be found in the gold market (see Chapter 5) and the money market.[6]

For the money market, Capie notes how the Bank 'tried to influence expectations and engaged in psychological warfare'. It also gave 'dark hints and by a variety of means nudged or indicated or otherwise tried to suggest the outcome it wanted'.[7] These tactics applied also to the foreign exchange market. Senior dealers took most decisions on intervention tactics. As we will see, they were often about trying to surprise the market. Decisions were made based on gut feelings.

---

[3] Michael D. Bordo, Ronald MacDonald and Michael J. Oliver, 'Sterling in Crisis, 1964–1967', *European Review of Economic History* 13, 3 (1 December 2009), 437–59.

[4] Foreign exchange and gold market reports (dealers' reports), various dates, London, Bank of England Archives, C8.

[5] Finance Act 1932 (London: HMSO, 1932).

[6] For more on the money market see Allen, *Monetary Policy and Financial Repression*; William A. Allen, *The Bank of England and the Government Debt: Operations in the Gilt-Edged Market, 1928–1972* (New York: Cambridge University Press, 2019).

[7] Capie, *The Bank of England*, 309.

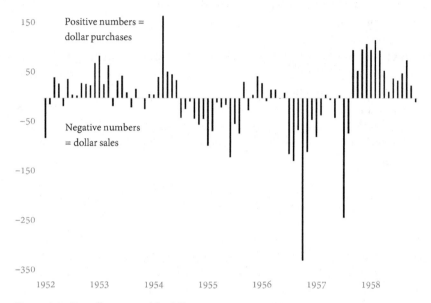

Figure 4.1. Overall net monthly dollar intervention, 1952–58
*Source*: Dealers' reports (C8).

Figure 4.1 illustrates the Bank's monthly net dollar intervention. The figure shows monthly dollar purchases (positive numbers) and sales (negative numbers).[8] Dollar purchases weaken sterling and increase reserves. Dollar sales strengthen sterling and use up reserves. The November 1956 Suez crisis stands out as the highest sales month. The figure shows trends over several months. After November 1957 (on the right-hand side of the graph), the Bank managed to increase its reserve position. From 1954 to 1957, there is a period of constant sales. It is indicative of pressure on sterling. Later we will look at daily figures. They present much more volatility.

To understand a typical day in the dealers' room, let us look at an outsider view. In 1961, the Bank of France sent M. Gouzerh to spend five days at the Bank of England. He recorded: '[Th]e information reported has not been communicated by the Bank of England, but are the results of

---

[8] For more analysis on this data, see also Alain Naef, 'Dirty Float or Clean Intervention? The Bank of England in the Foreign Exchange Market', *European Review of Economic History*, 2020, https://doi.org/10.1093/ereh/heaa011; Alain Naef and Jacob Weber, 'How Powerful Is Unannounced, Sterilized Foreign Exchange Intervention?', *SocArXiv*, 25, 1 (2021), 180–201, https://doi.org/10.31235/osf.io/bfehz.

observations I made.'[9] His report offers a detailed insight into the day-to-day business of the Bank and gives estimates of operations and a description of processes. This was a time of central bank cooperation and the French observer was welcomed. However, mistrust remained. The Bank wanted to keep some of its trade secrets. Gouzerh reported that he was asked to leave the dealing room every day just before 5 pm, under the pretence that he would disturb the dealers as they were busier then. He noted that 5 pm was the time when heavy sterling sales from the United States started. This kind of mistrust would eventually be resolved. In Chapter 14 on the ERM crisis, I rely on intervention data that was shared daily among European central bankers.

The intervention orders were given during business hours by telephone to four retail or commercial banks: Westminster, Lloyds, National Provincial and Société Générale. Westminster received the bulk of the orders. The goal was either to prevent the exchange rate from depreciating too quickly or to encourage or amplify an appreciation. The French observer estimated that during the five days he spent at the Bank, dealers intervened more than $150 million.[10]

The dealers, according to Gouzerh, feared both the opening of the market in Paris in the morning and the opening of the New York market at 3 pm. The Bank of England usually gave sterling a final push in the last half-hour of trading. After that, the Bank handed over the responsibility for intervention to the New York Fed in the evening. The Fed's operations were monitored by a 'principal' at the Bank of England. The principal stayed in touch with New York until the market closed late in the evening London time.

Another document shows how the Bank viewed its role in the market. Before the October 1959 general election, the Bank prepared a foreign exchange intervention plan. It reads:

So long as the outcome of the election remains unclear, confusion in the exchange market must be expected, some operations one way, some another. In that event we will endeavour to maintain relative stability in the sterling/dollar rate until the

---

[9] The original reads: 'Les renseignements consignées ci-dessous ne m'ont pas été communiqués par la Banque d'Angleterre, ils sont le résultat d'observations.' Extract of a letter from M. Gouzerh staying at the Bank of England to M. Floch, 19 May 1951, Paris, Archives of the Bank of France, 1495200501/564.

[10] Extract of a letter from M. Gouzerh staying at the Bank of England to M. Floch, 19 May 1951, Paris, Archives of the Bank of France, 1495200501/564.

results become more apparent, aiming provisionally at something like 2.79¾–2.80¾, i.e., a wider fluctuation than one normally sees during the day.[11]

After the election, the Bank had two scenarios in mind. In the event of downward pressure, the Bank would

> not offer much resistance but let the rate fall quite quickly to say, 2.78 1/16, testing the market periodically on the way down. There would be no point in spending much on the way down which would be expensive and encourage speculation against the pound. Later, when election influences had subsided, we would examine the possibility of bringing about an improvement in the rate.[12]

In the event of upward pressure, the Bank 'would let the rate go over 2.81 fairly easily; then we would begin to take in dollars on a rising market. If the demand proved to be large we would let the rate go to the upper limit'.[13]

This highlights the dual strategy of the Bank. In uncertain markets, it would maintain 'relative stability'. When the pound was falling, it would let the price reach a new equilibrium before trying to influence the direction of the exchange rate again. What emerges from these extracts is the 'cookbook' nature of intervention. The Bank treated fundamental economic variables as exogenous to its intervention decisions as it could not adjust fundamentals. Dealers could do no more than try to influence the Treasury or government. The Bank did not consider devaluation or changes in interest rates as options. Dealers were often forced to intervene in spite of the fundamental value of the currency.

Another feature during that period was that intervention was covert and had little signalling value for the market. Current literature stresses that a central bank can lead the market with signalling, when fundamental economic factors become fuzzy after an election or a global shock for example.[14] The Bank of England did not make public its interventions. Instead, it preferred surprise and changing tactics to try to win over the market. This sometimes worked as the reserves of the Bank were sizeable in comparison to the market. This is no longer the case today.

Changes in tactics are illustrated by the following intervention instructions given by Bridge to the Federal Reserve: 'I shall ask you to go into the

---

[11] Contingency plan, the exchanges – Friday, 9th October, 8 October 1959, London, Archive of the Bank of England, C43/32.

[12] Ibid.     [13] Ibid.

[14] Lucio Sarno and Mark P. Taylor, 'Official Intervention in the Foreign Exchange Market: Is It Effective and, if so, How Does It Work?', *Journal of Economic Literature* 39, 3 (2001), 839–68.

market after lunch. . . . Don't go before lunch. I thought it wise to change tactics a bit. It is a good thing.'[15] These instructions show how Roy Bridge was changing strategies every day to try to surprise the market, as opposed to trying to guide the market (as central bankers tend to do today). Bridge was at the heart of the Bank's foreign exchange strategy. He saw it as a game he played to try to fool or outsmart the market. Capie argues that this was one of the reasons why the Bank was so backward: 'One of the principal failings in the operation as far as the Bank was concerned was their obsession with psychological warfare. Their pride in market skills and the lack, for so long, of serious economic input contributed to a concentration on manipulating the market.'[16]

The Bank intervened in several dollar markets. The dealers' reports offer a detailed intervention classification. Intervention is broken down by different types of market in Figure 4.2. The figure underlines the fact that the bulk of interventions was made in the spot market. Spot interventions accounted for 72 per cent of the total dollar amount spent during the Bretton Woods period. Of the interventions, 89 per cent (72 + 17) were made in the spot or forward London market. Overnight interventions, representing 11 per cent (9 + 2) were in New York. Of the overall amount spent during the Bretton Woods period, 0.5 per cent was mainly in Switzerland in transferable sterling markets.[17]

The Bank was unfamiliar with the forward market. This reflected a general backwardness and rigidity when it came to defending the UK currency. The Federal Reserve almost exclusively used forward intervention.[18] The Bank was still struggling to understand this market fully. It struggled to leverage it to manage sterling. Reporting on a conversation with Earland and Preston at the Bank, Bodner was surprised to learn about 'the difficulties that they [the Bank] seem to find in narrowing the forward discount'.[19] According to Bodner,

[15] Telephone conversation with Mr Bridge, Bank of England at 11:15 am, H. L. Sanford to file, 10 August 1956, New York, Archives of the Federal Reserve, box 617015.

[16] Capie, *The Bank of England*, 243.

[17] Even if Switzerland was not a 'transferable sterling' country, it offered a transferable dollar/sterling market. Dealers were monitoring rates in this market, as can be seen in their reports. Percentages are rounded up and therefore do not add up to 100 per cent. The comparison for the whole period is biased because transferable sterling interventions occurred only between February 1955 and December 1958.

[18] On the Federal Reserve intervention policy, see Bordo, Humpage and Schwartz, *Strained Relations*.

[19] Telephone conversation with Messrs Earland and Preston of the Bank of England at 8:50 am, Bodner to file, with copy to Coombs and eleven others, 23 October 1967, New York, Archives of the Federal Reserve, box 617031.

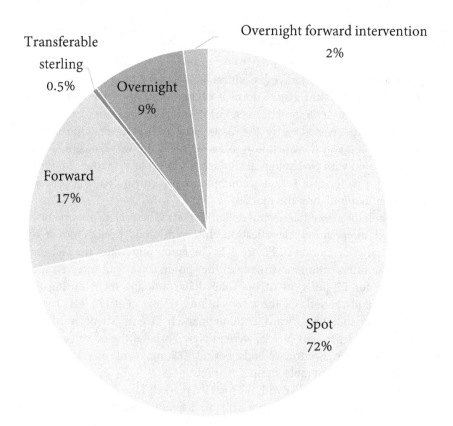

Figure 4.2. Total dollar sales by type, 1952–72
*Source*: Dealers' reports (C8).

'it seems clear from this conversation that there is, in fact, no technical reason why the Bank of England could not narrow the forwards sufficiently to create an incentive in favour of sterling'. Bodner thought the Bank just did not get it. He continued: 'The real limitation is the Bank of England's reluctance to take on a very large additional amount of forward commitments and their fear that this is what would result from any attempt to significantly narrow the forward discounts.' The Radcliffe Report did not favour forward market operations. The report stresses that 'operation in the forward market would not be an effective method of countering speculation against the pound'.[20]

Figure 4.3 shows daily forward operations from 1952 to 1972. The Bank only bought forward sterling in large quantities during the 1964–67

---

[20] The Radcliffe Report, para. 707, 257.

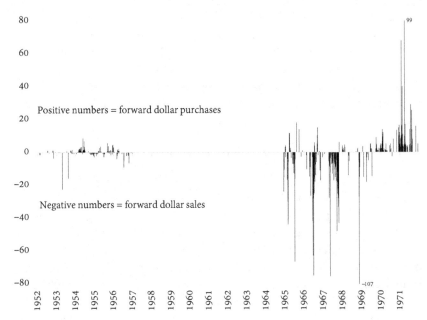

Figure 4.3. Forward market intervention
*Source*: Dealers' reports (C8).

sterling crisis. The Bank reacted strongly to the 1964 general election. The Labour Party had won the election and the ensuing crisis 'called for the deployment of every available technique, and forward intervention was one of these'.[21] After a hesitant start, the Bank increased its activity in the forward market. The increase was so rapid that before the 1967 devaluation, its oversold position stood at $7183 million.[22] At this point, the Bank wanted to back out of its outstanding forward position. But doing so would have signalled an imminent devaluation and triggered further speculation. Capie notes that experience gained in 1964–67 had scarred the Bank and Treasury. In the 1970s, the Bank was reluctant to engage in forward intervention.[23]

British reluctance was partly due to Governor Montagu Norman (1920–44). Norman had castigated the forward market as 'dominated by speculators'.[24] He called it an 'anathema' for the Bank. Only occasionally did the Bank intervene in this market during Norman's governorship – for

---

[21] Capie, *The Bank of England*, 205.     [22] Ibid., 247.     [23] Ibid., 372.
[24] Richard Sidney Sayers, *The Bank of England, 1891–1944* (Cambridge: Cambridge University Press, 1976), 420.

example, in 1926.[25] Immediately after the opening of the London forward market, Knoke asked the Bank: 'Are you operating officially in the forward market?'[26] Gurney of the Bank of England replied: 'No, we are not touching the forward market at all.' The word 'touching' is quite strong in this context. It highlights the Bank's reluctance to operate in this market. Its refusal to intervene in the forward market seemed to be based on tradition more than any valid economic argument.

### COOPERATION WITH THE FED

The literature often portrays the Bretton Woods period as the peak of central bank cooperation.[27] In practice, however, exchanging information and working hand in glove were longer processes for the Federal Reserve and Bank of England. The 1950s saw cooperation slowly unfold. The Bank of England was reluctant to share information. Most of what follows comes from archival records of telephone conversations. The archives of the Fed offer detailed daily telephone conversation for the period.

Cooperation meant that the Fed intervened on behalf of the Bank. The Bank still did not fully trust the Fed early in the Bretton Woods period. In 1951, the foreign exchange market reopened and the Bank gave the Fed general instructions, telling it 'to operate for us at the official limits, i.e., to buy sterling in the New York market at 2.78 and to sell it at 2.82'.[28] These were broad and official instructions. Between the bands, the Bank of England preferred intervening through other third parties in North America. The goal was to make the Bank's operations on the American continent more secret. The Bank of England's main concern was that Fed dealers were not 'regular operators in sterling nor are they what we would regard as "in" the market' and that 'when they do intervene the whole market appears to be immediately aware' of this.[29]

---

[25] Bordo, Humpage and Schwartz, *Strained Relations*, 36.

[26] Telephone call from Mr Gurney from the Bank of England to Mr Knoke 11:35 am, 18 December 1951, New York, Archives of the Federal Reserve, box 617031.

[27] For example, Borio and Toniolo, 'One Hundred and Thirty Years of Central Bank Cooperation'; Gianni Toniolo and Piet Clement, *Central Bank Cooperation at the Bank for International Settlements, 1930–1973* (Cambridge: Cambridge University Press, 2007).

[28] 'Aide Memoire for the Governor – Sterling Operations in the New York Market', 25 May 1956, London, Archives of the Bank of England, C43/319.

[29] Sir George Bolton's letter of 2 October, memorandum sent to Parson and Hawker with a copy to Tansley and Bridge, 15 October 1956, London, Archive of the Bank of England, C43/319.

Third parties the Bank hired to intervene in New York included the Bank of Canada. This led to some tensions between the Fed and the Bank. In 1956, the Fed became concerned that the Bank of England would use the Bank of Canada in New York instead of the Fed. The Fed wrote to the Bank to complain. The Bank of England wanted the operations to appear to be genuine demand, showing the strength of sterling, and not demand fabricated to support a weak sterling. The Bank of Canada was a natural player in New York. This made market participants less suspicious that the Bank of England was behind the operations. In theory, bank secrecy meant that any broker operating for a third party would withhold the identity of that third party (this applied to central bank dealers as well). In practice, however, dealers would share information and who was buying and selling would quickly become known to everyone. Introducing a third party such as the Bank of Canada added another tier, making it less obvious who was behind the orders, at least so the Bank thought. The issue was then discussed at length between the two central banks to try to channel British intervention in New York through the Federal Reserve.

This issue with the Bank of Canada was one example of the difficulties experienced in the 1950s for the two central banks. Another issue arose in the mid-1950s. The issue came from the Bank of England's reluctance to share foreign exchange market intervention data with the Federal Reserve. The Fed, in telephone call after telephone call, tried to get intervention figures from the reluctant Bank. This was a legitimate request as the Fed also operated at the other end of this market. Sharing information was to everyone's benefit. Sanford from the Fed started fishing for information. He asked Bridge about intervention amounts in 'round numbers'.[30] Bridge answered, 'it was less than we thought it would be in advance', a cryptic answer at best. This forced Sanford to guess: 'Would $40 million sound like a reasonable figure?', to which Bridge answered, 'Rather on the high side'. This shows how reluctant the Bank was to share information about foreign exchange operations. These exchanges took place frequently in 1955–56. And from 1957, the Bank began to share more information on its interventions. This indicates more cooperation than in the interwar years when such exchanges did not occur. Still, the Bank was reluctant to fully cooperate.

In the late 1950s, the Federal Reserve and the Bank of England were talking about the foreign exchange on most days. The records show a

---

[30] Telephone conversation with Mr Bridge, Bank of England, at 11:34 am, Sanford to file, 15 March 1955, New York, Archives of the Federal Reserve, box 617031.

progressive institutional and personal integration between the two institutions. Personal connections and open collaboration would become critical in the 1960s. At that point, sterling was in almost constant crisis and the United States started to play a more important role in the fate of the British currency.

## STRATEGIES AND TACTICS

Why did the Bank of England intervene? Its mission was to keep the London spot rate under control, but what about the other exchange rates? Here I show how the Bank reacted to movement in the various sterling rates. This is done by running a reaction function on the intervention dataset presented in this book.

To understand how central banks respond to exchange rate fluctuations, economists have estimated reaction functions.[31] Klug and Smith looked at the Suez crisis. They determined a reaction function of the monetary authorities, and found that the Bank of England intervened in reaction to variations in the transferable sterling exchange rate. This shows that the Bank was concerned not only about exchange rates in London but also abroad. Bordo et al. used a reaction function to study foreign exchange market intervention for the United Kingdom during the sterling crises of 1964–67.[32] They argue that the Bank of England reacted to the lower band of the exchange rate as well as within the Bretton Wood bands. Here I use a reaction function to determine which exchange rate was influencing the monetary authorities' policies.

When reading the dealers' reports, it seems clear that the Bank of England dealers intervened to avoid sterling depreciation against the dollar. Central bankers call this leaning against the wind; understand the wind as market forces. Bank dealers monitored both the official exchange rate in London and transferable sterling in New York and Zurich. Look at the first photograph of Bank of England dealers at the end of Chapter 7. The picture shows a chalk board in the background of the dealers' room.

---

[31] For a review of the literature on reaction functions, see Hali J. Edison, *The Effectiveness of Central-Bank Intervention: A Survey of the Literature after 1982*, vol. 18 (Princeton, NJ: Princeton University Press, 1993), 37–42; Christopher Neely, 'An Analysis of Recent Studies of the Effect of Foreign Exchange Intervention', Federal Reserve Bank of St. Louis working paper (1 June 2005), 2–3; Takatoshi Ito and Tomoyoshi Yabu, 'What Prompts Japan to Intervene in the Forex Market? A New Approach to a Reaction Function', *Journal of International Money and Finance* 26, 2 (March 2007), 193–212.

[32] Bordo, MacDonald and Oliver, 'Sterling in Crisis, 1964–1967'.

The chalk board displays exchange rate prices for both Swiss francs and even Swiss franc notes. This means that the Bank also monitored exchange rates abroad, including Swiss banknotes. The reaction function helps determine which of these different rates was more important in shaping the Bank's policy decisions.

The reaction function relates several exchange rates to Bank of England intervention. To reduce the issues associated with multicollinearity, the explanatory variables which relate to exchange rates are the differences from the lower bound instead of being actual exchange rates. The lower band is 2.78 until 1967, then 2.38 after the devaluation. By taking the difference from the lower band, the variables on the right-hand side become much less correlated than if they are used as sterling/dollar exchange rates directly. The Augmented Dickey–Fuller Unit root test confirms that all series are stationary when taken as the difference from the floor. Intervention data are stationary as they are.

Transferable sterling is relevant only in the period before 1958 as it later disappeared as a discrete sterling rate. Because the dealers' reports start reporting transferable sterling from 1953, a reaction function for the sub-sample from 1953 to 1958 is estimated (regression 1 in Table 4.1). The following equation shows the reaction function used in this book. It is similar to other reaction functions in the literature.[33]

$$I_t = \beta_0 + \beta_1 I_{t-1} + \beta_2 \Delta S_{t-1} + \beta_3 \Delta_{low} S_{t-1} + \beta_4 \Delta_{low} S_{t-1}^{TREND} + \beta_5 \Delta_{low} S_{t-1}^{NOTE}$$
$$+ \beta_6 \Delta_{low} S_{t-1}^{3FWD} + \varepsilon$$

where $It$ is intervention in dollars taking positive value for purchase of dollars and negative value for sales of dollars, $I_{t-1}$ is lagged intervention to allow for autocorrelation, and $\Delta S_{t-1}$ is the difference between the exchange rate at days $t-2$ and $t-1$, which is used in most reaction functions. The remaining four terms are the difference between the Bretton Woods lower band (2.78/2.38) and the four exchange rates: London spot rate, transferable sterling, Swiss banknote cross-rate and the three-month London forward rate. Three regressions are run for the full sample, one before and one after the introduction of convertibility in December 1958. The results are presented in Table 4.1.

What does the regression analysis tell us? The Bank of England was reacting to an increase in the spot exchange rate by buying dollars and

---

[33] This function is inspired by Ito and Yabu, 'What Prompts Japan to Intervene in the Forex Market?'; Bordo, MacDonald and Oliver, 'Sterling in Crisis'.

Table 4.1. *Sterling reaction function regressions*

| | Dependent variable: Bank of England intervention | | |
|---|---|---|---|
| | (1) Pre-convertibility including transferable sterling (1953–58) | (2) Post-convertibility to devaluation (1959–67) | (3) Whole sample (1952–72) |
| Intercept | −3.35 (0.63)*** | −9.81 (1.97)*** | −2.89(1.36)** |
| London spot sterling | 171.01 (33.97)*** | 326.08 (97.23)*** | 171.62 (82.98)** |
| Transferable sterling | 28.31 (9.75)*** | | |
| Three-month forward | 0.95 (25.67) | 217.37 (85.90)** | 47.49 (57.51) |
| Swiss offshore banknote cross-rate | 3.98 (3.33) | | 5.30 (3.22)* |
| Lagged intervention | 0.35 (0.07)*** | 0.38 (0.03)*** | 0.35 (0.03)*** |
| Previous day difference | 513.10 (162.90)*** | −260.70 (55.85)*** | −283.39 (70.97)*** |
| *Adjusted R²* | 0.321 | 0.258 | 0.194 |
| *Observations* | 1,000 | 2,249 | 4,966 |

*Note*: Standard errors are reported in parenthesis and are robust to heteroscedasticity and autocorrelation using heteroscedasticity and autocorrelation-consistent (HAC) estimators, using a Newey–West correction.
***signifies statistical significance at the 1% level; **signifies statistical significance at the 5% level; *signifies statistical significance at the 10% level.

to a decrease by selling dollars. This was expected. It is corroborated by qualitative evidence from the dealers' reports. A decrease in the spot rate of $0.01 per sterling (for example, $2.80 to $2.79/£) would have led to the Bank spending $1.71 million on any given day, other things remaining constant. Post-convertibility, the Bank would spend $3.26 million for a similar decrease in the spot rate. This is just short of double the amount before convertibility. The fact that lower exchange rates led to more intervention after convertibility is expected. With fewer controls on capital flows, the Bank needed more firepower after convertibility.

Before convertibility, the monetary authorities also reacted to transferable sterling. This is consistent with findings by Klug and Smith. The impact they found is greater, however.[34] For the pre-convertibility sample, the coefficient for the transferable sterling exchange rate is significant, but six times smaller than that for the official London sterling rate. This is consistent with evidence from daily telephone conversations between the Fed and the Bank.[35] During most of the period between 1952 to 1972, Bank of England and New York Federal Reserve officials would talk at least once a day to discuss market conditions as seen. These discussions also mentioned the state of transferable sterling in New York. The Bank prioritised the status of the official spot rate over other exchange rates.

What is interesting is that changes in forward rates triggered no reaction pre-convertibility as the coefficient is not significant (regression 1). Post-convertibility, forward rates seem to have played a role. The coefficient is significant only at 5 per cent (regression 2). The absence of significance in the forward market in regressions 1 and 3 highlights the reluctance of the Bank to engage in the forward market, as shown earlier. Finally, a more surprising result is the offshore banknote cross-rate in Switzerland. It does not seem to have influenced monetary authorities' decision-making. This could be because this is an artificial cross-rate and not a quoted rate. Or maybe authorities focused on official markets.

## INTERVENTION PERFORMANCE

The Bank of England spent most days in the foreign exchange market. How efficient was this intervention? There is a vast literature on measuring foreign exchange intervention effectiveness. Here I analyse how successful the Bank's interventions were by using the intervention data presented earlier. It also assesses what made interventions successful. This is relevant not only to the history of the Bank, but also is of interest to the literature on intervention and to central banking professionals.

I use a simple daily indicator to observe exchange rate behaviour the day after an intervention. The indicator tests whether the exchange rate appreciates after a dollar sale or depreciates less than on the previous day. The limitation of the indicator is that it captures only the short-term effect of intervention and does not offer information over a few days. It is inspired

---

[34] Adam Klug and Gregor W. Smith, 'Suez and Sterling, 1956', *Explorations in Economic History* 36, 3 (July 1999), 181–203.

[35] Telephone conversations between Bridge and Sanford, New York, Archives of the Federal Reserve, boxes 617015 and 617031.

by an indicator developed by Humpage and applied by Bordo, Humpage and Schwartz to the US case.[36]

During the Bretton Woods period, the Bank mainly tried to keep sterling from depreciating. This becomes clear when reading the dealers' reports and other internal memos. The Bank never tried to make sterling depreciate. If it was overvalued, it took the opportunity to build up reserves. Therefore, my assessment of the intervention only focuses on dollar sales. These operations were meant to make sterling appreciate. Intervention success in this context means that the Bank prevents sterling from depreciating.

I use three success criteria (SC). Exchange rate reversal (SC1) measures if dollar sales led to next-day appreciation of the exchange rate. Depreciation-smoothing (SC2) measures if selling dollars lessened the depreciation compared to the previous day. The sum of the two (SC3) combines reversal and smoothing to create a general measure of success. This last measure encompasses the two main reasons why the Bank would sell dollars on the market, either to smooth a fall or to reverse depreciation of the pound. Table 4.2 presents the results. The test suffers from not being able to establish the counter-factual in the absence of intervention. The Bank could have been intervening on a day when the exchange rate was reversing anyway. The test measures this as a success. However, as the Bank intervened mainly when the market was under pressure (against the wind), this should provide a reasonable account of the Bank's performance.

Table 4.2 highlights differences in success rates before and after convertibility. Before convertibility, the Bank managed to achieve desired outcomes (appreciation or smoothing) in half the days it sold dollars. The Bank had an impact on the exchange rate the next day, every other day. After convertibility, the success rate dropped to 36 per cent – a success in one in three attempts.

Market conditions became more adverse after convertibility. This becomes clearer when examining the intervention's size. Table 4.3 presents summary statistics of the Bank's daily intervention, comparing the pre- and post-convertibility period. The data come from the Bank of England dealers' reports. Before convertibility, the Bank spent $2.7 billion in the

---

[36] Owen F. Humpage, 'U.S. Intervention: Assessing the Probability of Success', *Journal of Money, Credit and Banking* 31, 4 (1999), 731–47; Owen F. Humpage, 'The United States as an Informed Foreign-Exchange Speculator', *Journal of International Financial Markets, Institutions and Money* 10, 3 (1 December 2000), 287–302; Bordo, Humpage and Schwartz, *Strained Relations*.

Table 4.2. *Intervention success*

| | Number of sales days | Exchange rate reversal the next day (SC1) | | Depreciation smoothing the next day (SC2) | | Reversal and smoothing (SC3) | |
|---|---|---|---|---|---|---|---|
| | Days | Days | Success rate | Days | Success rate | Days | Success rate |
| **Pre-convertibility** (1952–58) | 905 | 239 | 26% | 209 | 23% | 448 | 50% |
| **Post-convertibility** (1959–72) | 1,395 | 230 | 16% | 269 | 19% | 499 | 36% |
| **Overall** (1952–72) | 2,300 | 469 | 20% | 478 | 21% | 947 | 41% |

*Source:* Dealers' reports (C8).

*Note:* The methodology compares the movement of the exchange rate the day after an intervention. The percentages are success rates.

Table 4.3. *Bank of England intervention in the spot and forward markets, descriptive statistics*

| In $ million | Forward dollar sales | | Spot dollar sales | |
|---|---|---|---|---|
| | 1952–58 | 1959–72 | 1952–58 | 1959–72 |
| Mean | 1.5 | 33.6 | 3.8 | 31.6 |
| Median | 0.8 | 19.6 | 1.6 | 9.8 |
| Maximum | 22.4 | 211.4 | 54 | 1,229 |
| Minimum | 0.1 | 0.7 | 0.1 | 0.5 |
| Std. Dev. | 3.0 | 38.8 | 5.7 | 76.3 |
| Sum | 137 | 5,707 | 2,681 | 21,879 |
| Observations | 90 | 170 | 708 | 692 |

*Source*: Dealers' reports (C8).

market; after convertibility it was almost $22 billion. Despite intervening on only 170 days in the forward market after 1959, the Bank still managed to sell a total of nearly $6 billion. Table 4.3 does not show net interventions but only dollar sales, not purchases. On average, when the Bank was selling dollars in the market, the average spot sale was $3.8 before convertibility and $31.6 after convertibility, a ten-fold increase.

How large was Bank of England intervention compared to overall transaction volume in the sterling/dollar market? Data on market volume are hard to come by. To get a better idea, a telephone call report from the Federal Reserve archives gives a clue. The call mentions a market volume in New York of $47.6–64.4 million a day and $19.5 million in London.[37] It is unclear whether these days are typical or days with unusual trading volumes. But that would put the sterling/dollar trading volume at $67.1–83.9 million when combining New York and London volumes. Average spot operations were $3.8 million a day before 1959. This would put the average dollar sale by the Bank at around 5–6 per cent of the total market. The maximum sales of $54 million by the Bank during the whole period is around 64–80 per cent of the market size estimates. In other words, on a normal day the Bank was responsible for 5 per cent of the market. This is sizeable. During a crisis, the Bank had the power to deploy over three-quarters of the market turnover on a given day. Before convertibility, the Bank of England was a large player in the market.

---

[37] Telephone call, H. L. Sanford, 30 April 1954, New York, Archives of the Federal Reserve, box 617031.

Market size figures post-convertibility are not available, but it is likely that the influence of the Bank shrank. In 2016, as a comparison, the daily foreign exchange market volume for sterling was $649 billion and the total reserve of the UK government was $111 billion. This means that if the government spent all its reserves on one day in 2016, it would only reach 17 per cent of the market, as opposed to 80 per cent if it had spent only $54 million in the Bretton Woods period.[38] This is part of the explanation as to why the Bank of England avoids intervention today.

If the Bank was not always successful, what did make interventions successful? To reach a better understanding, I use a probit regression to differentiate which elements contribute to success. This methodology has also been used on modern data by Fratzscher et al. to derive the effect of intervention size and other variables to intervention success. In the regression, I test five variables that could explain intervention success. The variables are size of the intervention; exchange rate trend; exchange rate alignment with fundamentals; volatility of the exchange rate; and how far the exchange rate was from the Bretton Woods bands.

Before presenting the results of the analysis, what is the ex ante expectation? Larger interventions are expected to be more successful. Trend is also expected to be important. If the pound has been falling for ten days, making it appreciate would be more difficult. If it had been already appreciating for ten days, it would be easier to keep the trend going. Volatility can indicate stress on the currency; it is expected to make the dealers' task more difficult. Unsurprisingly, the closer to the lower band (Bretton Woods floor $2.78 or $2.38/sterling), the more difficult the intervention. Proximity to the lower band means a currency crisis can be expected, making investors more likely to sell sterling.

What about the alignment of the currency with its fundamental value? The hypothesis is that the more the exchange rate is misaligned vis-à-vis its fundamental value, the more difficult intervention is. For example, if poor balance of payments figures have just been published, the fundamental value of the currency is likely to go down. In this context, intervention would be less successful.

---

[38] Daily turnover for the pound today is 12.8 per cent of $5,067 billion or $649 billion (BIS, 'Triennial Central Bank Survey of Foreign Exchange and OTC Derivatives Markets in 2016'). The reserve data come from the Bank of England as the average for 2016 of the central government all foreign currency total reserve assets by instrument (in $ million) not seasonally adjusted, Reference PQMBAAR.

Fundamental value is difficult to pin down. Current literature focusing on floating rates uses three-year moving averages of the exchange rate. It is assumed that this indicates the currency's long-term fundamental value.[39] In the Bretton Woods context, moving averages performed poorly. They fail to show the fundamental value of sterling as the exchange rate is mean-reverting over three-year periods. A three-year moving average simply represents the average of the exchange rate during the Bretton Woods period. The average exchange rate from 1952 to 1967 is almost 2.80 (the official parity). It indicates that three-year moving averages probably offers no more than weak long-term trends in during Bretton Woods.[40]

While moving averages are a poor indicator of the fundamental value of a currency, the forward market offers a better proxy. Svensson argues that within exchange rate bands, the forward rate can indicate the credibility of the currency.[41] Remember, the Bank of England engaged less in this market. This makes it freer of outside influence. It offers an idea of the fundamental value of the currency, even if it is not perfect. In my regression, I use the difference between the spot and forward rates called the forward premium. This is our proxy for distance of the exchange rate from fundamental value. The probit equation is modelled as follows:

$$SC_t = \beta_0 + \beta_1 I_t + \beta_2 \left( S_t - S_t^{3FWD} \right) + \beta_3 TREND_t + \beta_4 VOLATILITY_{t-t10}$$
$$+ \beta_5 \Delta_{low} S_{t-1} + \varepsilon$$

where $SC_t$ is intervention success on day $t$, according to reversal (SC1), smoothing (SC2) and smoothing or reversal (SC3). $S_t - S_t^{3FWD}$ is the forward premium. $\beta_3 TREND_t$ is the ten-day trend, computed as a sum of the differences of ten-day exchange rates. $\beta_4 VOLATILITY_{t-t10}$ is the ten-day local volatility. $\beta_4 \Delta_{low} S_{t-1}$ is the gap between the exchange rate and the lower band (2.78 or 2.38).

The first striking feature in Table 4.4 is that intervention size has a negative effect on success for the reversal of the exchange rate. The larger the intervention the less likely it is to succeed in changing the direction of the exchange rate. This is probably due to a reverse causality issue. Bigger interventions are made during crises and are less likely to be successful.

---

[39] See, for example, Marcel Fratzscher et al., 'When Is Foreign Exchange Intervention Effective? Evidence from 33 Countries', *American Economic Journal: Macroeconomics*, 11, 1 (2019), 132–56. https://doi.org/10.1257/mac.20150317.

[40] The mean exchange rate is exactly 2.800219231 using daily data.

[41] Lars E. O. Svensson, 'Assessing Target Zone Credibility: Mean Reversion and Devaluation Expectations in the ERM, 1979–1992', *European Economic Review* 37, 4 (1 May 1993), 763–93.

Table 4.4. *Intervention success explained*

| | Dependent variable: Intervention success (1/0) – Probit regression | | |
| --- | --- | --- | --- |
| | (1) Reversal (SC1) | (2) Smoothing (SC2) | (3) Smoothing and/or reversal (SC3) |
| Intercept | 2.088 | –0.257 | 0.494 |
| | (1.09)* | (1.18) | (1.07) |
| Intervention size | –0.004 | 0.002 | –0.0007 |
| | (0.001)*** | (0.0009)* | (0.0009) |
| Spot with past two week's trend (1/0) | –0.028 | –0.903 | –0.575 |
| | (0.08) | (0.08)*** | (0.07)*** |
| Distance from fundamentals (forward premium/discount) | –30.423 | –9.916 | –36.698 |
| | (11.43)*** | (12.23) | (11.02)*** |
| Local volatility | –1.093 | –0.061 | –0.253 |
| | (0.39)*** | (0.42) | (0.38) |
| Distance from the Bretton Woods floor $\left(S_{floor}-S_{t-1}\right)$ | 3.806 | 4.406 | 1.436 |
| | (4.21) | (4.17) | (3.80) |
| *McFadden $R^2$* | 0.02 | 0.09 | 0.04 |
| *Observations* | 1,392 (1,106 failures/286 successes) | 1,392 (1,066 failures/326 successes) | 1,392 (890 failures/502 successes) |

*Note*: Standard errors are reported in parenthesis and are robust. A Huber/White correction has been applied. ***is statistical significance at the 1% level; **is statistical significance at the 5% level; *is statistical significance at the 10% level.

The biggest intervention in the sample occurred the day before the 1967 devaluation. At this point, intervention was unlikely to fool market participants. They were expecting and heavily gambling on a devaluation without the risk of a quick appreciation playing against them. Larger interventions, however, seemed to increase success when the Bank managed to smooth a depreciation. To relate that to the first point, greater interventions do not reverse exchange rates but might be able to smooth depreciation.

If the intervention is going against the trend of the previous weeks, or if it is taking place during a period of volatility, it is less likely to succeed. The distance from the lower band is not significant in any of the regressions.

The forward premium seems to make an impact. The direction of the impact is puzzling. First, it is worth noting that during most of the Bretton Woods period, there was a forward discount. This means that the forward rate was below the spot rate. Currency investors generally had a negative outlook on the British currency. The negative coefficient in the regressions seems to suggest that the lower the forward discount, the more likely interventions were to work. This could be due to higher discounts leading the Bank to intervene with larger amounts (and the data shows a correlation between lower discounts and higher intervention size). But the result remains somewhat surprising.

These results need to be read with caution. No clear trends emerge because of the frequency of interventions. The Bank was in the market on more than 80 per cent of the days. Several coefficients are not significant, a result that is in line with similar studies.[42]

### THE EXCHANGE EQUALISATION ACCOUNT

The Exchange Equalisation Account (EEA) is central to understanding for the Bank's foreign exchange interventions. It is the institutional link between the Bank of England and the Treasury. There is a limited amount of literature focused on the activities of the EEA. The following paragraphs review this literature and give a brief history of the EEA since its creation. I draw heavily on the work of Susan Howson, the first economic historian to explore its workings systematically.

The EEA was established in 1932 after Britain left the gold standard to manage the exchange rate. Its main purpose was to manage the floating pound from 1932 to 1939 after the sterling float of 1931.[43] The first operations of the EEA were meant to prevent rapid appreciation of the pound after the British economy recovered from the shock of leaving the gold standard.[44] The EEA was part of the Treasury, but the Bank of England was in charge of foreign market operations on its behalf. Figure 4.4 presents a schematic structure of the EEA. During the interwar years, the Treasury kept tight control over its operations. During the Bretton Woods period, the mandate of the Bank was simply to keep the exchange rate within the agreed IMF bands. This resulted in less involvement by the Treasury in its daily operations. As the Radcliffe Report put it, beyond its main mandate, the Bank had some room to manoeuvre when it

---

[42] Even with a much bigger sample, Fratzscher et al., 'When Is Foreign Exchange Intervention Effective?', have only few coefficients that explain intervention success.

[43] Susan Howson, *Sterling's Managed Float: The Operations of the Exchange Equalisation Account, 1932-39* (Princeton, NJ: International Finance Section, Department of Economics, Princeton University, 1980), 15.

[44] Leonard Waight, *The History and Mechanism of the Exchange Equalisation Account* (Cambridge: Cambridge University Press, 1939), 8.

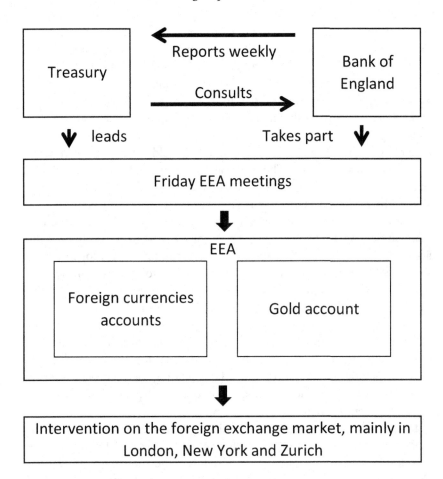

Figure 4.4. Schematic structure of the EEA
*Source*: Based on Howson, *Sterling's Managed Float* and the structure of the 'EEA ledgers', London, Bank of England archives 2A141/4 to 2A141/17.

came to daily exchange rate management. The Bank 'has discretion to operate' when the exchange rate was within the IMF limits and often intervened 'in order to prevent violent fluctuations of the rate'.[45]

The main role of the EEA was to buy or sell currencies on the foreign exchange market to manage exchange rates. Most operations were done by

[45] *Radcliffe Report*, para. 326.

the Bank in London. The New York Fed sometimes performed overnight operations in New York on behalf of the Bank. The EEA operated mainly in dollars and French francs until 1935. After that, it introduced Dutch florins, Swiss francs, Belgian francs, Swedish kronors, Norwegian kroners, Canadian dollars, Argentine pesos and Indian rupees.[46] During the Bretton Woods period, most of the interventions were in dollars. Rarer operations were in gold, French francs, Belgian francs, Deutschmarks and Canadian dollars. The EEA kept important reserves in gold. They were converted into dollars when needed. The goal was to ensure 'that exchange transactions within its territories do not differ by more than 1 per cent on either side of the parities declared to the [International Monetary] Fund'.[47]

The creation of the EEA was a result of the Bank's limited room to manoeuvre in its foreign exchange operations. As the Bank had to make its accounts public, it was decided to create a separate account for intervention. The EEA was able to act without having to disclose any reserve figures. This kept intervention activity hidden from the public.[48] The EEA was created as a loan from the Treasury to the Bank. Any unused funds from this loan would then be lent back to the Treasury in the form of Treasury bills.[49] This allowed for automatic sterilisation. In the interwar years sterilisation was not total but 'substantial', as Howson argues.[50] There were two limitations to sterilisation.[51] First, lending back excessive reserves to the Treasury was not automatic. Second, it depended on how the banking system reacted.

Imagine the Bank bought £10 million with the equivalent amount in dollars to defend the sterling exchange rate. These £10 million were withdrawn from the economy. This reduced the money in circulation. This could impact monetary conditions and interest rates. However, if the Bank then took these £10 million to buy Treasury bills, the money would have little effect on the amount of money in circulation or on

---

[46] Howson, *Sterling's Managed Float*, 36.
[47] *Radcliffe Report*, 111. This can also be found for example in Capie, *The Bank of England*, 59.
[48] Howson, *Sterling's Managed Float*, 7, for the details on how intervention could be deduced by the public.
[49] Treasury bills are short-term bills issued by the Treasury. They were either issued 'tap' or 'tender'. Tap bills are tendered constantly by certain government departments. Tender bills are tendered weekly for the best price. Waight, *The History and Mechanism*, 40.
[50] Howson, *Sterling's Managed Float*, 9–10.
[51] A detailed account of how an operation by the EEA would affect money supply can be found in Waight, *The History and Mechanism*, 40–3, and is summarised in Howson, *Sterling's Managed Float*, 9–10.

interest rates. This was built into the mechanism of the EEA as it was a loan from the Treasury, as we have seen. Without this purchase, the Bank would have simply written off the £10 million, thereby deflating the economy, not least because a significant amount of Treasury bills were issued 'on tap', or constantly, and not only periodically. Thanks to the initial loan, the EEA had an inherent sterilisation mechanism. According to the Radcliffe Report, the Bank only kept 'a working balance' in sterling and invested the rest 'entirely in "tap" Treasury Bills'.[52] Even if the purchase of Treasury bills was not simultaneous, it was close to perfect as tap Treasury bills were constantly available to the EEA.

The other channel for sterilisation has to do with the banking system and the provenance of the money inflow.[53] The Bank of England's *Quarterly Bulletin* explains the mechanism: 'An inflow of gold or foreign exchange added both to the cash reserves of the banks and to their deposits – enabling them to increase their domestic lending – unless offset by open market operations carried out by the authorities.'[54] A foreign gold or dollar inflow would potentially increase the money available. When the EEA acted as a counterpart of a foreign gold or dollar inflow, its operation would increase the reserves and deposits in British banks. Keeping a constant deposit ratio (around 10 per cent at the time), banks would be able to lend more after capital inflows from abroad.[55]

Take the example of a French investor wanting to buy sterling in London to avoid a possible French franc devaluation. Depending on the market for French francs in London, the EEA might have ended up buying these French francs. If the French investor kept this money in an account with a London bank, the EEA transaction would have the effect of increasing the British money base. To offset this inflow of capital for which the EEA had paid, it needed to undertake open market operations, selling Treasury bills on the money market.

Apart from the seminal contribution by Howson detailing the early years of the EEA, there are few studies on this topic, and most of these focus on the interwar years. In 1933, the economist Alzada Comstock described the EEA as 'Great Britain's little-known but successful

---

[52] *Radcliffe Report*, para. 325.
[53] Howson, *Sterling's Managed Float*; Waight, *The History and Mechanism*.
[54] Bank of England, 'The Exchange Equalisation Account: Its Origins and Development', *Bank of England Quarterly Bulletin*, December 1968, 379.
[55] This is explained in greater detail in Waight, *The History and Mechanism*.

experiment'.[56] Similar studies could be found at the time and highlighted the interest in this new tool. It was unknown to most economists and surrounded by secrecy. Noel Hall and Leonard Waight provide two early attempts to understand the EEA, but their approach is not based on archival data.[57] Howson presents the mechanisms behind the EEA and offers an interpretation of the EEA's actions based on the Treasury's archival records.[58] She examines how the exchange rate targets decided by the Treasury were implemented with EEA intervention. Between 1932 and 1939, the targets changed several times, from \$3.40/£ in 1932 to \$4.95/£ in 1936. This flexibility allowed the EEA and the Bank to amass substantial reserves. However, for the Bretton Woods period, the literature is limited to brief references to the EEA in histories of the Bank or of monetary policy.

American and French equivalents of the EEA have received more attention. Anna Schwartz presented a review of the Exchange Stabilisation Fund, and Bordo and co-authors offer an extensive review of US intervention.[59] Olivier Accominotti relies on data from the *Fond de Stabilisation des Changes* to justify the Bank of France's behaviour during the interwar period.[60] However, the EEA has not benefited from similar accounts in the literature. All three funds are similar in the fact that they belong to each country's treasury. The respective central banks were managing the funds. This included keeping detailed accounts of the funds.[61]

The EEA ledgers at the Bank of England record reserve data.[62] These daily ledgers have not been used in the prior literature in any detail.[63] They contain important information on the state of Britain's foreign exchange

---

[56] Alzada Comstock, 'The British Exchange Equalization Account', *American Economic Review* 23, 4 (1933), 608–21.

[57] Noel Frederick Hall, *The Exchange Equalisation Account* (London: Macmillan, 1935); Leonard Waight, *The History and Mechanism of the Exchange Equalisation Account* (Cambridge: Cambridge University Press, 1939).

[58] Howson, *Sterling's Managed Float*.

[59] Anna Jacobson Schwartz, *From Obscurity to Notoriety: A Biography of the Exchange Stabilization Fund* (Cambridge, MA: National Bureau of Economic Research, 1996); Bordo, Humpage and Schwartz, *Strained Relations*.

[60] Olivier Accominotti, 'The Sterling Trap: Foreign Reserves Management at the Bank of France, 1928–1936', *European Review of Economic History* 13, 3 (2009), 349–76.

[61] For open data on the Fond de Stabilisation des Changes and the EEA, see Alain Naef, 'Central Bank Reserves during the Bretton Woods Period: New Data from France, the UK and Switzerland' (SocArXiv, 18 January 2021), https://doi.org/10.31235/osf.io/he7gx; For more details on the US equivalent, see Bordo, Humpage and Schwartz, *Strained Relations*.

[62] 'Ledgers of the Exchange Equalisation Account, 1947–70', London, Archive of the Bank of England, 2A141/1–17.

[63] Capie presents some monthly and quarterly data on actual reserves, see Capie, *The Bank of England*, 389–93.

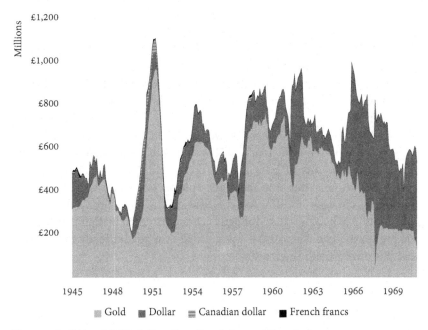

Figure 4.5. EEA gold, US dollar, Canadian dollar and French franc reserves
*Source*: 'General Ledger of the EEA', 1945–49 and 1949–52, London, Archives of the Bank of England, 2a141/6–2a141/17.

reserves at daily frequency. This information was unknown to contemporaries. It reveals manipulation of the reserves position or window dressing.[64] Daily data make it possible to track the extent of daily window dressing operations, as explained in Chapter 11.

As the Bank was executing orders on behalf of the Treasury, it kept ledgers on all EEA activity. The daily data span October 1939 to March 1971. Previous studies calculate reserve levels from proximate sources or use monthly or quarterly data.[65] They have not used EEA ledgers, which offer more accurate daily figures. Figure 4.5 offers a monthly overview of the EEA's largest holdings, namely gold, US dollars, Canadian dollars and French francs. Throughout the period, gold and US dollars were the account's main reserves.

---

[64] For more on window dressing and for open access reserve data, see Naef, 'Dirty Float or Clean Intervention?'; Naef, 'Central Bank Reserves during the Bretton Woods Period'.
[65] For example Bordo, MacDonald and Oliver, 'Sterling in Crisis'; Cairncross and Eichengreen, *Sterling in Decline*.

EEA reserves are a poor proxy of the Bank's foreign exchange operations. The EEA was used for more than just intervention. The Treasury
used it for all its foreign exchange needs. The Bank used it for customer
transactions. For example, say the Bank of Italy asked the Bank of England
to buy $100 million on its behalf to be stored at the Bank. Before or after
the transaction, the Bank of Italy would transfer dollars or sterling to the
EEA. Within the course of a few days, the EEA would proceed to execute
the $100 million gold purchase. It would spread the purchase over a few
days, to avoid moving the market. This means that such daily movements
in the EEA accounts of both the US dollar and gold would only reflect
customer business but not the intervention. John Fforde stresses that
estimating changes in EEA reserves was not a good proxy for market
intervention. He argues that 'foreign exchange ordered by Bank customers,
mainly central banks and HMG, was usually supplied directly by the EEA
and not put through the market'.[66]

---

[66] Fforde, *The Bank of England and Public Policy*, 416.

# 5

# The Reopening of the London Gold Market in 1954

## *Sealing the Fate of Sterling and the International System*

The London gold market was more than a local gold market. It played an important role in the international monetary system. In the 1960s, Charles Coombs, the vice president of the Federal Reserve Bank of New York, understood the issue. He wrote that the London gold market 'represented a time bomb resting at the very foundation of the Bretton Woods system'.[1] Here I examine how this bomb was set up. US policymakers allowed the London gold market to reopen without fully understanding what the consequences would be. The reopening established a direct link between sterling and gold. Thereafter, sterling crises could potentially turn into gold crises. This would threaten international monetary stability. In the 1950s, the United States still had substantial gold reserves and capital controls. In the 1950s, US confidence in its gold reserves was unshakable. The Fed therefore allowed the United Kingdom to open the gold market on the assumption that it was a minor issue. As discussed in Chapter 10, the London gold market would eventually play a central role in the demise of the Gold Pool and the creation of a two-tier gold market. This in turn contributed to the end of the Bretton Woods system.

The London gold market reopened on 22 March 1954. This was a major event in the unfolding of the Bretton Woods system. The market had closed at the outbreak of the war in 1939.[2] This hiatus 'deprived the international economy for fifteen years of one of its major institutions', the Bank of England wrote in a later memorandum.[3] The BIS celebrated an 'event which was not only of great potential significance but which also had

---

[1] Coombs, *The Arena of International Finance*, 68.    [2] Capie, *The Bank of England*, 158.
[3] Internal draft memorandum, September 1960, London, Archives of the Bank of England, C43/320, 1.

an immediate influence, since it coincided with steps taken by several countries to normalise their foreign exchange systems'.[4]

London was the central gold market during the Bretton Woods system. This important role was relatively new. Before the nineteenth century, the City was not at the centre of the gold trade. The leading global gold market moved from Genoa to Antwerp, then to Amsterdam before finally being established in London. Today London still offers the largest gold market. Despite London's leading role, when the London gold market was not functional other markets took over. These included Zurich, Paris and Hong Kong.

During the fifteenth century, African gold was sent to Genoa, Florence, Venice and Milan, where it was traded.[5] Florence fixed the price twice a day. This feature would be replicated in the London market.[6] Later, Antwerp, a central place of trade in the fifteenth and sixteenth centuries, hosted African gold sales. The Belgian city was an early global market for gold and other commodities.[7] This might not have formally been an integrated central global gold market yet, but it involved the trading of gold globally. In 1596 a default by the Spanish state led to a wave of bankruptcies in Antwerp, which at the time was exposed to Spanish loans.[8] This led to Antwerp's slow decline as a global financial centre and reopened the contest for leadership.

Amsterdam took a more prominent role as a financial centre in Europe in the seventeenth and early eighteenth centuries. It became the main market for silver and gold bullion. However, the Glorious Revolution of 1688 gave British finance a boost.[9] The shift of the leading gold market went through Moses Mocatta, a gold trader based in Amsterdam. Mocatta moved to London in 1671. At first gold was used as a way to pay for Mocatta's diamond business.[10] Progressively, gold increased in importance and the Mocattas started a subsidiary gold market in Amsterdam, which

---

[4]  BIS, Annual Report, 1954 (1 April 1953–31 March 1954), 14 June 1954 (Basel: BIS), 144.
[5]  Andrew M. Watson, 'Back to Gold and Silver', *Economic History Review* 20, 1 (1967), 19.
[6]  Timothy Green, *The World of Gold*, 2nd ed. (London: Rosendale Press, 1993), 16.
[7]  Peter Spufford, 'From Antwerp and Amsterdam to London: The Decline of Financial Centres in Europe', *De Economist (Netherlands Economic Review)* 154, 2 (1 June 2006), 152.
[8]  Ibid., 158.
[9]  There is an extensive literature on this topic starting with the seminal work by Douglass C. North and Barry R. Weingast, 'Constitutions and Commitment: The Evolution of Institutions Governing Public Choice in Seventeenth-Century England', *Journal of Economic History* 49, 4 (December 1989), 803–32.
[10] Green, *The World of Gold*, 17.

would progressively expand.[11] In 1799, the Mocatta firm was still under the family's control. It was now called Mocatta & Goldsmid, the name under which the firm operated during the Bretton Woods period.[12] Soon after the inauguration of the Bank of England in 1694, Abraham Mocatta, Moses' son, became the Bank's sole gold broker.[13]

In 1810, a select committee of the House of Commons surveyed the London gold market because of the 'High Price of Gold Bullion'.[14] With few participants, the market was subject to collusion. Mocatta & Goldsmid was the Bank's only broker until 1840.[15] Later in the century, other brokers were permitted to enter the market. During the mid-eighteenth century, the London and Amsterdam bullion markets were highly integrated, as demonstrated by Pilar Nogues-Marco.[16] However, London took precedence over Amsterdam. The Bank Charter Act 1844 gave the London market an advantage by providing a 'guaranteed market and a minimum purchase price for gold'.[17]

Gold became key in international transactions in the mid-nineteenth century and the Bank of England played a central role in the international monetary system. The rapid increase in countries joining the Gold Standard meant the metal was essential to public finance worldwide. London would at this point play a leading role as a global gold market, being 'the most liquid exchange for refined gold'.[18] Most newly minted gold was sold in London. The rules of the Gold Standard let gold flow freely in and out of the country. During this period, the Bank was the main dealer and acted with four others: Mocatta & Goldsmid, Sharps Wilkins, Pixley & Abell and Samuel Montagu & Co. Broker.[19] Most of these

---

[11] Spufford, 'From Antwerp and Amsterdam to London', 168.

[12] Paul H. Emden, 'The Brothers Goldsmid and the Financing of the Napoleonic Wars', *Transactions (Jewish Historical Society of England)* 14 (1935), 229.

[13] Green, *The World of Gold*, 17–18.

[14] Michele Blagg, 'Gold Refining in London', in *The Global Gold Market and the International Monetary System from the Late 19th Century to the Present: Actors, Networks, Power*, ed. Sandra Bott (Basingstoke: Palgrave Macmillan, 2013), 90.

[15] Green, *The World of Gold*, 18.

[16] Pilar Nogues-Marco, 'Competing Bimetallic Ratios: Amsterdam, London, and Bullion Arbitrage in Mid-Eighteenth Century', *Journal of Economic History* 73, 2 (June 2013), 446.

[17] Blagg, 'Gold Refining in London', 92.

[18] Stefano Ugolini, 'The Bank of England as the World Gold Market Maker during the Classical Gold Standard Era, 1889–1910', in *The Global Gold Market and the International Monetary System from the Late 19th Century to the Present: Actors, Networks, Power*, ed. Sandra Bott (Basingstoke: Palgrave Macmillan, 2013), 65.

[19] Ibid., 85.

participants remained until the Bretton Woods period. Rothschild took the place of the Bank of England as market-marker after the First World War. Also, Sharps Wilkins and Pixley & Abell merged and the metallurgical firm Johnson Matthey joined.

1919 marked the creation of the London Gold Fixing, which would survive with interruptions until 2014.[20] Fixing was the process of fixing the price of gold once a day. At the start of the Second World War the market was officially closed and would not reopen until 1954.

## BURGEONING COMPETITION

During the closure of the London market (1939–54) Zurich emerged as a competitor. Other so-called free markets emerged. They offered gold priced often in dollars, notably in Beirut, Bangkok, Cairo, Kuwait, Macao, Milan, Montevideo, Tangier and Hong Kong. The IMF disapproved of these markets as they suggested that the official dollar price of gold was not credible. The Fund feared that these markets could destabilise currencies.[21] In 1950, in a telephone call between the New York Federal Reserve and the Bank of England, Sir George Bolton estimated that the market in free gold was around $60 million a month ($585 million in 2017 dollars). This represented a turnover of around $2–3 million a day, mainly in Montevideo, Paris, Milan and Zurich. Bolton commented on different markets, noting that 'Beirut is just a tunnel in and out of the Middle East' and that 'Hong Kong is not a big factor'.[22] The Bank was aware of these free markets and was watching them closely in cooperation with the Fed. They drained international gold production and were a threat to the official gold price.

Coombs observed that these free markets were involved in private hoarding and did not cater to South African or Russian business.[23] Bott asserted that immediately after the war these markets offered substantial

---

[20] Anthony John Arnold, 'Business Returns from Gold Price Fixing and Bullion Trading on the Interwar London Market', *Business History* 58, 2 (17 February 2016), 283.

[21] Sandra Bott, 'South African Gold at the Heart of the Competition between the Zurich and London Gold Markets at a Time of Global Regulation, 1945–68', in *The Global Gold Market and the International Monetary System from the Late 19th Century to the Present: Actors, Networks, Power*, ed. Sandra Bott (Basingstoke Palgrave Macmillan, 2013), 111; Coombs, *The Arena of International Finance*, 43.

[22] Telephone call from Sir George Bolton from the Bank of England, telephone memorandum, L. W. Knoke, 8 December 1950, New York, Archives of the Federal Reserve, box 617031.

[23] Coombs, *The Arena of International Finance*, 43.

premia on the official gold price. In 1947, Bott reported prices reaching the equivalent of $80 an ounce. This led to arbitrage, as purchases 'were made in New York and Mexico, where the price was around US$43 per ounce. It was then resold in India for pounds sterling at a price equivalent to around US$80'.[24] The BIS calculated that, from 1946 to 1953, out of a global production of $6,600 million, one-third was privately hoarded.[25] This put pressure on central banks. It could hinder global growth as it limited the amount of fiat currency that central banks, mainly the Fed, could issue. Remember that gold was backing the dollar.

Paris was another contender for hosting a global gold market. The city had a financial centre and the French government had ambitions to be at the centre of the international monetary system. But gold trading in Paris never managed to compete effectively with Zurich or London. The Paris market remained a national retail market. It opened on 13 February 1948, against the wishes of the IMF.[26] Foreigners were still forbidden from trading in this market until January 1967, but it reopened to foreigners because of French ambitions to make Paris a larger international player.[27] The 1967 opening of the market to foreigners did not increase gold sales. Rather, the market shrank from FF8.5 million average daily transactions in January 1967 almost halving to FF5.4 million in February and FF4 million in April.[28]

The London market offered tighter spreads than Paris. As price depends on volume, it was difficult for Paris to catch up unless it increased its volume, which they it do only with better prices. The Fed put it simply: '[T]he low spread maintained by London bullion brokers between their buying and selling prices for gold makes London an attractive market for both buyers and sellers.'[29] Before the Second World War, London had a monopoly on South African gold sales, which increased transaction volumes.[30] After 1945, Zurich started to compete with the City for South

---

[24] Bott, 'South African Gold', 113.

[25] BIS, Annual Report, 1954 (1 April 1953–31 March 1954), 14 June 1954 (Basel: BIS), 153.

[26] Thi Hong Van Hoang, 'The Gold Market at the Paris Stock Exchange: A Risk–Return Analysis 1950–2003/Der Goldmarkt an Der Pariser Börse: Eine Rendite-Risiko-Analyse 1950–2003', *Historical Social Research/Historische Sozialforschung* 35, 3 (133) (2010), 389.

[27] Ibid., 390–1.

[28] French BIS Gold Expert meeting minutes, '30ème réunion des experts de l'Or et des Changes', 8 May 1967, Archives of the Bank of France, 467200501-74, 3.

[29] Alan Holmes, Research Memorandum on the Reopening of the London Gold Market (Foreign Research Division), 8 April 1954, New York, Archives of the Federal Reserve, 9.

[30] Bott, 'South African Gold', 109.

African business but only seriously challenged London after the market temporarily closed in 1968.

## THE GOLD MARKET REOPENING

The reopening of the gold market created a direct link between sterling and the London gold market. This link would eventually put stress on the international monetary system. Any shock to the sterling/dollar market could influence the gold price via the London gold market. The gold price was the barometer of the Bretton Woods system.[31] Having the market in London created a transmission channel via sterling. Harvey defines the London gold market as a 'status market'. She argues that beyond its market function, it was a global indicator of the price of gold.[32] Capie finds that the London gold price reflected 'international sentiment on the dollar and so affected other currencies'.[33] Central banks did not engage in arbitrage but, as Eichengreen has established, if the price increased to more than $35 an ounce, it created an opportunity. Central banks could buy cheaper gold at the federal window and sell it for more in the London market.[34] This would arbitrage the price in London down but deplete US gold reserves in the process.

When the Bretton Woods system was set up, private ownership of gold was forbidden in the United States and Britain. The Bretton Woods articles of agreements did not mention private gold markets, suggesting they did not foresee that these would become an issue. Coombs wrote: 'From the very beginning therefore, the official United States price of gold was vulnerable to speculative challenge by the private gold markets functioning abroad.'[35] Before the London market opened, some South African gold was sold directly in South Africa. The South African gold market was open to dealers from across the world, not only British.[36] Channelling all gold

---

[31] Bank of England, 'The London Gold Market', *Bank of England Quarterly Bulletin*, March 1964, 16–21; Bordo, Humpage and Schwartz, *Strained Relations*, 177.

[32] Rachel Harvey, 'Market Status/Status Markets: The London Gold Fixing in the Bretton Woods Era', in *The Global Gold Market and the International Monetary System from the Late 19th Century to the Present: Actors, Networks, Power*, ed. Sandra Bott (Basingstoke: Palgrave Macmillan, 2013).

[33] Capie, *The Bank of England*, 158.

[34] Barry Eichengreen, *Global Imbalances and the Lessons of Bretton Woods* (Cambridge, MA: MIT, 2007), 44.

[35] Coombs, *The Arena of International Finance*, 43.

[36] 'Procès-verbal du Conseil Général', 25 March 1954, Paris, Archives of the Bank of France, vol. 145.

through London created an official price for gold, which investors could locate in the financial press. What was the political process that led to the opening of this market and why did the Federal Reserve not stop this potentially harmful market from opening?

The London gold market opened as a result of a power play between the United States, the IMF, the United Kingdom and South Africa. US officials were constrained by their commitment to buy gold at $35 an ounce at the gold window, the IMF saw gold markets as destabilising, the United Kingdom wanted to increase the international role of both London and sterling, while South Africa wanted to sell gold at a fair price. Surprisingly, the United States displayed only limited interest in all this.

In 1947, the IMF worried that newly minted gold would escape the control of monetary authorities. It issued a statement to encourage members to 'take effective action to prevent external transactions in gold at premium prices'.[37] Sales at premium prices would disrupt exchange stability, the IMF believed. Its remarks were aimed at South Africa, which was trying to sell its gold at the best price. In 1947, the Bank of England had allowed a few licensed bullion dealers to trade gold as long as the premia on the official market did not exceed 1 per cent.[38] Following a request from the IMF, the British government withdrew this authorisation and refrained from developing a gold market in London.

British restraint was short-lived, as the French soon asked the IMF for a private gold market in Paris. It reluctantly agreed. The French were at odds with the IMF after trying to introduce a dual exchange rate system in 1948. They ended up leaving the Fund from 1948 to 1954 to fight what they thought were 'Anglo-American abuses *in the name* of Bretton Woods'.[39] France having its own gold market meant that the IMF could no longer oppose a similar market opening in London.

South Africa also challenged the IMF. The country started selling gold directly to manufacturing and artistic markets at a premium. In 1949, the *Wall Street Journal* announced that South Africa managed 'to sell 620,000 ounces of pure gold abroad at $38.52 an ounce'.[40] This represented about 5 per cent of the country's annual production. The price was '$3.52 over

[37] IMF, quoted in Coombs, *The Arena of International Finance*, 43.  [38] Ibid., 43–4.

[39] Eric Monnet, 'French Monetary Policy and the Bretton Woods System: Criticisms, Proposals and Conflicts', in *Global Perspective on the Conference and the Post-War World Order*, ed. Gilles Scott-Smith and Simon Rofe (Basingstoke: Palgrave Macmillan, 2017), 5.

[40] 'South African mines to sell gold abroad at $38.52 an ounce', press report, 28 June 1949, Washington, DC, Archives of the International Monetary Fund, PREP/49/183, 291273.

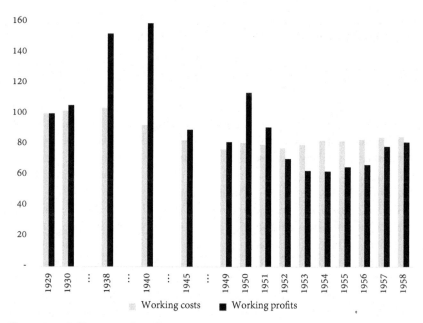

Figure 5.1. Gold costs and profits

*Source*: Productivity figures show all available data from BIS annual reports (1951, 1954, 1957 and 1958). The chart is deflated with inflation figures from Thomas Ryland, Sally Hills and Nicholas Dimsdale, 'The UK Recession in Context – What Do Three Centuries of Data Tell Us?', *Bank of England Quarterly Bulletin* 50, 4 (2010): 277–91.

*Note*: Index and inflation adjustment: author's calculation.

the $35 an ounce price set by the U.S. and the International Monetary Fund'. While visiting South Africa, a delegation from the IMF noted how South Africa 'used the argument that it is unreasonable for gold to remain at its present price while the price of all other commodities is greatly increased'.[41]

Adjusting for inflation, profits from South African mines fell consistently. This put pressure on production and left large amounts of low-grade ore unworked. The BIS closely monitored South African productivity and profitability in its annual reports. Figure 5.1 illustrates costs and profits per tonne in South Africa from 1929 to 1958. The gaps in the chart are for the years the BIS did not collect data. The index compares prices with 1929, which is set at 100. Despite reducing costs by over 20 per cent in real terms

---

[41] 'Discussion with South Africa – Gold Transactions and Balance of Payments, Memo from the Secretary to the Members of the Executive board, 4 April 1949, Washington, DC, Archives of the International Monetary Fund, EBS/49/56, 292237.

after the war, profits never reached pre-war levels. During the 1950s, profits were almost 40 per cent lower than in 1929. The nominal anchor of the gold price at $35 an ounce was a problem for South African producers.

In the 1950s, the United States controlled 64 per cent of the global gold reserves. US policymakers did not see the opening of the London gold market as a priority.[42] Allowing the market to open meant there would be two gold prices: A market price of gold in London and the official gold window price. Coombs revealed that despite seeing the risks, 'in Washington the official mood was not to worry unduly over such distant problems'.[43] The US gold reserves at the time were high enough for this not to be a pressing issue. US policymakers were confident that their reserves were large enough to weather any crisis. Evidence of this confidence is found in a telephone conversation transcript between Bolton and Knoke. Knoke said: 'We still have $23 billion in gold bars and even if present selling continues I see no danger of our [reserves] falling to a level where we might be scared.'[44] The 1960s would prove him wrong.

The United States did not see the gold market as an issue. It was 'far too early to say much about these problems, many of which may be purely academic since they deal with eventualities in a rather uncertain future'.[45] The United States did not think that it could lose large amounts of gold reserves on this market. The explanation for this nonchalant attitude was two-fold. Reserves were high enough. Also, the Federal Reserve was highly sceptical of theories advanced by academics, mainly Triffin. Triffin argued that international liquidity would become a problem in the future. He had been arguing, from 1947 onwards, that a system based on gold would eventually run out of gold for central banks to use as reserves. This in turn would slow economic growth. The Fed was critical of Triffin. Other academics, such as Despres et al., believed that the system could survive with smaller US gold reserves as long as there was sufficient trust in the dollar.[46] This is how the system works today, with the dollar as an international reserve currency despite having little gold backing. In 1954,

---

[42] Coombs, *The Arena of International Finance*, 44.    [43] Ibid., 45–6.

[44] Telephone call from Sir George Bolton of the Bank of England, telephone memorandum, L. W. Knoke, 8 December 1950, New York, Archives of the Federal Reserve, box 617031.

[45] Alan Holmes, Research Memorandum on the Reopening of the London Gold Market (Foreign Research Division), 8 April 1954, New York, Archives of the Federal Reserve, 9.

[46] Emile Despres, Charles Poor Kindleberger and Walter S. Salant, *The Dollar and World Liquidity: A Minority View* (Washington, DC: Brookings Institution, 1966).

this debate was still in its infancy and the Fed did not start to worry about it until the late 1950s.

Russian gold sales in 1953 eased the price in offshore markets. The United States started to see 'certain advantages in a free gold market, where South African and Russian supplies might well tend to outrun industrial and hoarding demand'.[47] Such a market could not be in New York if it were to accommodate Russian sales during the Cold War. When it came to the international monetary system, Russia and the United States had aligned interests. The Fed saw the opening of the market as an opportunity to improve global supply. Prior to the opening of the London market, the Bank of England had been dealing directly with the Russians for gold purchases.[48]

The United Kingdom wanted to increase its standing in global finance. The Treasury issued a press release stating that before the war, 'London was the premier centre of the world for dealings in gold'.[49] The reopening was meant to give 'growing opportunities for traders, merchants and bankers, so that they may make the fullest contribution towards the increased overseas earnings'.[50] Schenk argues that the Bank of England hoped to restore 'the status of the City of London and of sterling' by reopening the gold market.[51] The sterling area, and mainly South Africa, was producing 'about 60 per cent of world gold output outside the USSR'.[52] London's position at the centre of the sterling area made it 'a natural market for gold'.[53] The Fed for its part thought that this market would help London. It would be the 'reestablishment of London as the center of the world gold trade and fuller use of the technical skills of its gold and foreign exchange dealers'.[54] The Fed was more than happy to let the market open and did not foresee any associated problems.

---

[47] Coombs, *The Arena of International Finance*, 45.
[48] The governor 'referred to the proposed purchase of Russian Gold which he had already mentioned to the Committee, and said that firm arrangements had now been made to buy gold for the E.E.Account to the approximate value of £20 million. (Mention made informally on the 18th and 25th November 1953)', informal minutes of the Committee of the Treasury, quoted in the Extracts from Minutes of the Committee of the Treasury, London, Bank of England archives, reference G14/133.
[49] Press release from the Press Office of H.M. Treasury, concerning the reopening of the London Gold Market for the First Time since the Outbreak of the Second World War, 19 March 1954, London, Bank of England Archives, C43/159. Transcript available at www.gold.org/sites/default/files/documents/after-the-gold-standard/1954mar19.pdf.
[50] Ibid.    [51] Schenk, *The Decline of Sterling*, 111.
[52] Alan Holmes, Research Memorandum on the Reopening of the London Gold Market (Foreign Research Division), 8 April 1954, New York, Archives of the Federal Reserve, 8.
[53] Ibid., 8.    [54] Ibid., 2.

The London gold market opened as a result of South Africa's willingness to sell gold and Britain's interest in re-establishing the City as a leading trading centre. The IMF was opposed to opening the market, but US policymakers and Federal Reserve officials did not see it as an immediate threat. This was thanks to a favourable economic outlook in the United States and substantial gold reserves. With no opposition, the market reopened. It became the barometer for the health of the Bretton Woods system.[55] Later, it led to the creation of the Gold Pool in the early 1960s (see Chapter 7).

## BEHIND CLOSED DOORS

The gold market was consolidated around five main players in London. They processed all orders. It gave the Bank of England privileged access to the world's most important gold market. Here I use new archives to explain the details of the functioning of the London gold market. This is important in order to understand what role the Bank played before the market became the focal point of the crisis in the international monetary system in 1961 (Chapter 7). The gold market was vital for international finance, but setting the gold price only involved a handful of individuals behind closed doors.

The gold market was an over-the-counter (OTC) market, which meant it did not have a physical location during the day, except for the fixing. It operated throughout the whole day but the biggest volume usually went through at the fixing. The fixing started each day at around 10.30 am in the offices of N. M. Rothschild & Sons and a price was generally set at 11 am. Rothschild chaired and hosted these meetings.[56] The process was as follows: The five dealers were all in communication with their respective trading rooms. First, the chairman would 'suggest a price, in terms of shillings and pence down to a farthing; this price will be chosen at the level where it is thought that buyers and sellers are likely to be prepared to do business'. The price was then moved until 'there are both buyers and sellers in evidence'.[57] When buyers and sellers had agreed on a price, this became the fixing price.

The market was composed of two merchant banks – Samuel Montagu & Co. and Rothschild – two gold brokers – Sharp Pixley & Co. and Mocatta and Goldsmid – and a metallurgical firm – Johnson Matthey. Demand

---

[55] Bank of England, 'The London Gold Market'; Harvey, 'Market Status/Status Markets'.
[56] Bank of England, 'The London Gold Market'.     [57] Ibid.

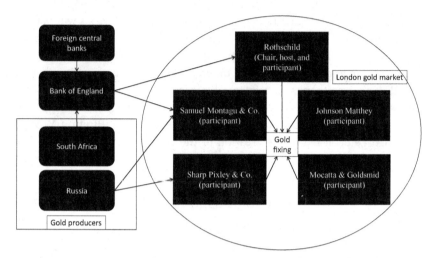

Figure 5.2. Schematic representation of the London gold market

*Source*: Bank of England, 'The London Gold Market', *Bank of England Quarterly Bulletin*, 1964, 16–21 and Bank of England dealers' reports.

*Note*: For readability, not all possible arrows are present. For example, foreign central banks were able to deal directly with market-participating investment banks. Russia probably also dealt with Rothschilds and other dealers.

came from central banks, industry and the arts, and hoarding. Supply was from new production, central bank sales, Russian sales and disposing of hoarding.[58]

Figure 5.2 is a schematic representation of the market. Access to the market was only possible through one of the five main dealers. The Bank of England often played the role of agent for official third parties and was South Africa's main dealer. Dealing with the Bank gave an informational advantage to customers. The Bank's dealers processed most of the South African supply and were active in the market all day so they knew when to sell and how to avoid oversupply. Unsold gold was often absorbed into the reserves of the Exchange Equalisation Account at market price. This was an advantage as it did not move the market price and was a direct transaction between the Bank and South Africa.

Rothschilds hosted the fixing and had the biggest market share. It also acted as an agent for the Bank. In May 1936, the governor suggested installing a direct line with the dealing room at Rothschilds. He was adamant to stress that it was not an endorsement. He wrote: '[A] private

[58] Ibid., 18.

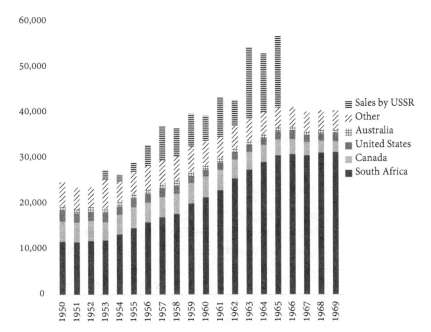

Figure 5.3. World gold production estimates by the BIS
*Source*: BIS annual reports, various years.

line be installed with Messrs. Rothschilds Bullion Room in view of the fact that the gold fixing takes place on their premises: this would in no way imply that Messrs. Rothschilds were regarded as being in a privileged position vis-à-vis the bank.'[59] In September 1938, the Bank decided that outside of fixing dealings, it should 'no longer deal exclusively with Rothschilds'. The Bank would also deal with Mocatta & Goldsmid. This was not due to 'dissatisfaction with the services most efficiently rendered by Rothschilds'.[60] It was in the interest of efficiency and competition. The Bank tried to maintain the appearance of a competitive market when Rothschilds was in a leading position.

If market demand came from the five main participants at the fixing, where did the supply of gold in the market come from? Figure 5.3 presents an estimate of world gold supply, combining new production and Russian sales. Data are from the BIS archive. Gold supply shows an upward trend

---

[59] Extracts from Minutes of the Committee of Treasury, 13 May 1936, London, Bank of England Archives, G14/133.

[60] Extracts from Minutes of the Committee of Treasury, 7 September 1938, London, Bank of England Archives, G14/133.

until 1965, when Russian sales ceased and South African production stopped increasing. Russian sales were dependent on the country's agricultural performance. When the country did not produce enough food (mainly wheat) to feed its population, it would sell gold to buy supplies from abroad. South African production depended on the price of gold. As the gold price never increased during the period, mining of lower ore tended to diminish. Equally, there were some productivity gains leading to more production. After 1965, South African production stagnated.

## BANK OF ENGLAND OPERATIONS

The Bank of England was responsible for the London gold market. Capie argues that after opening the gold market, the Bank of England intervened 'to steady prices and to keep orderly markets'.[61] It was about 'housekeeping', just as the Bank was doing in other London markets. Here I analyse the operations of the Bank of England in the gold market before the creation of the Gold Pool. Despite not having any formal or informal mandate from the Fed, the Bank was defending gold–dollar parity at its own expense.

What was a typical day like for the gold dealers at the Bank of England? What follows is the dealers' daily report for 15 March 1956, a typical day. The report read: 'Gold was fixed ½ d. lower at 249s.4.½d. at which price we sold 20 South African bars to the market and took 160 for H.M.T. The international price was marginally firmer at $34.96 ½. Against dollars we bought 240 bars from Montagus (= the Russians) and sold 120 to the Italians.'[62]

What does this mean in plain English? On that day, the Bank sold twenty bars of South African gold at a market price of 249 shillings 4½ pence an ounce of gold.[63] That amount is equivalent to $34.916, below the official Bretton Woods price. It bought 160 bars for the Treasury (or H.M.T.). This gold was for the reserves of the Exchange Equalisation Account. Remember that the account belonged to the Treasury but was the United Kingdom's reserve account. Still, on that day, the Bank acted as an agent for the Italians, who wanted 120 gold bars. This was part of their

---

[61] Capie, The Bank of England, 158.
[62] 'Dealers' report', 15 March 1956, London, Bank of England Archives, C8.
[63] The old accounting system was divided into pounds (£), shillings (s) and pence (d). The amount here is equivalent to £12.47 in modern notation.

customer business, where they acted as an agent. The bank also bought gold from Samuel Montagu & Co. Montagu was one of the five key market players. On this occasion, Montagu sold gold on behalf of Russia. This was one of the key functions of the gold market. It allowed Russian gold to relieve price pressure on gold in London. The Russians would always supply gold, never buy it.

The main quote for the gold price was always in sterling, but all market participants were aware of the equivalent dollar price. At $34.96½ on the quote analysed earlier, the price was lower than the gold window price of $35 an ounce. This explains why the Bank of England offered only twenty gold bars from South Africa to the market. It took all the rest for its customers and for the EEA. If the price of gold were higher, it would have sold all the gold to the market to meet the demand. The Bank was managing the price of gold to stay around the Bretton Woods official price at the gold window at $35 an ounce.

This lower price on that day was detrimental for South Africa, which wanted to maximise profit, but beneficial for the Treasury, which was able to buy gold cheaply. In a letter to the Federal Reserve, the Bank explained this selling process. The South African Reserve Bank would 'ship gold regularly to London and give us, as their agents, an order each week to dispose of a specified amount of the gold we hold for them'. Marketing of gold was the Bank's role. It managed 'both the timing of the sales and whether the gold is offered in the market or sold to other purchasers'.[64] The Bank decided whether to offer it to other central banks of the counter or to sell it to the market. It almost acted as a market maker.

Figure 5.4 summarises Bank of England operations in the gold market using data from internal daily dealers' reports. The data are presented for the first time here. The Bank classified dealings as 'customer' operations (shown here in grey) or 'market' operations (in black). The distinction was internal for the Bank. To market participants, all operations looked the same. After 1957, however, the Bank stopped distinguishing between the two and reported all operations in aggregated figures (also in black). In 1956, the Bank was still treating operations for South Africa and the Treasury/EEA as customer operations before aggregating them in March 1957. This was arguably a shift in the way the Bank understood its mission. It changed from that of a simple agent to a more holistic role. It was ensuring that the price was where the Bank wanted it to be: somewhere

---

[64] Letter from Sir George Bolton to Werner Knoke, 31 May 1954, London, Archives of the Bank of England, C43/319.

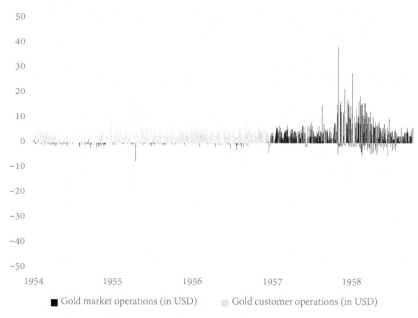

Figure 5.4. Market and customer gold transactions by the Bank of England, 1954–59
*Source*: Dealers' reports (C8).


between $35.08 and $35.20 an ounce. This role would be enhanced with the introduction of the Gold Pool. At that point, this became the official mission of the Bank of England.

The official Bretton Woods gold price was $35 an ounce. This is the price at which the Fed sold gold at the Fed window. There was a tax imposed by the US Treasury of 0.25 per cent. Adding the tax made the official price $35.0875. At this price, the gold would be delivered in New York. If investors then wanted to insure and transport the gold from New York to London, there were additional costs. Taking into account insurance and transport costs between London and New York, the price of gold in London from the Fed window was $35.20 an ounce. Above this price central banks could make an arbitrage profit. They could buy gold in New York and sell it in London. The Bank of England wanted to keep the price below $35.20 an ounce to avoid central banks speculating against the Fed. With a price of say $35.21, a central bank could buy gold at $35.0875 at the Fed and sell it on the London market, covering transport costs and making $0.01 profit an ounce. Even if central banks were unlikely to engage in arbitrage against the United States, the possibility of arbitrage sent a bad signal to market participants. It would cast doubt on the ability of the

Table 5.1. *Price preferences of the various market actors*

| Third party | Role of the Bank on behalf of the third party | Price preference of the third party |
|---|---|---|
| South African government | Gold selling agent | As high as possible |
| European central banks as buyers | Gold buying agent | As low as possible |
| European governments as Bretton Woods participants | No official role until the creation of the Gold Pool | Stable and lower than $35.20 per ounce |
| US government | No official role until the creation of the Gold Pool but implicitly guarantor of the price below $35.20 | Stable and lower than $35.20 per ounce |
| Treasury through the Exchange Equalisation Account as gold buyer | Gold-buying agent | As low as possible |
| Treasury through the Exchange Equalisation Account as currency policy setter | Ad hoc | Ad hoc |
| Bank of England as market housekeeper | Housekeeper/market intervener | Stable and lower than $35.20 per ounce |

*Source*: Author's judgement based on various archives.

United States to maintain gold parity. In the long run, this would threaten the credibility of Bretton Woods.

As we have seen, the Bank had many hats: Sometimes agent for the Italians, at other times helping the Treasury build reserves. The Bank marketed South African gold. It even took responsibility for the global gold price. The complex position of the Bank is summarised in Table 5.1. The table shows the Bank's preference for the gold price, depending on which hat it wore. The Bank had an incentive to keep the price from dropping in order not to lose South African business. But it also had an incentive not to let the price soar to keep the international monetary system from breaking down.

Only South Africa had an incentive to maintain a high gold price. It provided most of the world's gold supply and could threaten to sell its gold elsewhere. The Bank had to manage the conflicting interest of South Africa against its other customers. Russia and other producers shared South Africa's interest in a high price. They had the disadvantage not to deal

Table 5.2. *Bank of England gold operations in $ million*

| Unit: £ million., both sales and purchases are positive numbers | 1954–59 all operations | | 1961–68 all operations (Gold Pool) | |
|---|---|---|---|---|
| | Gold purchases | Gold sales | Gold purchases | Gold sales |
| Average | 4.2 | 1.8 | 2.4 | 5 |
| Median | 3.9 | 1.4 | 2.1 | 2.1 |
| Std. Dev. | 3.1 | 2.6 | 2.9 | 12.7 |
| Sum of sales/purchases | 3,734.3 | 206 | 1,994.3 | 3087 |
| Observations (number of days) | 883 | 117 | 827 | 619 |

*Source*: Bank of England dealers' reports (C8).
*Note*: Sales and purchases are presented as positive numbers.

with the Bank of England directly. In the context of the Cold War, Russia had little diplomatic clout. It was obliged to participate passively in this market. Its transactions were done through private dealers, as we have seen.

Table 5.2 categorises sales and purchase operations separately for two distinct periods: pre-convertibility and the Gold Pool period. Purchases are operations that increase the Bank's net gold position or transactions on behalf of customers. Sales are when the Bank sells gold against sterling or dollars. Apart from a handful of operations, most sales operations were on the Bank's own account and not for customers. Sales should mitigate market pressure by reducing the gold price.

Before 1959 convertibility, 88 per cent of the Bank's operations were net gold purchases. The Bank was not worried about an increase in the price and could buy gold on most days.[65] If buying was too strong, the price would rise and, therefore, the Bank joining buyers is a sign that the price was under control. After convertibility, purchases represented only 57 per cent of operations. Convertibility forced the Bank to sell larger amounts of gold on the market. Operations rose from $1.8 to $5 million a day on average. At the same time, the average purchase the Bank was able to make on a given day was almost halved. This meant that market conditions after convertibility were worse. The Bank was forced to sell more gold and was able to buy less. Before convertibility, the Bank spent just $206 million to defend the gold price in London from 1954 to 1959.

[65] The Bank purchased gold on 883 days and sold it on 117 days. 883/(117 + 883) = 0.883, or 88%.

After convertibility, the Gold Pool was forced to sell fourteen times more (just over $3 billion) from 1961 to 1968. This explains why it was no longer willing to manage the London gold price by itself but asked for US assistance. This led to the creation of the Gold Pool, the subject of Chapter 7.

London had been the leading global gold market since the mid-nineteenth century. British authorities had a strong desire to reopen this market after the Second World War. The context of Bretton Woods meant that the market was to play a central role in determining the credibility of the dollar peg to gold. It was going to be a barometer for the entire Bretton Woods system. If the dollar price of gold in London increased, it highlighted that the official gold dollar parity at the gold window was not credible. London became important for the international monetary system. It was the main international gold market, while US citizens were prevented from owning gold under the terms of the Gold Reserve Act 1934. As shown, US policymakers did not fully grasp the potential consequences of the reopening of the gold market. The IMF, on the other hand, did see it as a threat to the stability of the international monetary system. Bank of England market operations in the gold market until 1959 mainly involved purchases. There was little upward pressure on the price of gold. Convertibility and freer capital flows thereafter drastically increased pressure on the London gold market. In the early 1960s, market forces would prove too strong for the Bank of England to manage alone. It led to the creation of the Gold Pool, as we will see in Chapter 7. The first crisis came in October 1960 with the US presidential election and John F. Kennedy's pledge to 'get America moving again'. This was viewed as an 'inflationary policy that might force the United States to devalue its currency'.[66]

---

[66] Bordo, 'Bretton Woods', 69.

6

# 1958 Convertibility and Its Consequences

With convertibility, the Bretton Woods system was finally able to operate as intended. The 'real' Bretton Woods put to the test the ideas elaborated in 1944 at the Mount Washington Hotel, Bretton Woods. Theory was meeting practice. Convertibility was a seamless process. It did not trigger a crisis, but changed the structure of the whole international system. Convertibility put an end to parallel markets. It made arbitrage unnecessary and removed the different types of sterling presented in Chapter 2. Transferable sterling became redundant and was merged with official sterling. Swiss markets no longer offered opportunities for profitable arbitrage. Here, I analyse the direct effect of convertibility on the currency market. Using new data, I show how this important institutional change had little effect on the day-to-day functioning of the currency market. However, it did change how governments would manage their economies.

The trilemma of international finance forced policymakers to choose two of the following three policies: free capital flows; a fixed exchange rate; and monetary policy independence. Before convertibility, the United Kingdom had relative control of capital flows and fixed exchange rates. The government could set its monetary policy somewhat independently. Convertibility brought freer capital flows. The United Kingdom now had to choose between leaving the Bretton Woods fixed exchange rate system or relinquishing the right to set its own monetary policy.[1] They wanted neither. Leaving the Bretton Woods system and floating was only briefly considered in the ROBOT and collective approach schemes. These never saw the light of day. Prime Minister Harold Wilson (1964–70) explained what fixed exchange rates and free capital flows meant for the government.

---

[1] Many controls on capital flows remained, most of which survived until the 1980s. The trilemma simplifies reality.

He wrote that 'every action we took had to be considered against a background of the confidence factor, particularly against our assessment of what speculators might do'.[2] Wilson's speculators were overseas sterling holders pondering whether to sell their sterling before a possible devaluation. Convertibility put pressure on UK policymakers and reduced their freedom of action.

## WHAT IS CONVERTIBILITY?

After restrictions from the war years were lifted, the Exchange Control Act formalised capital controls. The Act divided the world into four sterling regions, as we have seen. Many of the controls introduced in 1947 were lifted in 1958. The relevance of the different sterling regions diminished. The world would be divided only into the sterling area (the United Kingdom and its former colonies) and the non-sterling area (the rest of the world). Investors from Europe, the United States and many other non-sterling area countries could now freely move sterling in and out of the sterling area. Residents of the sterling area were not allowed to convert sterling into dollars or any other currency.

The timing of introducing convertibility was difficult. The United Kingdom had to coordinate the move with a French devaluation. Convertibility was finally agreed at the end of 1958.[3] The French devaluation was carried through on 26 December 1958. The United Kingdom was free to follow suit by unifying transferable and official sterling. Non-resident sterling was now transferable anywhere. There would no longer be two prices for sterling: one in London, the other in other trading places such as Zurich and New York. On Saturday, 27 December 1958, the UK Treasury issued the following statement: 'From 9 a.m. on Monday, December 29th, sterling held or acquired by non-residents of the sterling area will be freely transferable throughout the world. As a consequence, all non-resident sterling will be convertible into dollars at the official rate of exchange.'[4] Non-residents of the sterling area were now allowed to transfer sterling, say from New York to London. Sterling area residents were still not allowed to convert their sterling abroad without a valid reason

---

[2] Harold Wilson, *Labour Government, 1964–70: A Personal Record* (London: Michael Joseph, 1971), 32–3.

[3] Fforde, *The Bank of England*, 566–606.

[4] Sterling was divided into different types, and resident sterling was the currency held by residents of the sterling area. See 'Exchange Control Retained', *Manchester Guardian*, 29 December 1958, 5.

(for example, for import/export or for travel). Convertibility meant that businesses and individuals could buy goods abroad without limit. The aim was to facilitate trade within Europe and with the United States.

Convertibility was a European move. The BIS explained that the reason behind this new setting was 'to promote genuine economic integration'.[5] The new framework forced 'each country to keep its domestic monetary policy more closely in line with that of other countries, for no country can embark alone on an inflationary policy if it wishes to maintain convertibility'.[6] What sounded like a good thing to the BIS was a major concern to national governments. Wilson later complained about having to factor in 'what speculators might do'.[7] Overall the press was enthusiastic. The *Manchester Guardian* explained: 'The currency changes by the leading European countries were regarded yesterday in many parts of the world as a sign of complete economic recovery in the nations concerned.'[8] With this recovery came more pressure on European currencies. Pressure started on sterling first.

## THE POLITICS OF CONVERTIBILITY IN EUROPE

Convertibility was a condition of Marshall Aid just after the war. In 1947 the United States wanted to establish European currency convertibility. The goal was not only to have an economically strong Europe opposing the Soviet Bloc. The United States also wanted to make Europe a strong trading partner. Negotiations for convertibility took place within the framework of the Organisation for European Economic Co-operation (OEEC).[9] The organisation was set up to implement the Marshall Plan. The *Manchester Guardian* explained: 'Negotiations about this week-end's changes in international currency relations began, in fact, at the O.E.E.C. meeting a fortnight ago, when the wreck of the plan for a Free Trade Area caused an ugly outburst of Anglo-French ill-feeling.'[10] The negotiations were mainly among three leading European countries. The *Guardian* noted: 'It ought to be made clear that the new policy was discussed between

---

[5] BIS, Annual Report 1959, 8 June 1959, 27.          [6] Ibid.

[7] Wilson, *Labour Government, 1964–70*, 32–3.

[8] 'A Sign of Full Recovery: How the Changes Are Regarded', *Manchester Guardian*, 29 December 1958, 5.

[9] The predecessor of the Organisation for Economic Co-operation and Development (OECD), a rich country club as the *Economist* likes to call it.

[10] 'Europe in Concert', *Manchester Guardian*, 29 December 1958, 4.

the French, British and German Governments and then submitted to the other members of the O.E.E.C.'[11]

Once convertibility was established, European countries were divided into two groups. 'Weak-currency countries lobbied for more generous IMF quotas and increases in international reserves. Strong-currency countries objected that additional credits encouraged deficit countries to live beyond their means.'[12] Britain was in the weak-currency group. It was the most successful country in receiving international aid. This was because of the importance of sterling. Germany, on the other hand, would have lobbied for more rigour and smaller quotas, but after the war the country was under the control of the United States. It was the 'poster child' of US policy in Europe and one of its strongest allies. France, another strong-currency country in the early 1960s, was lobbying for more rigour. President de Gaulle's claims to go back to gold were made in this spirit. The French wanted a more rigorous international system.

The IMF was a strong proponent of convertibility. It was one of the reasons for the its existence. The IMF was bound by the Article of Agreements, Article I, section 4. The article stipulated that the IMF was to 'assist in the establishment of a multilateral system of payments in respect of current transactions between members'.[13] The article also mentions 'the elimination of foreign exchange restrictions which hamper the growth of world trade'. Convertibility was one of the reasons the IMF had been set up.

## AN END TO PARALLEL MARKETS

Convertibility offers a unique example of capital controls being lifted suddenly. With this sudden shock, exchange rates were disrupted. I study the effect of this disruption using new exchange rate data. The data show that parallel and offshore markets became obsolete. Sterling became both fungible and transferable. There was no reason to have different prices in different places. Leland Yeager argues that convertibility 'unified and broadened the markets in spot and forward exchange, made competition in them more keen, narrowed the spreads between buying and selling quotations'.[14] On the market, the transition to convertibility was smooth.

---

[11] Ibid.    [12] Eichengreen, *Globalizing Capital*, 112.

[13] Bretton Woods Conference, Final Act, Washington, Archive of the IMF (hereafter IMF), 22 July 1944, GD-48, 8329, 1944, 21.

[14] Yeager, *International Monetary Relations*, 376.

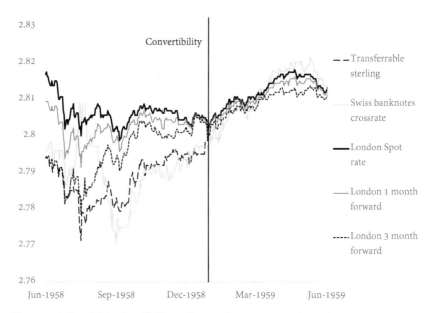

Figure 6.1. Parallel sterling/dollar exchange rates
*Source*: Accominotti et al., Swiss National Bank Archives and Bank of England dealers' reports (see text).

It did not trigger an immediate crisis as might have been expected with more capital flowing in and out of London. The Bank of England dealers' report of 29 December 1958 noted that the 'first day of convertibility found markets a little confused at the start but later there was considerable activity here [in London] especially in dollars, French Francs and Swiss Francs'.[15] There was no major crisis or speculation against a specific currency. Market participants saw convertibility as the harbinger of recovery in Europe.

Figure 6.1 highlights the effect of convertibility. Exchange rates were moving relatively independently before convertibility. After convertibility they moved closely together. They were now all part of the same global market. I present several different rates. The data for transferable rates and the Swiss cross-rate have been collected from manuscript ledgers in the archives of the Swiss National Bank and the Bank of England. Forward and spot data come from Accominotti et al.[16] Transferable sterling ceased to

---

[15] 'Dealers' report', 29 December 1958, London, archive of the Bank of England, C8.
[16] Accominotti et al., 'Currency Regimes'.

exist with convertibility, which unified the different sterling rates, reducing the scope for arbitrage.

Convertibility lowered the forward premia. Here I measure the rate ninety days before and after convertibility as a comparison. Looking at the average daily forward rate, discounts decreased 63 per cent for the one-month forward (from −0.06 to −0.04 per cent). The decrease was similar for the three-month forward at 67 per cent (from −0.15 to −0.09 per cent). There is little evidence that the exchange risk diminished after convertibility. The risk of a sterling devaluation was just as high as before convertibility, if not higher. The lower discount came from the more liquid market with more arbitrage possibilities in Europe and New York. The Swiss banknote market no longer was the only arbitrage opportunity. Speculators no longer needed to travel to Zurich with a suitcase full of cash to convert their unwanted sterling. They could now place orders in London or New York, where the prices were the same.

Foreign exchange markets across the world became far more integrated. Convertibility also had an impact on the London foreign exchange market. Just as in 1951, it would be reasonable to expect buying and selling spreads to diminish. The market became more liquid and more integrated with global markets. But evidence of spread reduction is not as marked as in 1951. I use the same bid–ask spread index as I employed in Chapter 3. Bid–ask spreads in the two years leading up to convertibility were, on average, 9.5 per cent higher than after convertibility. It is unclear whether this was driven by convertibility alone. The decrease in spreads is not comparable with the spot market reopening in 1951. In 1951, spreads decreased by 70 per cent between December 1951 and December 1953. Convertibility, on the other hand, had a limited effect on spreads in a comparable timeframe. Dealers did not change their behaviour.

Why did spreads not decrease significantly? In theory, convertibility increased the turnover. A more liquid market should have led to lower spreads. However, this ignores the different forces at play. Lyons has shown that the foreign exchange market today is dominated by few players and a decentralised structure.[17] This applies also to the 1950s. Higher turnover did not increase competition as the main market participants did not change. A few large commercial and investment banks were still making the price. This explains the relatively stable spreads at this point.

---

[17] Lyons, *The Microstructure Approach to Exchange Rates*.

In summary, convertibility was quite a smooth process. It did not trigger a run on sterling, as might have been expected with capital flow liberalisation. Convertibility did not make spreads diminish significantly, as did the 1951 market reopening. However, it did reduce the discount of alternative markets when compared with the London spot market. If convertibility took place quite smoothly in terms of the market reaction, its consequences for the international monetary system were profound, as we will see.

# 7

# The Gold Pool

The Gold Pool was a buying and selling syndicate created in 1961 to manage the price of gold in London.[1] It was intended to support the London gold price, reinforce the stability of the international monetary system and allow the United States to maintain its commitment to keep the price of gold at $35 an ounce. The Gold Pool started as a gentleman's agreement. It emerged during monthly meetings of central bankers at the Bank for International Settlements. The Gold Pool is one of the most ambitious examples of central bank cooperation ever. It involved the pooling of reserves, the sharing of profits and losses, and constant information-sharing among central banks.

Recall that after the opening of the gold market in 1954, the gold price was kept under control by the Bank of England.[2] Convertibility, however, changed everything. The London gold market was no longer immune to outside pressure as capital controls were lifted. A steady gold price was important to the Bank of England, but even more important to the Federal Reserve as the guarantor of the official gold price. The question of who would bear the cost of selling gold in London when excess demand arose. Initially, the Federal Reserve worked directly with the Bank of England. Later the Fed involved other European countries under the umbrella of the Gold Pool.

---

[1] This chapter is based on joint work with Michael Bordo and Eric Monnet. I offer new data and information not presented in the joint work. The text has also been substantially revised. See Michael D. Bordo, Eric Monnet and Alain Naef, 'The Gold Pool (1961–1968) and the Fall of Bretton Woods: Lessons for Central Bank Cooperation', *National Bureau of Economic Research Working Paper*, no. 24016 (2017); Michael D. Bordo, Eric Monnet and Alain Naef, 'The Gold Pool (1961–1968) and the Fall of the Bretton Woods System: Lessons for Central Bank Cooperation', *Journal of Economic History*, 79, 4 (2019), 1–33, https://doi.org/10.1017/S0022050719000548.
[2] See Chapter 5.

The gold crisis of 1961 was the first test for the Bretton Woods system with freer capital flows. The rise of the gold price put the Bank under pressure. Policymakers understood that the cost of maintaining the price at around $35 an ounce could become extremely high. The Bank started to question the role of the United Kingdom in maintaining the gold price. Negotiations with the Federal Reserve opened. If Bretton Woods was about cooperation, as Toniolo and other scholars claim, this is where cooperation started to assume centre stage.[3] Practical questions now arose: What information was the Bank willing to share with the Fed? Who should one call at 4 am in New York if there was a run on gold? I show how the Bank was often reluctant to cooperate, even though it was pushed to do so by the Federal Reserve. If US–UK cooperation started slowly, cooperation with other European powers took even longer. France felt side-lined from the start and progressively followed its own path. The French suggested an alternative monetary system. Their ideal was closer to the gold standard and more rigorous, in line with French policy since the interwar years.[4]

Earlier literature mentions the creation of the Gold Pool, but mainly using secondary literature.[5] I draw on the archives of the Bank of England, New York Fed and BIS. The chapter also gives a detailed overview of cooperation between the Fed and the Bank. The literature simply takes for granted that Bretton Woods was a period of cooperation. Here I delve into the details of this cooperation and how it slowly evolved.

The Gold Pool was initially a covert scheme, but its existence soon leaked to the public. It made the link between the credibility of the US dollar and the London gold market apparent to all. This was an endorsement by the United States of the London gold price as a barometer of the health of the international monetary system. Once that was made public, there was no going back. Gold Pool members supporting the gold price would have to unite or abandon the Bretton Woods agreement altogether.

---

[3] Toniolo and Clement, *Central Bank Cooperation*.

[4] Monnet, 'French Monetary Policy and the Bretton Woods System'; Michael D. Bordo, Eugene N. White and Dominique Simard, 'France and the Breakdown of the Bretton Woods International Monetary System', in *International Monetary Systems in Historical Perspective*, ed. Jaime Reis (New York: St Martin's Press, 1995); Eichengreen, *Globalizing Capital*, 113–14.

[5] For a description based on secondary sources, see, for example, Barry Eichengreen, *Global Imbalances and the Lessons of Bretton Woods* (Cambridge, MA: MIT Press, 2007). The creation of the Gold Pool is also described in Toniolo and Clement, *Central Bank Cooperation*.

## COOPERATION WITH THE FED

The 1961 US presidential election put a strain on the gold price. This forced the Bank of England to cooperate with the Fed. The Bank had been responsible for monitoring the London market since 1954. As I showed in Chapter 5, the cost of maintaining this market was around $2 million a month. The Bank sold that amount of gold to the market every month.[6] This was a reasonable cost, considering all the advantages the market gave both the City and sterling. After convertibility, pressure started to rise. So did the cost of intervening in the market. In late August 1960, in the run-up to the US presidential election, gold gained value in London. Speculators feared the dollar was going to be devalued.

The presidential candidate, John F. Kennedy, had delayed his commitment to keep the official $35 an ounce price of gold until the end of October 1960. Coombs noted that for that reason many central banks – the Bank of Italy especially – were buying large quantities of gold in London.[7] They were reluctant to speculate openly against the dollar by going to the US gold window. This would have been politically damaging. London gold was more expensive than gold at the US gold window. But it allowed central banks to remain anonymous buyers and avoid pressure from United States.

In the September 1960 IMF meeting, the Bank of England started to complain. It informed the Fed of the situation 'having assumed some responsibility for selling gold to maintain orderly market conditions', Coombs later wrote.[8] The Bank was essentially doing the Fed's job. The Bank was 'in the awkward position of being squeezed out of the market by other central bank buyers whenever gold became available'.[9] Because of heavy central bank buying, the Bank had to stay out of the market to keep the price from rising too much. On 13 September 1960, as the gold market started to heat up, the Bank of England contacted the Fed. It informed the Fed of a rise in the 'international price of gold', as the Bank worded it.[10] The word 'international' hinted that it was not the sole responsibility of the Bank of England. The Bank warned that the price

---

[6] This was not an actual cost the Bank was obliged to pay, but the price it decided to spend to avoid 'undue fluctuation' in the market. This mission was something the Bank thought was necessary.

[7] Coombs, *The Arena of International Finance*, 49–50.     [8] Ibid., 50.     [9] Ibid., 50.

[10] 'Letter from H. C. B. Mynors to Alfred Hayes', 13 September 1960, London, Archives of the Bank of England, C43/420.

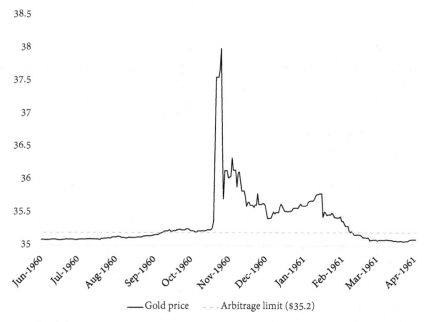

Figure 7.1. Daily London gold price (11 am fixing) and gold price arbitrage limit
*Source*: Dealers' reports (C8).

had reached '$35.15, the highest level since the London market was reopened in 1954'.[11]

Figure 7.1 illustrates the price reaching $35.20 in early September 1960.[12] The Bank identified four main causes: the Bank of Italy buying gold; few sales from other central banks; 'tension in the international situation, i.e. Cuba, Congo, Berlin'; and demand 'from the Middle East' growing after 'the assassination of the Jordanian Prime Minister'.[13]

In October 1960, the intra-day gold price reached $40/oz. The 11 am fixing was set as high as $38. Roy Bridge commented: '[T]this was the

---

[11] Ibid.

[12] $35.20 was the price at which it was profitable for central banks to buy gold at the Fed and sell it in the London gold market.

[13] In Cuba, Fidel Castro had just taken power, thereby increasing US concerns; in Congo (later renamed Zaire), Sese Seko Mobutu gained power; in Berlin, the idea of a wall was making its way after a five-day ban on West Germans entering the East on 1 September; and in Jordan, Prime Minister Hazza' Barakat al-Majali, who had taken power in 1959, was assassinated. The quotes are from a letter from H. C. B. Mynors to Alfred Hayes, 13 September 1960, London, Archives of the Bank of England, C43/420.

Table 7.1. *Gold sales by country*

| Sales to. . .<br>(in gold bars) | Week ending 22 October 1960 | Week ending 29 October 1960 |
|---|---|---|
| Switzerland | 2,180 | 1,245 |
| Canada | 240 | 488 |
| USA | 145 | 269 |
| France | 68 | |
| Germany | 47 | 23 |
| Middle East | 40 | 20 |
| Far East | 37 | 77 |
| Paraguay | 20 | |
| Italy | 20 | |
| Belgium | 4 | 7 |
| Argentina | | 9 |
| TOTAL | 2,801 | 2,138 |
| Total turnover | $39 | $31 |

*Source*: Letter from Preston to Roche, 1 November 1960, London, Archives of the Bank of England, C43/320.

really rough period during which turnover was very large and the price surpassed $40 on Thursday, 20th October.'[14] The run in October is best explained by an insider, E. E. Mocatta, a dealer and descendant of the Mocatta who founded the London gold market in 1671.[15] He was replying to questions from the New York Federal Reserve:

I feel that the week-end of the 14th October was the turning point in the gold market. During that week-end the Continent and, in particular, Switzerland, as well as Canada, seem to have decided that Senator Kennedy was going to be elected with a good majority. They considered that this would bring about more inflation in your Country [the United States] and, as a result, your balance of payments would suffer further. They considered, therefore, that a devaluation of the dollar in the first half of next year was a real possibility, and done soon, it could be blamed on the former Republican administration.[16]

Who bought gold during this run? Table 7.1 summarises the destination of gold purchases on the London market. It is likely that the majority of

---

[14] 'Roy Bridge to Charles Coombs', 24 November 1960, London, Archives of the Bank of England, C43/320.

[15] See Chapter 5.

[16] 'Draft letter from Mocatta (gold dealer) to Roche (FRBNY) held at the Bank of England for information', 22 November 1960, London, Archives of the Bank of England, C43/320.

these went exclusively to private customers in the countries listed.[17] Most of the purchases in question went to Switzerland, Canada and the United States. Most of the Canadian sales and around 20 per cent of the Swiss sales went to private US speculators. Mocatta commented: 'We feel, however, that the majority of the Canadian sales were ultimately being purchased by citizens of the United States, and a proportion of the Swiss ones also.'[18] This would mean that a third to half of the sales during the run went to US private citizens. They speculated on Kennedy winning the election and a potential devaluation of the dollar.[19] The rest was probably speculators operating through Switzerland, or Swiss nationals. Central banks did not seem to be the main buyers. For the whole of 1961, estimates by the Bank of England show that of the $1,600 million of new gold placed on the London gold market, 37.5 per cent went to central banks and 62.5 per cent to 'hoarders, Industry and the Arts'.[20]

After circulating a copy of the estimates in Table 7.1, Preston from the Bank of England had second thoughts. He wrote to Parsons of the Bank of England to express his concern about sharing information with the New York Federal Reserve. He wrote: 'If we were to give new production as well as the other figures our own operations could be calculated.'[21] His concern sprang from the different activities of the Bank. As seen in Chapter 5, the Bank was at the same time seller for South Africa and buyer for the Exchange Equalisation Account (EEA). The Bank had privileged access to South African gold. It did not want the United States to know how it used this privilege as the Bank was not obliged to reveal the scale of its operations on behalf of South Africa. It was important to the Bank not to lose its South African business to Swiss competitors, something that eventually happened in 1968.

---

[17] Even if it were possible that some of the orders were passed by central banks through private banks in their respective countries, this is certainly not the case for US transactions and probably not for the Swiss and Canadian either. Bank secrecy meant that, in theory, the end buyer was unknown to the London dealers (and to the Bank of England) but in practice this information always leaked to the public.

[18] 'Draft letter from Mocatta (gold dealer) to Roche (FRBNY) held at the Bank of England for information', 22 November 1960, London, Archives of the Bank of England, C43/320.

[19] Actually, 29–47 per cent. This is computed from Mocatta's estimate, who guessed that 20 per cent of Swiss sales went to the United States.

[20] 'L. T. G. P. to Bridge', 17 April 1962, London, Archives of the Bank of England, C43/320.

[21] 'Letter from Preston to Parsons', 3 November 1960, London, Archives of the Bank of England, C43/320. A typo in the original text has been amended (replacing 'are' with 'our').

Increased market pressure would soon force the Bank to be more cooperative and transparent. The United States was willing to help, but needed to know how much the Bank of England was spending on intervention. On 16 November 1960, Coombs and Roche gave their private telephone numbers to the Bank of England. They wanted to be available 'out of normal telephone contact' at the Federal Reserve.[22] This shows how seriously the New York Federal Reserve took the price of gold in London at that time, as Coombs asserted.

A few days later, in November 1960, Bridge wrote to Coombs to report on the crisis over the past weeks. From 26 October to 2 November, Bridge reported: 'Demand continued but we managed to introduce some stability into the market around 256s. [£12.16] and $36 at a cost which we did not regard as exorbitant.'[23] At this point the Bank of England was still bearing the cost of intervention alone. It was also lobbying for US support.[24]

The following week (3–9 November), Bridge had to intervene heavily. He wrote to Coombs: 'So on the Thursday we decided to get all our weapons out in an endeavour to get a grip on a market which we were afraid might otherwise again run out of control as it had done two weeks before.'[25] But the pressure was too strong. Bridge continued: 'As we expected, there was pretty heavy buying; we had to let the price up to around $36 3/8, and to give a good deal of gold to prevent it from going up much farther.'[26] This was the Bank's strategy – defending the price, but not at any cost. Once the pressure was too great, the Bank would let the price rise before attempting to push it down again.

Speculation was the main issue, not increased demand from industry, the arts or foreign central banks. As an illustration of this frenetic speculation, Bridge reported an anecdote. A 'fellow' flew overnight from Chicago to buy five bars of gold before travelling by 'car to the airport and flew straight home again!'[27] In reaction to increased speculation, on 14 January 1961 the United States introduced a ban on US citizens holding gold outside of the country. Holding gold within the United States was already illegal for most citizens under the Gold Reserve Act 1934. Private gold

---

[22] 'Note from Preston to Bridge and Parsons on information and emergency contacts', 16 November 1960, London, Archives of the Bank of England, reference C43/320.

[23] 'Roy Bridge to Charles Coombs', 24 November 1960, London, Archives of the Bank of England, C43/320.

[24] Coombs, *The Arena of International Finance*, 51–2.

[25] 'Roy Bridge to Charles Coombs', 24 November 1960, London, Archives of the Bank of England, C43/320.

[26] Ibid.    [27] Ibid.

ownership was allowed under certain conditions – for example, for coins with 'sentimental or collectors' value' and uses for the industry.[28] The new interdiction against holding gold abroad was a consequence of the outflows during the October 1960 run.

In February 1961, the Bank was still not completely transparent with the Fed. Roche from the Fed queried whether the Bank of England knew of any central banks buying and selling on the market.[29] This was forbidden under the rules of the Gold Pool. Before the Pool was set up, the Federal Reserve had justified suspicions that the Italians were buying gold in London, thereby propping up the price.[30] In reply, the Bank official told Roche in a telephone conversation that they were 'not free to discuss the details of business transacted with the Bank's customers'.[31] Customers could buy and sell gold without having their identity revealed, as is the case of private banking today. Roche was 'obviously embarrassed' and 'then said that it was hoped in the Federal [Reserve] that in view of the closer relations now existing we would tell him when we sold gold to central banks'.[32]

The Fed was hoping that the Bank would breach customer confidentiality for them. The Fed was more liberal with such information. It was openly discussing the operation of the Bank of Canada on behalf of the Bank of England, as we have seen in Chapter 4. However, the Bank of England did not seem ready to cooperate fully with the Federal Reserve at this stage. This was despite trying to make a case for US support to maintain the price of gold. The Bank feared that revealing too much would lead the Americans to cut the British privileged access to South African gold, or worse, have South Africa move its business to Zurich. At the same time, the burden of supporting the gold price in London was rising and help was needed.

---

[28] This information comes from an article in the *Wall Street Journal*: 'Back in "Circulation": The $20 Gold Piece, Now Selling for $70', *Wall Street Journal*, 18 March 1968, 6.

[29] Hand-signed note to Bridge and Parsons, 28 February 1961, London, Archives of the Bank of England, C43/320.

[30] In a memorandum, Assistant Secretary of State for Policy Planning Smith wrote that more international monetary coordination 'might have been instrumental in dissuading the Italians from converting their dollar reserves into gold'; Glenn W. LaFantasie, ed., *Foreign Relations of the United States, 1958–1960, Foreign Economic Policy, Volume IV. Office of the Historian* (Washington, DC: United States Government Printing Office, 1992).

[31] 'Hand-signed note to Bridge and Parsons', 28 February 1961, London, Archives of the Bank of England, C43/320.

[32] Ibid.

In August 1961, pressure on the gold market mounted again. Bridge reported that it was 'probably the biggest day since January' and that there had been 'some central bank buying' but also heavy demand from Berlin.[33] Bridge shared his concerns with the Federal Reserve. He wrote: '[U]nless there was a detente on the political front, demand was expected to continue and I personally saw little prospect of holding the price below $35.20 for long, short of selling very large amounts.'[34] This was a threat. Bridge would let the price of gold increase, knowing very well that this would have negative consequences for the credibility of the dollar. Sanford from the Fed offered to earmark $40 million of gold in New York for the Bank of England's account. This meant in effect that the Federal Reserve was paying for the Bank of England's intervention in the London gold market. At this point the Gold Pool became a solution. Instead of losing gold on the London gold market, the Fed and the Bank could pool reserves with other countries.

## THE POLITICS OF THE GOLD POOL CREATION

The Gold Pool was a project between the United States and most of the European nations. All participated with different quotas. The proposal was first made by France at the end of 1960 but was rejected in Basel.[35] Later, the United States made a similar proposal. US policymakers realised that this would be necessary to keep their commitment to convert dollars into gold at $35/oz at the gold window. In autumn 1960, British officials approached the United States to ask whether the Fed would assist the Bank in monitoring the London gold market.[36] However, until the Gold Pool was formally settled it would take almost another year. During this year, the Bank of England continued to manage the gold market with some financial support from the Federal Reserve, as we just saw. The BIS took a leading role in facilitating talks on the creation of the Gold Pool and providing a venue for discussion.

Negotiations took place at plenum meetings at the BIS and in bilateral negotiations. Discussions started in October 1960 after the spike in the

---

[33] 'Telephone record', Bridge to Sanford, 30 August 1961, London, Archives of the Bank of England, C43/320.

[34] Ibid.

[35] Eric Monnet, 'French Monetary Policy and the Bretton Woods System'; Eric Monnet, 'Une Coopération à La Française. La France, Le Dollar et Le Système de Bretton Woods, 1960–1965', *Histoire@Politique. Politique, Culture, Société* 19 (2013).

[36] Coombs, *The Arena of International Finance*, 51–2.

gold price. France suggested in a BIS meeting that they should 'coordinate central bank interventions on the gold market at the international level by means of a gentlemen's agreement, and to reactivate the 1936 Tripartite agreement'.[37] The Bank of England opposed this. It believed that coordinated intervention would threaten the role of sterling as a reserve currency. The Federal Reserve, for its part, opposed any return to a tripartite agreement, which would have 'opened the door to a potential devaluation of the dollar'.[38]

In a private meeting with BIS officials, Alfred Hayes, president of the New York Federal Reserve, explained the Fed's position. The Fed would sell gold only for reasons pertaining to monetary stability. Gold in the London market would eventually 'flow into hoarding channels'.[39] This would be unfair to US citizens, who were not allowed to buy gold. The United States did not want to take part in an official scheme that would potentially supply gold to hoarders. It was willing to operate anonymously on the gold market with the Bank of England. The French leveraged the fact that the United States and United Kingdom intervened alone in the market. They argued it was proof that 'the international monetary system was used by the United States and the United Kingdom for their own policy objectives'.[40]

In January 1960, the BIS issued a memorandum evaluating what at the time was called the gold club. At this early stage, members of the club would not have to pay 1 per cent tax for buying gold at the Federal Reserve. The memorandum mentioned the possibility of the Federal Reserve intervening in London. It read: 'If the Federal [Reserve] should decide to supply gold loco [located in] New York at $35 for shipment to London to feed the London Market, it should be easily possible to reduce the price of gold in the latter centre.'[41] The BIS was still sceptical of putting such a club together. McDonald of the BIS banking department wrote that he was unsure whether the club was 'a good thing or equally favourable to all participants' and even that 'direct interests of the B.I.S. [could] suffer'.[42]

---

[37] Monnet, 'French Monetary Policy and the Bretton Woods System'.     [38] Ibid.

[39] Extract of minutes from visit to New York, meeting between Hayes, Holtrop, Roosa, Sanford, Guindey and Mandel, H. H. Mandel, 3 October 1960, Basel, BIS Archives, BISA 2/1, vol. 4.

[40] Monnet, 'French Monetary Policy and the Bretton Woods System'.

[41] 'The Gold Club', internal note signed Donald H. McDonald, 11 January 1962, Basel, Archives of the Bank for International Settlements, BISA 7.18 (15), HAL2, 1.

[42] Ibid.

## HOW THE GOLD POOL WORKED

The Gold Pool started operating informally. It was piloted by the international expert commission on gold and foreign exchange at the BIS. This was a meeting of the heads of the foreign exchanges of the member central banks every two months. Operations of the Pool started before final quotas were set in a spirit of cooperation and informality characteristic of the Basel meetings of the BIS. The scheme started as an experiment that could be disbanded at any point. It was expected to be temporary in nature. Eventually, it ran from 1961 to 1968. This was impressive for such a scheme. The Gold Pool had no formal enforcement mechanism. It relied on the good faith of its members to commit not to buy gold on the London market. But in any case, the Bank of England was generally informed of the origin of the transactions. And no central bank would have risked being noticed buying gold in London.

The Gold Pool comprised two syndicates. One was a gold-buying syndicate, the other a gold-selling syndicate. Initially, the Pool started as a gold-selling syndicate to prevent the price of gold from rising. The buying syndicate was set up later to allow central banks to buy gold in London at a competitive price and without adding pressure to the London market price. The Bank of England had discretion on how to manage the market. Bridge and his team of dealers were in charge of operations to avoid any purchases upsetting the price.

Member central banks elected to keep the existence and operations of the gold syndicate secret. But secrecy could only last so long. On 8 March 1962, the scheme was leaked to the press.[43] Publicity probably worked in favour of the Pool. No single speculator was willing to gamble against all the Western central banks combined. Single intervention operations were not communicated to the public.

Members had different quotas, representing their initial contribution to the scheme. The quota was also important at the end of each month when the Pool settled its accounts, to decide how much each country was entitled to purchase from the Pool surpluses. The United States was the main contributor, followed by Germany, which was sympathetic to US efforts after the war. Thus, if the syndicate purchased $100 million in a month when the gold price was low, Belgium, for example, could choose to take up to 4 per cent or $4 million (see Table 7.2).

---

[43] 'Clip of an article published in the *Journal de Genève*', sent to Roy Bridge, 8 March 1962, London, Archive of the Bank of England, C20/3.

Table 7.2. *Respective quota by member and initial share*

| Gold Pool initial quotas | | |
|---|---|---|
| | Percentage | Million US$ |
| United States | 50% | 135 |
| Germany | 11% | 30 |
| United Kingdom | 9% | 25 |
| Italy | 9% | 25 |
| France | 9% | 25 |
| Switzerland | 4% | 10 |
| The Netherlands | 4% | 10 |
| Belgium | 4% | 10 |
| **Total** | | **270** |

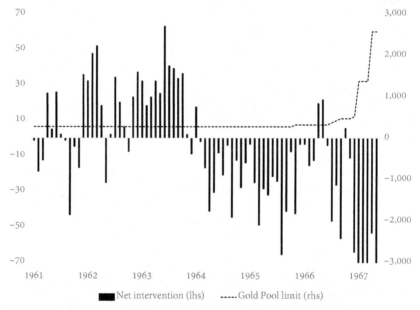

Figure 7.2. Bank of England net monthly operations on the London gold market and upper limit of the Gold Pool, November 1961–March 1968
*Source*: Dealer's reports for gold intervention (C8).
*Note*: Most of these operations would have been done on behalf of the Gold Pool.

The original limit for the gold-selling syndicate was set at $270 million. That was the maximum the Bank of England could spend to support gold. Periodically, from 1965 onward, the limit was increased (see Figure 7.2). When the Gold Pool closed in March 1968, the limit had reached $2,570 million, close to ten times the initial amount. Figure 7.2 shows the Bank of

England's net monthly interventions during the Gold Pool period. After its creation in 1961 the syndicate was mostly involved in accumulating gold. It started losing gold to the market from 1964 onwards. Losses intensified at the end of the scheme.

## THE CREATION OF THE GOLD POOL AND THE GLOBAL PRICE OF GOLD

How successful was the Gold Pool? Did it immediately impact the price of gold? Here I study two events which could have impacted the gold price. The first is the date the selling syndicate was created: 6 November 1961.[44] On that day, central banks brought reserves together to maintain the price of gold. More importantly, they committed not to buy gold on the London gold market, easing the pressure. Without central banks buying gold, the demand side of the market would fall and the price would likely decrease. It is impossible to know the exact amounts the central banks were purchasing directly in London, so this is not quantifiable. Once created, the syndicate was still secret. The market did not know it existed. So, it had no signalling value to private market participants. On this date, the expectation would be to see the price fall if many central banks withdrew from the market. Or the price could remain steady if central banks were not buying heavily before their commitment to stay out of the market.

The second key date is the day the existence of the Gold Pool was leaked: 8 March 1962. This signalled to the market that most Western countries were now united behind a gold price of $35.20. Operationally, gold operations were still the same, with the Bank of England dealers trying to avoid sharp rises in price. The only difference was that they now operated on behalf of the Gold Pool and no longer on behalf of the Bank of England with some support from the United States.

It would be reasonable to expect the gold price to fall after the creation of the Pool and after the leak. The Gold Pool would have a positive effect. Looking at the gold price only on these two dates provides little evidence of the Pool having a significant effect. The creation of the Gold Pool was followed by a fall in the gold price (see Figure 7.3). It is unclear whether this was a direct consequence of intervention. Equally, the leak might have caused a slight downward trend in the price, but the effect is not obvious.

What is more difficult to demonstrate is the counterfactual. If the Gold Pool had not been created and central banks had bought gold on the

---

[44] At this point, France and Belgium had not officially joined, but it is unlikely that they bought gold on the London market at this stage.

Figure 7.3. London gold price around two key dates
*Source*: Dealers' reports (C8).

London market in a disorderly fashion, what effect would this have had on the price of gold? This is, of course, impossible to answer. It would have been unlikely for central banks to purchase large quantities of gold in London without any coordination or without triggering political intervention by the United States.

It might not be surprising that the Gold Pool had a limited effect on the gold price once put in place in November 1961. The Bank of England continued to intervene as before. The gold reserves of the Bank at that time were $1.3 billion. They had a backing of $17 billion from the United States.[45] These amounts dwarf the $270 million in the initial Gold Pool. Before November 1961, the Bank was defending the price of gold on its own account with support from the Federal Reserve. After the creation of the Gold Pool the same dealers were operating. The only difference being that the funds now also came from European countries and central banks did not operate in the London gold market directly.

---

[45] UK reserve figure from the 'EEA ledgers', 6 November 1961, London, Archives of the Bank of England, 2A141/13. US reserve figures from FRED, M1476CUSM144NNBR for November 1961.

Bank of England dealers, 1942. Credit: The Bank of England Archive, reference 15A13/1/1/42/1.

Bank of England dealers, 1965. Credit: The Bank of England Archive, reference 15A13/1/1/42/2.

Bank of England dealers, 1965. Credit: The Bank of England Archive, reference 15A13/1/1/42/2 (3).

Bank of England dealers, 1974. Credit: The Bank of England Archive, reference 15A13/1/1/42/3.

8

# Cooperation and the Fed Swap Network

The Gold Pool was the first palliative measure put in place after the introduction of convertibility. The second was the US swap network. Swaps refer to one central bank exchanging domestic currency against foreign currency with another central bank. For example, the Bank of England could exchange sterling against dollars with the Fed. The two central banks would decide to reverse the transaction at an agreed forward exchange rate. The goal of these swaps was to provide foreign currency when needed. The main swap partner for the Bank of England during the Bretton Woods period was the Federal Reserve. Bordo et al. estimated that almost 57 per cent of all the $15.3 billion swap contracts of the Fed between 1962 and 1971 were with the Bank of England.[1] The Bank was the Federal Reserve's biggest customer when it came to swaps. The benefits of swaps were mutual, as Capie stressed: 'The essence of the swap network that revolved in the main around the Federal Reserve was to provide, in the case of the Bank, dollars for intervention purposes and the Fed with sterling with which it could purchase dollars that otherwise might be converted into gold.'[2]

The Federal Reserve international swap network was initially designed to ease the pressure on US gold reserves. Reserves were under pressure because of the US commitment within the Bretton Woods Agreement. Swaps ended up being a tool for managing sterling. The Bank agreed to join the network as a favour to the Federal Reserve. Within a few years, swaps had become the centrepiece of British foreign exchange management. They were part of a complex network of loans put in place to help maintain the fixed exchange rate of the pound. This loan network was the

[1] Bordo, Humpage and Schwartz, *Strained Relations*.
[2] Capie, *The Bank of England*, 228.

joint effort of the United States and the United Kingdom. The two countries often ended up negotiating further loan agreements with the rest of
Europe. Robert McCauley and Catherine Schenk have recently shown that
the swap network in the 1960s was not solely used for exchange rate
management.[3] They also helped manage Eurodollar funding liquidity and
Libor yields.

Why was the United States so keen to grant the United Kingdom access
to loans? US policymakers recognised that sterling was the dollar's first line
of defence. A sterling crash would trigger a run on the dollar. It would
reveal the weakness of sterling as an international currency. As a consequence, investors would in turn fear for the stability of the other international currency, the dollar. Under normal circumstances, it would be
reasonable to expect that a depreciation of sterling would lead to an
appreciation of the dollar. However, this mechanism did not apply. In
the context of the Bretton Woods system, the two currencies had a similar
function. Leadership for the main international reserve currency was
moving from the pound to the dollar. It was clear to investors that if
sterling fell, the dollar would come under pressure. The United States
wanted to avoid a run on the dollar at all costs.

The Bank was in a position where it needed help, and this led to a
warmer relationship with the Federal Reserve, unlike in the early 1950s.
The Bank and the Fed were in contact by telephone every day. I present
new records of these conversations to trace the evolving relationship. The
swap network enhanced the stability of the international monetary system,
but only in the short term. The long-run liquidity problem raised by the
Triffin dilemma remained. The dollar and sterling supporting each other
made the currencies inherently prone to instability. Both currencies were
liable to speculative attacks. This mutual dependency made the Bretton
Woods system more unstable.


## THE BANK OF ENGLAND'S USE OF SWAPS

The 1960s marked the rediscovery of swaps. Central bankers in Europe had
used them in the 1920s.[4] Swaps re-emerged when the Swiss National Bank

---

[3] Robert N. McCauley and Catherine R. Schenk, 'Central Bank Swaps Then and Now: Swaps
and Dollar Liquidity in the 1960s', 1 April 2020, www.bis.org/publ/work851.htm.

[4] Capie, *The Bank of England*; Richhild Moessner and William A. Allen, 'Banking Crises
and the International Monetary System in the Great Depression and Now', *BIS Working
Papers*, 333 (December 2010), 25.

suggested that the Federal Reserve establish a swap line because the Swiss National Bank was experiencing large dollar inflows. The Federal Reserve did not want these dollars converted into gold. After this initial try, the practice was broadened. The Fed established a swap network with most European central banks to act as a buffer for its gold reserves.[5] The Fed wanted to keep these banks from using the gold window to convert their dollars into gold. The Fed could use the swap line to borrow in a European currency and buy dollars back from a European central bank that had accumulated them. The United States would also put political pressure on European countries to hold a larger proportion of their reserves in dollars. The aim was to avoid too heavy a gold drain from the United States. A gold drain would have undermined the credibility of the dollar. From 1962 onwards, swap lines were key to the US policy to defend gold and provided dollar liquidity to European central banks.[6] They were rediscovered by central bankers in the wake of the 2008 global financial crisis.

The Federal Reserve took the initiative in creating its first swap line with the Bank of England. At the time, the Bank only agreed as a gesture of good faith. It did not see any advantage in taking part in the network. Soon, swap contracts would become the pound's lifeline. Since the fate of the pound and the dollar were interlinked, the Federal Reserve provided this support with the aim of keeping a crisis from contaminating the dollar. The Bank of England first agreed to a $50 million swap line with the Fed, which was later increased to $500 million. A note from the governor in March 1962 about a discussion with Sir Denis Rickett from the British Treasury reads: 'Sir Denis agreed that there was no merit in this but that it might be necessary to go along with the American proposal as a symbol of international co-operation.'[7]

Despite early reluctance for their use, swap agreements became the centrepiece of British exchange rate policy in the 1960s. The swap line started with a small drawing by the Federal Reserve on the $/£ swap line in 1962–63. After that, drawings were only made by the Bank of England to acquire dollars until 1971. Table 8.1 presents annual drawings by the Bank. It highlights the relative importance of the United Kingdom when compared with the other fourteen participants in the network.[8] From 1964 to

---

[5] Coombs, *The Arena of International Finance*.

[6] Bordo, Humpage and Schwartz, *Strained Relations*, 149.

[7] 'Extract from the governor's note dated 21 March 1962 on a talk with Sir Denis Rickett', 21 March 1962, London, Archive of the Bank of England, C43/742.

[8] Other participants were Austria, Belgium, Canada, Denmark, France, Germany, Italy, Japan, Mexico, the Netherlands, Norway, Sweden, Switzerland and the BIS.

Table 8.1. *Bank of England drawing on US swap networks*

| In million dollars | BoE drawing % of all countries drawing | BoE drawing | All countries drawing |
|---|---|---|---|
| 1962 | 0% | 0 | 0 |
| 1963 | 0% | 0 | 50 |
| 1964 | 88% | 1,370 | 1,550 |
| 1965 | 100% | 1,765 | 1,765 |
| 1966 | 69% | 625 | 910 |
| 1967 | 66% | 1,650 | 2,487 |
| 1968 | 58% | 2,045 | 3,503 |
| 1969 | 46% | 795 | 1,719 |
| 1970 | 22% | 400 | 1,834 |
| 1971 | 0% | 0 | 30 |
| 1972 | 0% | 0 | 19 |

*Source*: Bordo, Humpage and Schwartz, *Strained Relations*. Calculations by the author.
*Note*: The table does not show US drawings from other countries.

1967, the United Kingdom constituted on average 80 per cent of the Federal Reserve dollar lending of the fifteen nations able to draw from the Federal Reserve loan facility.

The use of swap lines and the creation of the Gold Pool led to a warmer relationship between the Federal Reserve and the Bank. As described previously, in the 1950s the Bank had been reluctant to share information with the Fed when it came to foreign exchange intervention. The Bank also avoided using the services of the Federal Reserve for intervention in New York. The two institutions had always been in close contact, but the Bank had been unwilling to share too much information. This changed in the 1960s and even more so when the Bank started to use the swap network to support sterling. In 1964, the Bank had more telephone conversations with the Fed. It was more willing to share information on its intervention strategy and pass intervention orders to the Fed. The Fed even gained discretionary power on operations.[9] The Bank would give the Federal Reserve a limit and leave operations to the discretion of the Fed operators. An extract of a telephone conversation memorandum best exemplifies this shift. Fousek, of the New York Fed, reported on a conversation with Preston of the Bank:

[9] These observations come from the various daily telephone conversation records at the Federal Reserve from 1964 onwards (New York, archive of the Federal Reserve, box 617015).

Preston called to say that he will be sending us an order to buy for their account up to £5 million at 2.7900. They hope they will have some beneficial effect from the announcement coming out of London (incomes policy). Should the spot rate move up, they would like us to use this opportunity and push up the 3 month forwards. For that reason, he is giving us a discretionary order for £10 million, value March 18, between 2.7714–25. If spot should start moving, depending on the situation, by moving up the forwards a little further, we might thereby get a beneficial effect for the spot rate. Should the spot really start moving, Blackler should be informed at home after 2:30 our time.[10]

In this telephone call the Bank delivered instructions for operations to be done overnight in New York. The Bank gave the Fed discretion. It gave permission for Blackler to be called at home if the situation became extremely worrying. In the 1950s the Federal Reserve could intervene only at the $2.78 lower band when things were going badly. In this quote, there is an order for $2.79 on the spot market. The Bank shared its strategy to try to benefit from good news and push the pound up. On the forward market the Federal Reserve was given discretion over £10 million. The goal was to improve the forward market with expected positive spill-over effects on the spot market. The spot market remained the Bank of England's main focus. The total discretion of over £15 million is quite substantial, as the average daily intervention (including in New York and London) in 1964 was £6.4 million. The Federal Reserve had discretion to spend double the average daily intervention if it felt the situation required it.

This unique example is only anecdotal but is representative of changes in the daily telephone conversations between the two central banks. From 1962 to 1963 onwards cooperation strengthened, as reflected in many similar memoranda. The Federal Reserve was given both more discretion and more information about the intentions and activities of the Bank of England. Capie mentions that the 1964 Bank Rate rise was the first time that the Bank consulted the Fed in advance.[11]

On a daily basis, agreements to swap currencies were made informally and quickly. For example, on 11 September 1964, Fousek reported that Blackler 'informed [him] that he will be needing $15 or 20 million for Tuesday and will send us a cable on Monday. (This will be another swap drawing.)'[12] Fousek wrote in his note that he was 'informed' that the Bank

[10] 'Telephone conversation with Mr. Preston of the Bank of England', Fousek to files, 16 December 1964, New York, Archives of the Federal Reserve, box 617015.

[11] Capie, *The Bank of England*, 193.

[12] 'Telephone conversation between Fousek and Blackler', Fousek to files, 11 September, August 1964, New York, Archives of the Federal Reserve, box 617015.

needed swaps, giving the impression that such a request was never denied. Once the limit was agreed, the swap lines were an easy facility for the Bank of England to use. Amounts were agreed by telephone and confirmed via telegraph. It was easy for the Bank to obtain dollars within a day or sometimes less. The Federal Reserve noted in a 1964 memorandum that 'undrawn amounts under swap arrangements with [the Bank of England, the German Federal Bank and the Netherlands Bank] may be considered available without prior consultation'.[13] Swaps became one of the Bank's preferred ways of accessing dollar credit.

Swaps were almost risk-free for the two parties. They included a collateral in currency backed by the other country. From the point of view of the Federal Reserve, the swaps were not only repayable in dollars and hence did not bear any currency risk. They were also backed by a collateral in pounds. If the Bank of England were to devalue while swap lines were still open, there was no risk to the Federal Reserve. The repayment would be in the original dollar amount. In the unlikely event of a British default, the Fed would still hold sterling as collateral. The low risk associated with swap contracts explains the low interest rates. Bordo et al. explain how interest payments worked: 'The creditor central bank invested the foreign currency that it acquired from the debtor central bank for the term of the swap in a time deposit or in some other interest-earning asset. (The debtor would do likewise with any unused balances.)'[14] In addition to bearing little interest, the unused balances could be reinvested, offsetting part of the interest payment.

Swaps between central banks were off-market accounting operations. They were a simple trade of IOUs. They had no impact on the foreign exchange market. They did not affect the money supply in either country opening a swap line or drawing on it (as long as the funds were not used). The Bank of England could then decide to use the money drawn from the swap line to intervene in the foreign exchange market. This would influence exchange rates and the money in circulation. Until the funds were used to intervene or pay a third party, swaps remained purely theoretical operations. They bore no consequences in the real world. This changed if the Bank decided to communicate the opening of a new swap line. This was the case in some rescue packages in the 1960s. The purpose of these

---

[13] 'Market offers of foreign currencies in case of emergency', B. E. MacLaury to file with copy to Coombs, Sanford, Fousek and Roche, 5 March 1964, New York, Archive of the Federal Reserve, box 616110.

[14] Bordo, Humpage and Schwartz, *Strained Relations*, 151.

rescue packages was to communicate to the market the willingness of the Bank of England to defend the pound. Otherwise, swaps were simply international reserves created 'out of thin air', as Coombs described it.[15]

## SHORT-TERM SWAPS?

Swap contracts provided dollar liquidity to the Bank to defend the pound. They were designed as a short-term solution to temporary imbalances. Swap contracts were issued for three months but could be rolled over, as they often were. Table 8.2 highlights that, between 1964 and 1968, the Bank drew close to $1.5 billion on average every year, giving it a large dollar-denominated debt. This was not temporary, as the Bank constantly rolled over swap contracts. The press was aware of the short-term nature of the swap facilities. In 1963, the New York Federal Reserve reported comments in the British press: '[T]he agreement increases only short-term liquidity, and that it should be followed by greater Anglo-American cooperation in permanently increasing world liquidity.'[16]

Table 8.2. *Annual summary of swap limits, drawings, repayments and outstanding debt*

| In million dollars | Swap line limit | Bank of England drawing | Bank of England Repayment | Outstanding debt to the Federal Reserve System |
|---|---|---|---|---|
| 1962 | 50 | 0 | 0 | 0 |
| 1963 | 500 | 0 | 0 | 0 |
| 1964 | 750 | 1,370 | 1,170 | 200 |
| 1965 | 750 | 1,765 | 1,490 | 475 |
| 1966 | 1,350 | 625 | 750 | 350 |
| 1967 | 1,500 | 1,650 | 950 | 1,050 |
| 1968 | 2,000 | 2,045 | 1,945 | 1,150 |
| 1969 | 2,000 | 795 | 1,295 | 650 |
| 1970 | 2,000 | 400 | 1,050 | 0 |
| 1971 | 2,000 | 0 | 0 | 0 |
| 1972 | 2,000 | 0 | 0 | 0 |

*Source*: Bordo, Humpage and Schwartz, *Strained Relations*.

---

[15] Coombs, *The Arena of International Finance*, 76.
[16] 'Foreign Press Comment on the Dollar–Sterling Swap', memorandum from Kotsonis and Serex to Coombs and 35 others, 5 June 1963, New York, Archives of the Federal Reserve, box 617015.

Table 8.2 demonstrates that the Bank of England had an outstanding swap position with the Federal Reserve in most years. From 1964 to 1969, the average outstanding was $646 million. During the same period, the Bank's dollar reserves were $476 million on average and total reserves were $1,479 million on average. This meant that 43 per cent of the Bank's reserves were short-term swap borrowings.[17] Almost half of the reserves the Bank owned during that period were short-term US credit. Swaps thus came to be much more than a temporary liquidity facility. They were an inherent part of British reserves. The United Kingdom was treated favourably, as Table 8.1 highlights. It demonstrates the importance of sterling for the Federal Reserve.

The confusion on the maturity of swap credit lines was widespread. In 1966, even the UK government, in pretence or in fact, did not know that these instruments were temporary. In January 1966, James Callaghan, Chancellor of the Exchequer, met Coombs. According to a note, he 'tended to assume that the Fed. swap could be rolled over beyond six months'.[18] The Chancellor had only recently learnt that 'the concept of the swap was that it should be for three months in the first instance with one extension of a further three months'.[19] This highlights the privileged position of the United Kingdom when it came to swaps. The strategic importance of the pound meant that US policymakers, and especially Coombs, were extremely lenient when it came to dollar credit. The Chancellor's surprise that these facilities were short-term reflects the extent to which these instruments gave the government breathing space. Efforts to improve the balance of payments and balance the budget could easily be deferred. There was an unlimited supply of cheap dollars. This meant that the United Kingdom had to make fewer sacrifices on fiscal and monetary policies than other countries. It was still able to maintain its Bretton Woods parity.

Swaps were more than a short-term liquidity solution for the United Kingdom. They were a feature of the Bretton Woods system. Did this enhance the stability of the international monetary system? Certainly, it helped avoid immediate crises. But did it improve the inherent stability of the Bretton Woods system? This is unclear. Contemporary observers noticed how it could increase the instability of the international monetary system. In a press review, the Federal Reserve noted how the UK Labour

[17] Data are computed using daily figures from the EEA.
[18] 'Note for the Record', I. P. Bancroft to the record, with copy to Walker, Rickett, Goldman and Galpin, 7 January 1966, London, Archive of the Bank of England, C43/49.
[19] Ibid.

Party, before gaining power in 1964, was critical of swaps. The memorandum noted that the press was echoing 'Labour's reservation about the effectiveness of the [swap] agreement on the ground that it "placed us in a position in which two currencies, both liable to attack, were trying to support each other".[20] The dollar was inherently weak and prone to attack, as Triffin and others revealed. The dollar was then used to support sterling. In turn, a weak sterling could trigger attacks on the dollar. Swap networks certainly were a useful short-term fix, but they did little to increase the long-term stability of the international monetary system.

## AN ARSENAL OF CREDIT

Swaps with the Federal Reserve quickly became the Bank's preferred credit instrument. Swaps were not communicated to the public, did not involve conditionality and could be agreed upon quickly and informally. The following paragraphs review the different sources of foreign exchange (mainly in dollars) available to the Bank of England. I present their advantages and drawbacks. Table 8.3 presents the sources of foreign currency at the disposal of the Bank of England. Privacy was a major concern for the Bank. It wanted to avoid communicating any losses or emergency loans unless they were significant enough to reassure the market.

Credit sources in Table 8.3 are classified from left to right in order of increasing term. The short-term instruments are on the left, longer-term instruments on the right. The Bank had reserves that were immediately available. But they were both limited and published regularly (see Chapter 11). Publication meant that any change would be noted by the market. It had the potential to trigger a run on sterling. Using most of the Bank's reserves, even to successfully defend sterling, was pointless as it would eventually bite back when reserves were published showing serious losses.

Swaps were favoured for their convenience, as we have just seen. They were one telephone call away and they offered total privacy. The Federal Reserve would communicate to the public only the limit of the swap line with the Bank of England. The amount drawn was secret. This meant that a swap could be raised without the market being informed.

---

[20] 'Foreign Press Comment on the Dollar–Sterling Swap', memorandum from Kotsonis and Serex to Coombs and 35 others, 5 June 1963, New York, Archives of the Federal Reserve, box 617015.

Table 8.3. *Schematic view of the Bank of England's foreign currency credit instruments*

| | Own reserves | Federal Reserve swaps | BIS facilities or 'Basel Arrangements' | IMF facilities (SBA, GAB and SDRs) | Private loans |
|---|---|---|---|---|---|
| Amount available (1960–71) | Up to reserve amount (average $1,773 million) | $50–$2,000 million | $200–$2,000 million | Up to $2,000 million | Up to third party's willingness to lend |
| Conditionality | None | None | None | None in the early 1960s but progressive introduction of conditionality | None |
| Process | Internal | Telephone call and written confirmation | Request at Basel meeting or directly to members | Formal process | Private or through Eurodollar syndicate |
| Availability | Instantaneous | One day or less | Relatively quickly | Longer process | Relatively quickly |
| Public/private | Published every three months in the Quarterly Bulletin | Drawings completely private | Private or communicated when needed | Public or often disclosed/leaked to the public | Often leaked or public |
| Term | No term | Three months renewable | Short-term | Medium to long-term | Negotiable |
| Cost/interest | None or interest-bearing for US Treasury bills | Close to Treasury bills | Negotiated on ad hoc basis | 1.5% per year on SDR | Market rates (usually higher than other forms of credit) |

The third dollar credit instrument was BIS agreements, otherwise known as Basel Arrangements. These were first used by Britain in March 1961 when sterling came under stress after a revaluation of the German mark and Dutch guilder of 5 per cent.[21] It started as a short-term loan agreement. The loan was to be repaid by 'the reflux of speculative funds or, if the reflux did not occur reasonably quickly, by recourse to the IMF'. These loan facilities were the last step before having to publicly apply for funds at the IMF. In addition to the Basel Arrangements, the United Kingdom also had access from 1965 to a Basel Group Arrangement. This special facility was intended to counter the effect of the conversion of sterling balances held overseas. The facility took the form of a swap agreement between the United Kingdom and the central banks of Austria, Belgium, Canada, Germany, Italy, Japan, the Netherlands, Sweden and Switzerland, as well as the BIS.

The IMF was the lender of last resort, in its most literal sense. The United Kingdom approached the institution only when strictly necessary, generally alongside other measures. The IMF offered various lending facilities that the Bank used: the Stand-By Arrangement (SBA) from 1952; the General Arrangement to Borrow (GAB) from 1961; and Special Drawing Rights (SDRs) from 1969. The SBA was available quite quickly and stood at $1 billion in 1964.[22] The GAB offered a lending facility of $6 billion.[23] SDRs were created to expand international liquidity. They were one of the Bank's least favourite credit tools. Because they involved a lengthy process, they could only be used as pre-emptive measures. The Bank had to request help from the IMF, which then needed to find a counter-party willing to provide dollars against SDRs. The counter-party was notified of the identity of the requestor. When used during a crisis, they would intensify the run against sterling by publicly admitting a position of weakness.

Private loans were at the disposal of the United Kingdom. They were not used frequently in the Bretton Woods period, but were used more frequently in the 1970s and 1980s. They were issued by banking syndicates on the Eurodollar market. The Eurodollar market is a dollar lending market

---

[21] F. T. Blackaby et al., *British Economic Policy 1960–74: Demand Management*, 2nd ed. (Cambridge: Cambridge University Press, 1979), 12.

[22] Scott Newton, 'The Two Sterling Crises of 1964 and the Decision Not to Devalue', *Economic History Review* 62, 1 (2009), 76–7.

[23] Bordo, Humpage and Schwartz, *Strained Relations*, 108.

located in London which emerged in the late 1960s.[24] In theory, these loans on the Eurodollar market had the advantage of being private and secret. However, in regard to the amounts borrowed, they were usually subscribed through a syndicate of private banks on the Eurodollar lending market. Schenk mentions the British government borrowing $2.5 billion from a syndicate including Chase Manhattan Bank in April 1974.[25] Schenk adds that public sector borrowers, including other countries, 'raised $44.4 billion on the Eurobond market between 1963 and 1980'.[26]

In 1964, Governor Cromer shared his intention to approach the private market for a loan with president of the New York Fed, Alfred Hayes:

Lord Cromer also mentioned the fact that Mr. John M. Meyer, Jr., Executive Vice President, Morgan Guaranty Trust Company, had just been visiting with him and proposing possible credit arrangement for the U.K. Lord Cromer had not of course informed Mr. Meyer of his earlier talks with Chase Manhattan. Lord Cromer and I agreed that while the credit idea had considerable merit, it would be well to keep it in abeyance at least for a little while longer.[27]

It is noteworthy that the governor of the Bank of England openly discussed the matter with the Federal Reserve. The Fed at the time was another important creditor for the Bank.

---

[24] For more on the Eurodollar market, see the recent exciting scholarship by a new generation of economic historians: Carlo Edoardo Altamura, *European Banks and the Rise of International Finance: The Post-Bretton Woods Era* (London: Routledge, 2016), https://doi.org/10.4324/9781315640426; Sebastian Alvarez, *Mexican Banks and Foreign Finance: From Internationalization to Financial Crisis, 1973–1982* (Houndmills: Palgrave Macmillan, 2019), https://doi.org/10.1007/978-3-030-15440-0; Ioan Balaban, 'International and Multinational Banking under Bretton Woods (1945–1971): The Experience of Italian Banks' (PhD thesis, European University Institute, 2021), https://doi.org/10.2870/429226; Seung Woo Kim, 'The Euromarket and the Making of the Transnational Network of Finance 1959–1979' (PhD thesis, University of Cambridge, 2018), https://doi.org/10.17863/CAM.23876.

[25] Schenk, *The Decline of Sterling*, 237.     [26] Ibid., 237.

[27] 'Telephone call between Cromer and Hayes', Hayes to files, 7 December 1964, New York, Archives of the Federal Reserve, box 617015.

# 9

# The 1964–1967 Currency Crisis

'This book is the record of a Government all but a year of whose life was dominated by an inherited balance of payments problem which was nearing a crisis at the moment we took office; we lived and governed during a period when that problem made a frenetic speculative attack on Britain both easy and profitable.'[1] This is how Harold Wilson (UK Prime Minister 1964–70) opened his autobiography. Simultaneously with the election of the Labour Party to power in 1964 (which itself added to pressure on sterling), a string of recurring currency crises began that would not be resolved until well after the 1967 devaluation.

After the 1964 general election, the fate of sterling and gold were increasingly intertwined. At this stage, the link between the two reserve currencies (sterling and the dollar) became apparent. US policymakers started to turn their attention to protecting sterling. The 1964 sterling crisis highlighted the role sterling still played in the stability of the international monetary system. Aware of the systemic importance of the British currency, the United States dedicated significant resources towards supporting the currency until 1967. This support would eventually prove insufficient.

From 1958 to the 1964 election, the influence of sterling was not visible on the gold market. Sterling was still relatively stable, bar a minor sterling crisis in 1961. Other international events related to the Cold War (the Cuban missile crisis and the Berlin Wall, among others) took centre stage. This put pressure on both the dollar and gold. The 1964 sterling crisis would reveal that sterling still played a role in global currency markets. Starting in autumn 1964 and continuing through to 1971, pressure on gold

[1] Wilson, *Labour Government, 1964–70.*

did not abate. The pressure was reinforced by the problem of rising inflation in the United States from 1965 onwards.[2]


## THE 1964 CRISIS

The Labour Party won the general election in October 1964. The new government was faced with fears over the devaluation of sterling. The previous administration had already been struggling with balance of payments deficits. The victory of Labour, which was 'not known for its friendliness towards the markets', made things worse.[3] Wilson himself was aware of market animosity, as he later wrote: '[W]e had always underestimated the power of the speculators against a Government of whose politics, policies and even personalities they did not approve.'[4] The literature is unanimous in stating that Labour did not want to be the party of devaluation.[5] The party was held responsible for the 1949 devaluation. Wilson did not want the electorate to 'permanently associate economic incompetence with his beloved Labour Party'.[6] Even if, as the then Chancellor of the Exchequer, James Callaghan, wrote, there was a reason for markets to expect it: 'We had been out of office for thirteen years, and there would be speculation that our first step might be to devalue sterling.'[7] However, Callaghan, like Wilson, was against devaluation because the 'Conservatives would have crucified' the Labour Party.[8]

The United States supported the decision not to devalue sterling. This meant that the United Kingdom had a strong hand in negotiating financial aid. As Schenk puts it: '[T]he key role of sterling in the international monetary system did allow Wilson and his Chancellors of the Exchequer to garner repeated large doses of international support for the sterling exchange rate both before and after the devaluation of 1967.'[9] This assistance was vital. When Callaghan was appointed Shadow Chancellor, he

---

[2] On inflation see Michael D. Bordo and Barry J. Eichengreen, 'Bretton Woods and the Great Inflation', in *The Great Inflation: The Rebirth of Modern Central Banking*, ed. Michael D. Bordo and Athanasios Orphanides (Chicago, IL: University of Chicago Press, 2013).

[3] Newton, 'The Two Sterling Crises of 1964', 78.

[4] Wilson, *Labour Government, 1964–70*, 33.

[5] Ibid., 6; Cairncross and Eichengreen, *Sterling in Decline*, 167; Raj Roy, 'The Battle for Bretton Woods: America, Britain and the International Financial Crisis of October 1967–March 1968', *Cold War History* 2, 2 (1 January 2002), 36; Schenk, *The Decline of Sterling*, 76.

[6] Roy, 'The Battle for Bretton Woods', 36.

[7] James Callaghan, *Time and Chance* (London: HarperCollins, 1987), 154.          [8] Ibid., 159.

[9] Schenk, *The Decline of Sterling*, 204.

visited the New York Fed. During his visit, he heard Hayes from the Fed speak 'very frankly about the strains on the dollar'.[10] Hayes also 'repeated more than once his belief that the best prospect for effective action in monetary matters depended upon Britain and America working together'. This was the Labour government's guarantee of US support.

There is a debate in the literature on whether 1964 witnessed one or two sterling crises. The interest of dividing the sterling crisis into sub-crises is limited. All these events were closely interlinked. Here I review the debate in the literature in the light of new evidence. What becomes clear from the data is that the Labour government not only inherited a balance of payments crisis from the previous government but was also naive in its approach to the currency market. It had been out of power for a long time. The policy goal was to avoid a devaluation. The government struggled to improve the balance of payments, despite the National Plan which was aiming to curb spending abroad and improve productivity. In this context, US support is the only reason for sterling to have avoided devaluation from 1964 to 1967.

On one side of the debate, Newton suggests that there were two sterling crises in the autumn of 1964 and that Labour handled the first one 'efficiently'.[11] The second crisis, Newton argues, was 'provoked by speculation stemming from market expectations'.[12] According to Newton, there was one crisis 'which coincided with the election result and another one which started three weeks later'. This would place the first crisis around 15 October and the second around 5 November. I analyse these dates against new data below.

On the other side of the debate, Michael Oliver wrote a reply to Newton's article.[13] Oliver posits two critiques. First, there was only one sterling crisis in the autumn of 1964. Second, the new Labour government did not display a 'textbook reaction' to the crisis but failed to react appropriately to stem speculation.[14] Using forward rates from *The Times*, Oliver argues that 'The behaviour of the 90-day forward rate suggests that sterling was not credible from September 1964'.[15] I agree with this timing.

---

[10] Callaghan, *Time and Chance*, 157.     [11] Newton, 'The Two Sterling Crises of 1964', 73.

[12] Ibid.

[13] Michael J. Oliver, 'The Two Sterling Crises of 1964: A Comment on Newton', *Economic History Review* 65, 1 (1 February 2012), 314–21.

[14] Newton, 'The Two Sterling Crises of 1964', 88; Oliver, 'The Two Sterling Crises of 1964', 314.

[15] Oliver, 'The Two Sterling Crises of 1964', 315; Bordo, MacDonald and Oliver, 'Sterling in Crisis, 1964–1967'.

Figure 9.1. Spot exchange rate, 1960–66
*Source*: Accominotti et al., 'Currency Regimes and the Carry Trade', 2017.

In fact, in September 1964 sterling had hit a three-year low and this was reported in the press at the time.

However, Oliver then argues that 'the daily dealers' reports from the Bank can be used to reconstruct changes in the reserves and allow a more accurate picture of reserve movements'.[16] This is problematic, as Bank of England reserves were not affected by intervention recorded in the dealers' reports only, but also by many other factors, as argued in previous chapters. But intervention figures from the dealers' reports, if not fully informative on reserve amounts, are an excellent tool to understand the Bank's operations. Further, I set out the actual reserve figures from the EEA. These were not available to Oliver.

When looking at the sterling exchange rate, it appears that the currency was beginning to decline in 1962 (see Figure 9.1).[17] This coincides with a period when the government accelerated its efforts to stimulate the

---

[16] Oliver, 'The Two Sterling Crises of 1964', 315.
[17] The price moved from the upper band of $2.82 per £ sterling to the lower band of $2.78 per £ sterling.

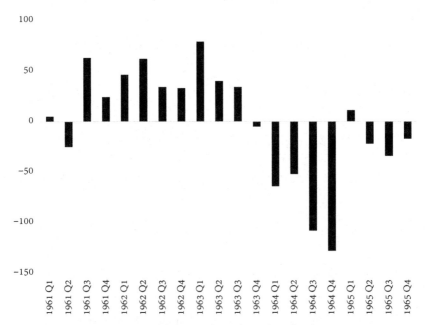

Figure 9.2. UK current account balance of payments (£ million)
Source: Office for National Statistics.

economy by its fiscal and monetary policy.[18] 1964 marked an acceleration of this decline, and sterling hit its lowest point in six years (1960–66) on 26 November at $2.7806. This rate was dangerously close to the Bretton Woods official lower band ($2.78).

The underlying issue was the balance of payments. It turned negative from the last quarter of 1963 and continued to worsen (see Figure 9.2). Yeager argues that at the beginning of 1964, 'the general picture was one of a booming home economy and weakening balance of payments'.[19] In January 1964, Yeager continues, the publication of an 'all-time record monthly deficit in merchandise trade' started to increase pressure on the pound. This pushed the government to increase the Bank Rate from 4 to 5 per cent. Coombs attributed the balance of payments problems to the 'overstimulative budget introduced by Chancellor Maudling'.[20]

[18] William A. Allen, 'The British Attempt to Manage Long-Term Interest Rates in 1962–1964', *Financial History Review* 23, 1 (April 2016), 47–70.
[19] Yeager, *International Monetary Relations*, 392.
[20] Coombs, *The Arena of International Finance*, 112.

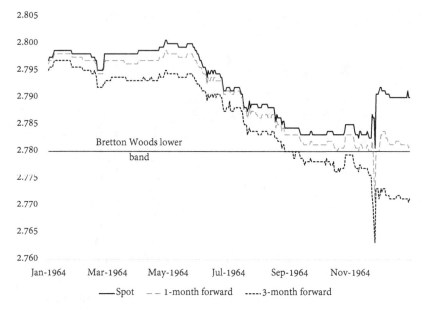

Figure 9.3. Sterling spot and one- and three-month forward rate, 1964
*Source*: Accominotti et al., 'Currency Regimes and the Carry Trade', 2017.

Articles in the *Economist* in February 1964 give a better understanding of the prevailing mood. The weekly paper expected a current account deficit of less than £100 million for the whole of the second half of 1964. The actual balance of payments deficit was much higher than that only for the last quarter of 1964, when the sterling crisis started.

Well before the 1964 election, the current and capital accounts were already deteriorating. Investors had reason to expect a further decline. Figure 9.3 highlights sterling's downward trend starting in May 1964. The prospect of a Labour victory five months ahead was most probably not the only reason for the fall. As early as late May 1964, however, the *Economist* seemed to be arguing that the prospect of a Labour win could have weighed on investors' expectations:

The fact is that many institutional investors are remaining out of the market in the belief that despite some revival in the Conservative Party's fortunes there is going to be a Labour victory at the October election and that the best investment policy in the intervening month is to build up liquid funds.[21]

---

[21] 'Adverse Trade Wind', *Economist*, 23 May 1964, 867.

Even if there was little coverage of the British election in the US press, some reports in the financial press can be found. In July 1964, the *Wall Street Journal* reported that the 'worst' could happen in an article entitled 'Capitalism under Fire': 'nationalization can be expected to become an increasingly important issue. And one with highly significant overtones for the American businessman and investor', and further that 'unions have settled on an approach that strongly attacks free enterprise'.[22] There are good reasons to believe that the worsening of sterling starting at the end of May might have been due in part to fears of a Labour victory in the context of weak fundamentals.

Sterling weakened both because of the disappointing balance of payments figures presented in Figure 9.2 and the prospect of a Labour win. Press reports from August to November 1964 give a better understanding of what information investors could receive. On 19 August, forecasts from the National Institute of Economic and Social Research announced deficit figures. The current account deficit 'could well be around £500 million', a disappointing figure.[23] The same day, the *New York Times* reported that sterling had hit a three-year low.[24] Sterling would again hit a new three-year low a few days later, as reported in the *Wall Street Journal*.[25] At this point, sterling was under stress, with negative press reports published on most days. Most simply mention pressure on sterling but rarely link this with the election campaign.

On 18 September, more negative trade figures were published, though these did not trigger a noticeable market reaction.[26] The weak state of the economy started to put pressure on Labour. The party would have to deal with the consequences if elected (which was the most likely outcome). Wilson had to 'present the country with a more grim financial picture' to avoid taking full blame for a possible currency crisis if elected.[27]

When Labour did win on 15 October, it did not have much of an impact on the foreign exchange market. The market had already factored in the

---

[22] Ray Vicker, 'Capitalism under Fire: British Unions, Sensing a Labor Victory, Mount Attack', *Wall Street Journal*, 2 July 1964, 10.

[23] 'Deficit of £500 m. Forecast: Sterling Drops Again', *Guardian*, 19 August 1964, 11.

[24] 'Pound Continues Slump in London: Sterling Declines to Lowest Level in Three Years', *New York Times*, 19 August 1964, 51.

[25] 'Sterling Rate Steadies after Fall to $2.7847, Lowest in Three Years', *Wall Street Journal*, 26 August 1964.

[26] Clyde H. Farnsworth, 'Britain's Deficit in Trade Deepens', *New York Times*, 18 September 1964, 45.

[27] Nora Beloff, 'Wilson Pressed to Sound Crisis Alarm', *Observer*, 27 September 1964, 2.

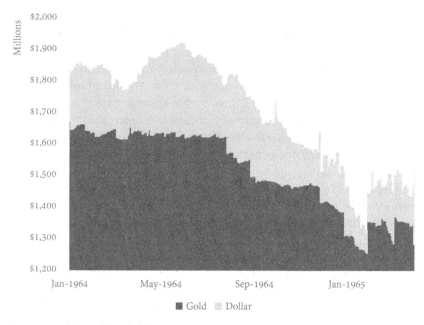

Figure 9.4. EEA gold and dollar reserves
*Source*: EEA ledgers.
*Note*: Scale starts at $1,200 million.

Labour win. The Bank of England dealers reported dollar sales of $10.24 million on the Friday following the election.[28] This is around 2.5 times the average daily intervention of previous years. A few days later, on 23 October, dealers at the Bank had to intervene for $31.5 million, eight times the average intervention. Pressure had increased. Overall, however, there seems not to have been a major crisis. The election of Labour was indeed factored into the market price of sterling.

The period between the election and early November (the point when Newton sees a second sterling crisis) was a quieter period. This lends some support to his thesis of two distinct sterling crises. The exchange stayed steady, albeit close to the lower band. However, when looking at reserve figures from the EEA (see Figure 9.4), British reserves were continuously worsening. This reveals constant pressure on the Bank of England. The Bank lost reserves from June 1964 onward. Sterling was effectively in crisis from late August 1964 to the 1967 devaluation, and even beyond that. Wilson echoed this when he later wrote: 'It is difficult to describe what it

---

[28] The comparison is with the average for 1952 (when the sample starts) to 15 October 1964.

meant to live against a background of this persistent speculation, speculation in the main made possible only by the balance of payments deficit. Indeed it virtually disappeared as a threat once we moved into strong surplus some five years later.'[29] Sterling was consistently close to the $2.78 lower band, with the government lurching from one rescue package to another.

What happened in Newton's 'second crisis'? Wilson mentions a 'run on sterling which began, following the Chancellor's Ways and Means statement on 11th November'.[30] The run, according to Wilson, was 'easy to explain': international companies in London feared devaluation because of the balance of payments deficit and therefore decided to move their sterling into safer currencies (mainly the dollar). This led to a run on sterling, leading to additional pressure. Wilson argued that markets did not like a 'Government concerned, even at a difficult time, with payments of the old-age pensioners and others in need, concerned to provide charitable largesse which our foreign critics felt Britain could not afford'.[31] Wilson's explanation describes the channel speculators took and not why they feared for their assets, other than the state of the balance of payments. By pursuing an expansionary domestic policy while still wanting to maintain a fixed exchange rate, the government was violating the macroeconomic trilemma. Beyond the deficit, it appears that the market did not trust the Chancellor's plans expressed on 11 November. This matches the timing of the 'second crisis' posited by Newton.

The press was critical of Chancellor Callaghan's budget. The *Wall Street Journal* reported the 'initial reaction to the special budget from businessmen was that it isn't likely to help much in solving the nation's most pressing problem, the serious deficit in the international balance of payments'.[32] This fell short of the currency market's expectations, which hoped more drastic changes would be introduced to redress the situation.

Callaghan himself admitted that his handling of the City was a learning process: 'I did not learn the ways of the City until I had held the post for some time, and consequently made mistakes.'[33] One of his first mistakes was made on 11 November. The City was sceptical of his ability. Callaghan did nothing to alleviate their doubts in his Ways and Means speech. His emergency budget fell short of expectations. The budget was meant to calm

---

[29] Wilson, *Labour Government, 1964–70*, 32.     [30] Ibid., 33.     [31] Ibid., 34.
[32] 'Britain's Budget Raises Benefits and Income Taxes', *Wall Street Journal*, 12 November 1964, 6.
[33] Callaghan, *Time and Chance*, 153.

the markets. But it contained few fundamental reforms for this purpose, apart from a new tax on petrol, which would raise £93 million. Most measures proposed were to take effect much later. The *Economist* noted: 'A disturbing point about Mr Callaghan's first emergency budget is that it contains an unduly large proportion of just such post-dated measures.'[34]

To sum up, the 1964 crisis started before Labour took office. It cannot only be blamed on Labour. The crisis became strongly accentuated in the run-up to the general election by fears of the party's victory. Once elected, the government failed to solve the crisis until well after the 1967 devaluation. Dividing the crisis into sub-crises does not help us make sense of the events. This long currency crisis put a strain on the economy.

The crisis also put pressure on the dollar, as we will see. In Callaghan's words: 'Sterling's devaluation would add to the difficulties of the dollar and might dislodge the Bretton Woods system, as in fact happened when sterling was eventually devalued in 1967.'[35]

## THE GOLD CRISIS

1964 marked the beginning of a four-year crisis for the London gold market.[36] The crisis only ended with the creation of a two-tier gold market in March 1968. The crisis started in September 1964. At that point, the Gold Pool was no longer able to accumulate gold and the gold price started to rise (see Figure 9.5). Three factors played a major role: first, the US election, followed by fears of inflation in the United States; second, the French attempts to discredit the international monetary system; and third, the crisis in the secondary reserve currency, sterling.

The start of the gold crisis coincides with both the US and UK elections. It is difficult to disentangle the effect of the 15 October 1964 UK general election from the influence of the 3 November US presidential election. Both played a role in the worsening of the London gold price. The market feared a sterling devaluation and Lyndon Johnson's campaign for a 'Great Society' could have caused inflation which might have led to pressure on gold–dollar parity. To make matters worse, in February 1965 French President Charles de Gaulle delivered a speech attacking the foundation of the international monetary system.

---

[34] 'Labour's Tanner', *Economist*, 14 November 1964, 671.

[35] Callaghan, *Time and Chance*, 160.

[36] This part draws heavily on joint work with Bordo and Monnet: see Bordo, Monnet and Naef, 'The Gold Pool (1961–1968) and the Fall of Bretton Woods'.

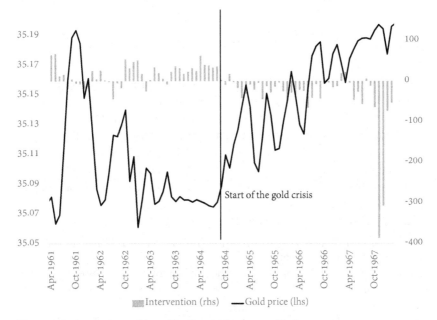

Figure 9.5. Average monthly gold prices and net monthly intervention
*Source:* Dealers' reports (C8) and author's calculations.

The 1964 sterling crisis exacerbated the contagion from sterling to the dollar. Sterling is an important explanatory factor in the gold crisis. This does not mean that the US election (and later US inflation in the context of the Vietnam War) and French calls for reform played no role. The timing of the events presented here seems to give more importance to the role of sterling than previously assumed. The sterling crisis needs to be reconsidered as an important explanation for the increase in the gold price starting in 1964. The literature has focused on both US and French influences, but the role of sterling has not yet been examined by economic historians in detail. This is what I do here.

1961–64 witnessed crises for the dollar emanating from the Cold War. The trend changed in 1964. 1964–67 were crisis years for sterling and this indirectly affected the dollar. Here I review the timing of the contagion from sterling to gold and determine the impact of the sterling crises on the Gold Pool. Normally, a depreciation of sterling, the second most important reserve currency, should have led to an appreciation of the dollar. Investors would normally move from one reserve currency to another when faced with a fall in sterling. However, on this occasion they did not. Econometric evidence shows the opposite. When sterling depreciated, the dollar lost value against gold. More pressure on sterling meant that the gold price rose against the dollar. In response, the Gold Pool had to invest more resources to defend it. This is interpreted as contagion from sterling, the secondary reserve currency, to the dollar, the main reserve currency.

The argument is not new. In 1964, Coombs warned the Federal Open Market Committee (FOMC) of the disastrous consequences of a sterling devaluation. He used the fear of a global collapse to persuade the FOMC to lend more funds to the Bank of England. He argued: '[T]he British might decide to devalue sterling. This would probably precipitate an international financial crisis of the first magnitude. He [Coombs] would expect to see a major speculative drive on the London gold market and sooner or later an even more dangerous attack on the US dollar.'[37]

Despite Britain not devaluing sterling, as Coombs had feared, the situation of the London gold market worsened in parallel to the run-up to the 1964 sterling crisis. After the initial crisis of September–October 1964, sterling experienced almost continuous downward pressure until the 1967 devaluation. This had an impact on the international monetary system. The Gold Pool's losses started in autumn 1964. The losses caused fundamental disagreements among Gold Pool members on the goals of the syndicate. Toniolo and Clement note that at the March 1965 gold experts' meeting at the BIS the French and Belgian delegates were unhappy. They 'did not join their colleagues in giving solemn assurances as to the medium-term continuation of Gold Pool operations'.[38] At the same venue in November 1964, Coombs reported that central bankers across Europe and the United States worried about the impact of sterling on the international monetary system. At the November meeting Coombs reported: 'In private conversations all the foreign department men from European central banks I met that weekend felt that we faced an explosive situation in both the gold and foreign exchange markets. They were particularly fearful that a massive speculative attack on sterling would react back on the dollar as well.'[39]

The pressure on the gold market was visible in two indicators: the price of gold and the cost of intervention. The more the Bank of England had to intervene to keep the price of gold under control, the more pressure there was. The Bank could either let the price rise, or waste Gold Pool reserves and intervene to keep it in check. These two indicators can be combined to

---

[37] Coombs, *The Arena of International Finance*, 118.
[38] Toniolo and Clement, *Central Bank Cooperation*, 411.
[39] Coombs, *The Arena of International Finance*, 114.

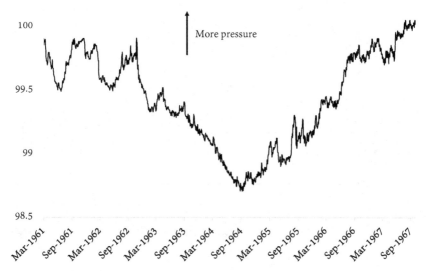

Figure 9.6. The Exchange Market Pressure index for gold
*Source*: Dealers' reports (C8) for the gold price and gold interventions.

form a rudimentary Exchange Market Pressure index for gold.[40] EMPs help give a more detailed idea of the market pressure. They can be sensitive to calibration and yield a picture that can be biased by the choice of variables. Instead of using daily intervention figures, the index is computed by using the cumulative intervention of the amount of gold bought or sold by the Gold Pool. This shows trends rather than noisy daily changes and helps identify trends and breaks in trends. The index is plotted in Figure 9.6. The average values for 1961 are set at 100. Higher values indicate more pressure on the gold market.

The index shows declining pressure at the end of 1962. The lower the index, the less the pressure. A downward trend indicates both that the price of gold was not rising and that the Gold Pool was able to accumulate gold for its members. The Gold Pool was successful in keeping the gold market under control during the early years of the syndicate. There is a

---

[40] EMPs usually have an interest rate component, but because this index is not for a currency, but for gold, there is no interest rate. For literature on EMPs, see Eichengreen, Rose and Wyplosz, 'Speculative Attacks on Pegged Exchange Rates'; Eichengreen and Gupta, 'Tapering Talk'.

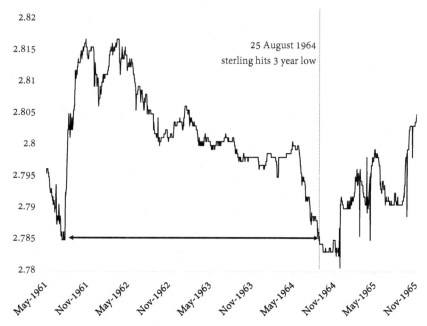

Figure 9.7. Sterling spot exchange rate, May 1961–November 1964
*Source*: Accominotti et al., 'Currency Regimes and Carry Trade'.

reversal of the trend in September 1964. At this stage, the Gold Pool started selling more gold than it was accumulating and the gold price tended to rise as pressure on the market was mounting. What prompted this sudden reversal? Both the US election and speculation against sterling increased pressure on the London gold market. These factors increased in 1964–65. They progressively put pressure on the gold price. This threatened the stability of the international monetary system.

It is uncontroversial to assume that investors were influenced by the press. Therefore, press reports at the beginning of the gold crisis provide partial answers. The trend of the EMP shown in Figure 9.6 reversed on 14 September 1964. The trend for the gold price alone reversed on 25 August.[41] On 25 August, the *Wall Street Journal* published an article entitled 'Sterling Rate Steadies after Fall to $2.7847, Lowest in Three Years'.[42] This can be seen in Figure 9.7. The *Wall Street Journal* attributed

---

[41] Reversal here is chosen as the troughs (or low points) which are never reached again for the rest of the sample.

[42] 'Sterling Rate Steadies after Fall to $2.7847, Lowest in Three Years', *Wall Street Journal*, 26 August 1964.

the fall to 'the mounting British trade deficit, the prospect of future deterioration in the international balance of payments and uncertainties caused by the upcoming parliamentary election'.[43]

On the same day that sterling hit a three-year low, the gold price started its continuous climb from 25 August to September 1969. This analysis does not exclude other explanations. US inflation or French pressure could also be at play. But the negative news about sterling is likely linked to an increase in the gold price. The situation in the United States certainly also played a role. For example, on 15 August the *Economist* reported that the London gold market was exposed to 'uncertainties over the Vietnam crisis which had carried the price to a five-month high'.[44] After this announcement, however, the gold price recovered rapidly.

The mounting pressure on the gold market was not noticed by the Bank of England at the time. On several occasions the Bank told the Fed by telephone what it thought caused the gold price increase. One day it was 'the demand of gold was ... still in good volume' because of 'the long weekend because of the holiday in New York' (8 October 1964)[45]. Another day it was 'reflecting the usual Thursday demand and the long weekend because of the holiday here on Monday' (3 September 1964). The reasons for the increase were not clear to Bridge, who also attributed the 'gold buying to the situation in Vietnam' (27 August 1964). The Bank was looking for excuses for the rise in the gold price. With the benefit of hindsight, we can see that it was a trend reversal and not occasional events that moved the gold price. The change of trend in August 1964 was a fundamental change, not a succession of small events as the Bank thought. The Vietnam War certainly put pressure on the gold price, but it was not clear why this started in August 1964.

After taking office, the new Labour government was advised by the Bank to raise interest rates to support the pound. The new government was hesitant. It delayed the rate hike until 23 November and imposed a sharp 2 per cent hike. This increase took place on a Monday instead of the usual Thursday, and informed the market that the situation was serious.[46] Sterling recovered on the morning of the rate rise, but by midday panic had returned.[47] The rate hike had consequences beyond the United

---

[43] Ibid.    [44] 'Money and Exchanges', *Economist*, 15 August 1964, 686.

[45] All the quotes in this paragraph and the next are from telephone records for various dates, 1964, New York, Archives of the Federal Reserve, box 617015.

[46] Harry G. Johnson, 'The Sterling Crisis of 1967 and the Gold Rush of 1968', *Nebraska Journal of Economics and Business* 7, 2 (1968): 6.

[47] Coombs, *The Arena of International Finance*, 115.

Figure 9.8. Cumulative Gold Pool interventions in million dollars from the creation of the Pool (6 November 1961) to November 1966
*Source*: Dealers' reports (C8)

Kingdom. It also prompted a rate increase in the United States. According to the Federal Reserve, the rate hike was agreed on 'to maintain the international strength of the dollar'.[48] Chairman Martin admitted: 'If it hadn't been for the British action, the Federal Reserve Board wouldn't have increased the discount rate at this time.'[49] For the New York Fed, the British move triggered an 'emergency session' of its directors. It was the 'first increase in 30 years that didn't come at a regularly scheduled directors' meeting'.[50] If a 2 per cent increase in the United Kingdom had been expected to trigger a reaction in the United States, the last-minute and dramatic nature of the United States' reaction shows the influence of sterling on the dollar. This certainly did not reassure investors and helps explain their flight out of sterling and out of the dollar into gold.

After showing the impact of sterling, Figure 9.8 offers an overview of cumulative Gold Pool intervention. When the figure increases, it means

---

[48] 'Discount Rate in 5 Districts Lifted to 4% after Britain Boosts Bank Rate to 7%', *Wall Street Journal*, 24 November 1964, 3.
[49] Ibid.     [50] Ibid.

that the Gold Pool is faced with mild market conditions and is able to buy gold. A decrease means more pressure on the gold market. The figure also highlights key dates in the three possible causes of the gold crisis starting in 1964.

As the EMP (see Figure 9.6) illustrates, the gold market started to worsen in mid-September. In a first sequence, from around September 1964 to January 1965, interventions were limited while the price was increasing. The cumulative surplus of the Pool stabilised, but was not yet starting to decrease (see Figure 9.8). In other words, the Gold Pool was no longer able to buy gold without upsetting the price. It was not yet forced to sell gold to the market. From the 1964 sterling crisis onwards, the cumulative surplus of the Gold Pool decreased. Gold Pool members increasingly had to contribute to the Gold Pool instead of simply being allowed to buy the excess gold.

De Gaulle's speech undoubtedly worsened the situation in February 1965. On 4 February, he declared that France would systematically convert excess dollar reserves into gold at the Fed Window. This speech was followed by France's conversion of dollars into gold at the Fed. French conversions were concentrated from early 1965 to mid-1966.[51] After 1966, France had run out of dollars to convert into gold. During this time, France remained a member of the Gold Pool.

The Bank of England dealers were, at best, unimpressed by the speech. Their daily report reads: 'The statement on the gold exchange standard by General de Gaulle did not create any fresh activity in the gold market; it came after effective dealing hours for Continental operators.'[52] The next day, dealers noted that 'buying was rather heavy' on the gold market.[53] The report continues: 'General de Gaulle's discourse had little effect upon the exchange market although there was at first a disposition for dollars to be offered in Switzerland.'

A closer look at the London gold price and the intervention operations by the Bank of England in 1965 lead to a similar conclusion. While the speech was followed by one month of general gold price increases, interventions during this time do not seem to show that the Gold Pool was in distress. It is difficult to disentangle the effects of events in the United States and United Kingdom from de Gaulle's speech. The French announcement happened on an upward trend in the gold price. One

---

[51] This is analysed in more detail in Figure 10.2.
[52] Daily dealers' reports, 4 February 1965, London, Archives of the Bank of England, C8/29.
[53] Daily dealers' reports, 5 February 1965, London, Archives of the Bank of England, C8/29.

month after the speech, the Bank of England spent \$54.6 million on behalf of the Gold Pool. The month before it had only spent \$7.7 million. The effect was only short-lived as the net losses of the Pool were \$18.2 million during the three months before and \$19.2 million during the three months after de Gaulle's speech. The speech was not a game changer. Later in 1965, Gold Pool operations suffered from the worsening of the US balance of payments and the rise in US inflation.[54]

It is not possible to disentangle quantitatively the exact contribution of sterling from the worsening conditions in the United States and the attacks by the French president. All three factors certainly played a role in the gold crisis. Next we will see how to quantify this impact.

STERLING AND GOLD

There was contagion from sterling to gold.[55] These two prices were linked, but the relationship is different from what might have been expected. A downward shock to the price of sterling tended to make gold appreciate against the dollar. A shock to sterling led to global instability. This led investors to withdraw from the dollar and invest in gold, which was seen to be a safe haven. This in turn put pressure on US gold reserves, adding to the crisis. This link had been described and understood by some, but not all, contemporaries.[56]

From the 1964 crisis to the 1967 devaluation, there is a negative correlation between the three-month sterling forward rate and the gold price in dollars. Forward rates show the situation of sterling and offer a better proxy than spot rates. They were less subject to intervention by the Bank of England.[57] They also present more volatility, which helps the interpretation. In Figure 9.9, the relationship seems to show that the lower the three-month forward sterling rate, the higher the London gold price. Troubles for sterling with larger forward discounts seem to affect the gold

[54] Bordo and Eichengreen, 'Bretton Woods and the Great Inflation'; Francis J. Gavin, *Gold, Dollars, and Power: The Politics of International Monetary Relations, 1958–1971* (Chapel Hill, NC: University of North Carolina Press, 2007).

[55] This part draws heavily on joint work with Bordo and Monnet: Bordo, Monnet and Naef, 'The Gold Pool and the Fall of Bretton Woods'.

[56] Coombs often mentioned the risk of contagion from the pound to the dollar through the London gold market. See Coombs, *The Arena of International Finance*.

[57] See Chapter 4 as well as Alain Naef, 'Dirty Float or Clean Intervention? The Bank of England in the Foreign Exchange Market', *European Review of Economic History* 25, 1 (2 February 2021): 180–201, https://doi.org/10.1093/ereh/heaa011.

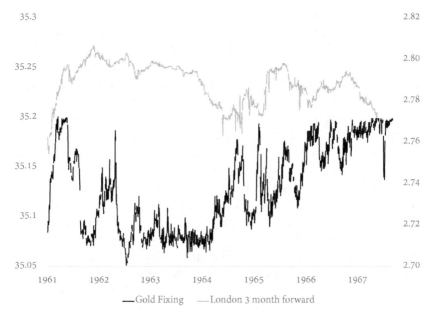

Figure 9.9. Gold fixing price at 11 am and London dollar/sterling three-month forward rate
*Source*: Forward data Accominotti et al., 'Currency Regimes and the Carry Trade'.

market negatively. This is most apparent after the election of Labour at the end of 1964. The election marked the beginning of a volatile period for sterling, with sustained pressure on the London gold market. It also appears in 1962 and 1963, although variations then were more modest.[58] Starting in June 1967, the gold price stabilised near its maximum. It reached a ceiling of $35.20, the level at which the Gold Pool intervened constantly. At the same time, the sterling forward rate continued to depreciate.

Why is a negative correlation between the two series evidence of contagion between the two reserve currencies? During Bretton Woods, currencies were all subject to one-way speculation. If a currency was under stress, shorting that currency involved practically no risk as it could only be devalued or stay at the existing parity. There was no risk of sudden appreciation of the currency. This made shorting a risk-free bet. Sterling and the dollar were the two most traded currencies at the time. Rumours of

---

[58] When running the regressions yearly, 1962 and 1963 also show a negative coefficient, but not 1961.

devaluation on sterling would lead to a flight out of sterling into the dollar. Equally, when rumours of a dollar devaluation were circulating, investors would sell dollars and seek refuge in the second largest currency, sterling. This is what you would expect. If this does not happen, however, it means that investors running out of sterling do not see the dollar as a safe enough currency. That means there is contagion from sterling to the dollar.

Is there a negative correlation between the gold price and the sterling forward rate? To test this, the London price of gold is regressed on the forward sterling rate with a one-period lag. Data are daily, the gold price comes from the Bank of England archives and the forward rates from Accominotti et al.[59] Using a lag is a way to cope with the fact that the value of the exchange rate is determined at the end of the day, whereas fixing the gold price takes place in the morning. The estimated equation includes a constant. The estimation is corrected for auto-correlation using the Huber–White procedure. Over the full sample (January 1961 to November 1967 or March 1968), the London price of gold is stationary. The data are in levels in the estimation and not as a difference. There is no co-integration relationship between the two variables.

The first estimation sample excludes the 1967 devaluation and stops on 15 November 1967. It yields a coefficient of –0.58. This means that when the forward exchange rate depreciates by one basis point, the gold price increases by approximately 0.6 basis points. Put differently, a decrease in the forward exchange rate from 2.8 to 2.75 is associated with an increase in the price of gold from 35.08 to 35.11. The second column in Table 9.1 shows that the coefficient is smaller when December 1967 to March 1968 is included. During this period, despite large variations in the sterling exchange rate, the gold price was kept constant at the upper band thanks to Gold Pool interventions.

Different sub-samples were analysed to determine whether this relationship was constant over time. This raises an econometric issue. The price of gold was not trend-stationary over 1964–66 when the Gold Pool allowed a continuous increase until it reached the upper bound of \$35.20. The Augmented Dickey–Fuller Unit root test confirms that the series is trend-stationary between the October 1964 sterling crisis and the November 1967 sterling devaluation. For this sub-sample, a linear trend is added to the estimation (labelled Trend in Table 9.1). The negative relationship holds. It is still significant over 1964–67 but not over the

[59] Accominotti et al., 'Currency Regimes and the Carry Trade'; 'Dealers' reports', London, Archives of the Bank of England, C8.

Table 9.1. *The relationship between the gold price and the sterling forward rate (daily data)*

| | Dependent variable: London gold price (fixing) | | | |
|---|---|---|---|---|
| | January 1961–November 1967 | January 1961–March 1968 | January 1961–October 1964 | September 1964–November 1967 |
| Sterling forward rate (–1) | –0.58*** | –0.16*** | 0.64** | –0.89*** |
| | (0.17) | (0.02) | (0.31) | (0.09) |
| Trend | | | | 0.01*** |
| | | | | (0.01) |
| Constant | 36.75*** | 35.57*** | 37.10*** | 37.10*** |
| | (0.48) | (0.05) | (0.26) | (0.26) |
| Adjusted R-square | 0.01 | 0.04 | 0.01 | 0.12 |
| No. observations | 1,708 | 1,788 | 790 | 919 |

*** signifies statistical significance at the 1% level; ** signifies statistical significance at the 5% level; * signifies statistical significance at the 10% level.

previous sub-sample (January 1961–October 1964). The period 1961–63 is not uneventful, but sterling troubles in 1961 and 1963 are short-lived. As argued earlier, the period was marked by international political crises. These crises did not foster contagion between dollar and sterling. The sterling effect on the gold–dollar price only really emerges with the 1964 sterling crisis.

# 10

# The 1967 Devaluation and the Fall
# of the Gold Pool

The 1967 devaluation triggered the collapse of the Gold Pool, setting the stage for the demise of Bretton Woods.[1] Policymakers at the time feared that a sterling devaluation would have consequences for the stability of the international monetary system. What they did not expect was the strength of the run on gold that followed. The devaluation, more than anything else, was the main cause of the run on gold starting at the end of November 1967. Less than four months later, the Gold Pool was disbanded. Subsequently, US policies were more isolationist. It was the first breach in the Bretton Woods system. It would eventually end some 150 years of (sometimes interrupted) gold-backed systems. If the gold standard started with Britain in 1821, it ended in Britain with the 1967 devaluation. US inflation and external imbalances played an important role in the end of the Bretton Woods system, but the 1967 devaluation was the spark that triggered it.

Economist Harry Johnson argued in 1968 that if the sterling devaluation had occurred in 1964–65 or even in 1966, it might not have triggered a run on gold.[2] In 1967, however, inflation in the United States was growing rapidly, and therefore the 1967 devaluation did trigger a run on gold. In Johnson's view, 'The immediate source of the gold rush was the belief that, like the pound, the dollar was overvalued and would have to be devalued.'[3]

What is the link between sterling devaluation and the disbanding of the Gold Pool? Econometric analysis will help us better understand the relationship between the two events. I also show the minor role France played,

---

[1] This part draws heavily on joint work with Bordo and Monnet: Bordo, Monnet and Naef, 'The Gold Pool (1961–1968) and the Fall of the Bretton Woods System'.
[2] Johnson, 'The Sterling Crisis of 1967', 10.　　[3] Ibid., 15.

contrary to the claims made in earlier literature.[4] Daily Gold Pool intervention figures and Fed gold window operation data help make the case here. These data are withheld in the archives of the New York Fed. But documents from the BIS allowed the reconstruction of operations at the Fed gold window, offering a new story. Finally, relying on the press at the time, I give an overview of the timing of the run on gold.

## A BRITISH TRIGGER TO AN INTERNATIONAL CRISIS

Existing literature mentions the link between the run on gold and the 1967 devaluation. Gavin cites a study by the Federal Reserve in the summer of 1966. The study anticipated that a sterling devaluation of 15 per cent would produce 'serious market uncertainties about the viability of other exchange rates, including those of the dollar'.[5] This fear was shared by policymakers such as Secretary of the US Treasury Henry Fowler. He stated a few weeks before the devaluation that 'if sterling falls, there will be great monetary unrest. The dollar will be affected strongly'.[6]

In its 1968 annual report, the Federal Reserve noted that the 'devaluation of the pound sterling on November 18th, 1967 was a major shock to the world's financial system'.[7] Later, the report argued that a week after the devaluation, 'the private demand for gold surged to record levels in the London and other foreign markets'. This was because 'confidence in exchange parities was badly shaken'. In 1968, the economist Harry Johnson noted a similar link between devaluation and gold price collapse. He wrote that 'purchase of gold for private use was rising rapidly in the period up to immediately before the speculation associated with the devaluation of sterling'.[8] Bordo and colleagues remarked that the dollar started to weaken after the sterling devaluation.[9] Bordo notes mounting pressure on the dollar 'via the London gold market'.[10] Schenk observes that Gold Pool losses in the wake of the devaluation put the syndicate under

---

[4] Allan H. Meltzer, 'U.S. Policy in the Bretton Woods Era – Review – St. Louis Fed', *Federal Reserve Bank of St. Louis Review*, 73 (May/June) (1991), 54–83; Eichengreen, *Global Imbalances and the Lessons of Bretton Woods*.

[5] Gavin, *Gold, Dollars, and Power*, 168.     [6] Ibid., 171.

[7] Federal Reserve Bank of New York, Annual Report 1968, 28 February 1969.

[8] Harry G. Johnson, 'The Gold Rush of 1968 in Retrospect and Prospect', *American Economic Review* 59, 2 (1969), 346.

[9] Bordo, White and Simard, 'France and the Breakdown of the Bretton Woods International Monetary System', 16.

[10] Bordo, 'Bretton Woods', 70.

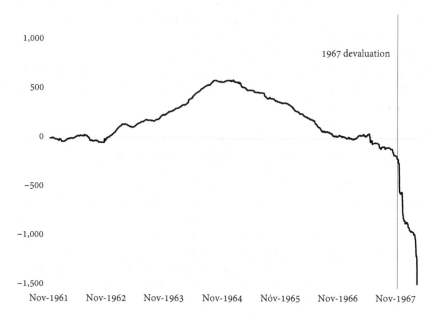

Figure 10.1. Cumulative Gold Pool interventions in million dollars from the creation of the Pool (6 November 1961) to its fall (14 March 1968)
*Source*: Dealers' reports (C8).

stress, even while the syndicate released a joint statement on 26 November in support of the $35 an ounce price.[11] Eichengreen also writes that, after the Middle East crisis of early 1967, the devaluation 'further undermined confidence in the remaining reserve currency, the dollar'.[12] There is broad agreement in the literature that after the devaluation, pressure on the gold market increased.

The US authorities anticipated that the sterling devaluation would be a shock to the gold–dollar market. But they did not prepare enough to absorb this shock fully. Or maybe they overestimated their ability to handle the situation. That the 1967 devaluation would cause instability in the international monetary system was clear to contemporaries. What was not clear was how this contagion would take place.

Figure 10.1 shows the impact of the sterling devaluation on Gold Pool operations. It was a rapid and violent shock. After the devaluation, the Gold Pool lost in excess of $1,238 million over just a few months, according to the dealers' reports.

---

[11] Schenk, *The Decline of Sterling*, 182.    [12] Eichengreen, *Global Imbalances*, 57.

The increase in Gold Pool interventions after the sterling devaluation is associated with a decrease of an unprecedented scale in US reserves. I use a Bai–Perron autoregressive test on monthly US monetary gold reserves. The test reveals a break in December 1967, the month following the sterling devaluation.[13] The results are robust whether the sample covers the whole Bretton Woods period (1944–71) or only the 1960s.[14]

## THE FRENCH OR STERLING?

After seeing the importance of sterling, what role did France play? The consensus is that France played a substantial part in the fall of the Gold Pool. France's role was minor at best compared with the impact of the 1967 devaluation. If de Gaulle's 1965 speech had an impact on the Gold Pool, by 1967 France had little influence on the international monetary system. A commonly held belief in the literature is that France was instrumental in the fall of the Gold Pool. This might not be true at all. New data on the activity of central banks at the Federal Reserve gold window show that France only played a role until 1966. In 1967 when the Gold Pool started to lose significant amounts of gold, France was out of the picture. The French gave the Gold Pool bad press on occasions, but never threatened the institution. The French stayed in the Pool until the end, and their influence was minor. They even voluntarily avoided any action that would have directly endangered the syndicate.

The literature mentions the role of France in the fall of the Gold Pool. But there is no clear indication of how the country affected the gold syndicate. Coombs mentions the 'Gaullist attack on the dollar and sterling' as one of the causes of the fall of the Gold Pool.[15] Eichengreen mentions the attack by the French president as one of many contributing factors to a deteriorating situation after 1964.[16] Meltzer argues that '1967 is the peak for France's accumulation of gold'.[17] This claim is contradicted by new data to which Meltzer did not have access. The French themselves were

---

[13] Using a sample from 1960–70. The break is robust in many different settings (trimming: 10–25%, significance: 1%, maximum breaks: 1–5).

[14] The break is also found in the 1947–70 specification (trimming 10%, maximum breaks: 2–5, and 5% significance).

[15] Coombs, *The Arena of International Finance*, 155.

[16] Eichengreen, *Globalizing Capital*, 52.

[17] Meltzer, 'U.S. Policy in the Bretton Woods Era, 63.

eager to claim that what they did was powerful enough to shape the destiny of the international monetary system.[18]

Let us first see how the gold window worked. Only central banks had access to the Federal Reserve gold window, not private customers. It gave central bankers direct access to US gold stocks at $35 an ounce. The window prevented central banks from buying gold directly in private gold markets such as the London gold market. By keeping central banks out of the market, gold window operations left the gold price unaffected. The facility directly depleted US gold stocks. The United States was guaranteeing the price of gold in the Bretton Woods system. If US gold stocks ran low, there was a risk of a run on US gold. This is just as depositors would precipitate a run on a bank if they believed it did not have enough capital. This explains why, when de Gaulle announced in 1965 that France would convert its dollar holdings at the Fed gold window instead of holding them as reserves, it put pressure on the United States. What was never established in the literature, because the data were kept secret, is when the French converted dollars into gold at the gold window. Also unknown was the magnitude of their purchases. We knew about their words, but not their actions.

Here I present new data on the Fed gold window from two indirect sources of institutions which both collected the information from the New York Fed. The Fed is still unable to share these data more than half a century after the events.[19] This highlights their sensitive nature. The first and main source of the quarterly numbers is a report on gold consumption and production from the BIS.[20] This report was first written in 1962 and new data were added yearly. The second source is the minutes that the Banque de France kept of the gold experts' meetings in Basel. Recall that the Gold Pool was managed by a group of experts from participating central banks during monthly meetings in Basel. During these meetings, the state of US gold reserves was occasionally discussed. The Banque de France kept detailed minutes of these meetings. Sometimes gold window operations were reported. The data for the last quarter of 1966 are missing from both these sources.

---

[18] Monnet, 'French Monetary Policy and the Bretton Woods System'.

[19] The Fed was very helpful but, for legal reasons, was unable to share anything that relates to gold transactions with foreign central banks unless they received explicit consent from the given institution. They confirmed that even through a request invoking the Freedom of Information Act (FOIA), the data would be redacted.

[20] Report on gold consumption and production, 30 November 1962, addendum 8 February 1969, BISA 7.18 (12) DEA 20.

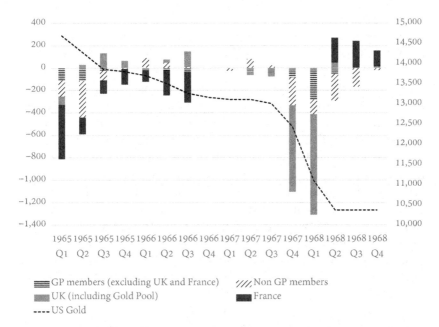

Figure 10.2. US gold window customer operations

*Sources*: gold consumption and production, Archives of the BIS, BISA 7.18 (12) DEA 20. Q3 1966 comes from the 'Minutes of the gold experts meeting', 5 November 1966, Archives of the Banque de France, 467200501-74. During the Gold Pool, sales and purchases by the United Kingdom are those of the Gold Pool.

*Note*: Positive values represent US purchases of gold against dollars, negative values represent US sales of gold against dollars. Data for Q4 in 1966 are missing.

Figure 10.2 presents the Fed gold window data. Positive numbers indicate a foreign central bank selling gold to the Fed and receiving US dollars in exchange. This is expected, other things held constant, to have a positive effect on the confidence in the United States. It increases US gold reserves. Negative numbers indicate a foreign central bank buying gold from the United States. This diminishes US gold reserves. For the case of the United Kingdom, most of the values come from Gold Pool operations that were managed by the Bank of England on behalf of the syndicate.

The data show two features. First, France played no major role in the fall of the Gold Pool in 1967 and second, most of the drain on US gold reserves during the period comes from the United Kingdom. The United Kingdom is visible because it managed the Gold Pool.

France was accumulating gold from the Federal Reserve only until the end of 1966. After that, the French stopped buying gold from the Fed. From the second quarter of 1968, they even started replenishing US gold reserves by exchanging French gold for US dollars. This challenges findings in the literature about France playing a significant role in the fall of the Gold Pool. It also revises claims by Meltzer about French operations at the gold window in 1967.[21] It is likely that the French stopped converting dollars at the gold window simply because they had no more dollars to convert. Monnet argues that France stopped converting dollars into gold in 1966 because this policy had failed. The French wanted more power in international negotiations on the international monetary system. Their influence was limited. They had realised this when the French proposal to create an international reserve asset linked to gold was rejected in 1966.[22] After the demise of the Gold Pool, France became a net contributor of gold. The country needed dollars to defend the French franc in the spring of 1968. This was due in part to the events of May 1968. Meltzer suggests that the Paris riots forced France to sell $1.4 billion of gold between March and December 1968, part of which went to the United States.[23] The US gold reserve came under stress between 1967 and 1968. At that point, France played a minor role for US gold reserves.

The second feature that appears in the data is a drain on US gold in the last quarter of 1967 and the first quarter of 1968. Figure 10.2 reveals that in Q4 1967 and Q1 1968, the principal purchaser at the US gold window was the Bank of England. The Bank was acting on behalf of the Gold Pool. There was no central bank run on the US gold window as might have been expected. If central banks feared the dollar was going to be devalued, they could have converted their dollars into gold. There was little pressure on the Fed gold window before the devaluation of sterling; the United States was leaning on other governments not to use the gold window. There was also a mutual understanding that such operations would be detrimental to the international monetary system. Note that Q1 1968 shows more demand from Italy. Italy was a Gold Pool member. Since figures are quarterly, it is impossible to be certain which part of the demand occurred between 15 March and 31 March, when the Gold Pool was no longer operating. And which part was an actual run on gold. In any case, the

---

[21] Meltzer did not have access to these data and there was therefore reason to believe that the French pursued their offensive on the international monetary system through gold purchases at the gold window. Meltzer, 'U.S. Policy in the Bretton Woods Era', 63.

[22] Monnet, 'Une Coopération à La Française'.

[23] According to gold window data, $600 million of these sales went to the United States, implying that another $800 million must have gone to private markets. Allan H. Meltzer, *A History of the Federal Reserve, Volume 2, Book 1, 1951–1969* (Chicago, IL: University of Chicago Press, 2010), 542.

amount converted by Italy in March 1968 is relatively trivial compared to the losses of the Gold Pool after the sterling devaluation.

During the last quarter of 1967, the largest gold demand other than the Gold Pool came from Algeria. Algeria is labelled as a non-Gold Pool member in Figure 10.2. Past literature claimed that this was an indirect operation on the part of the French. For example, according to Robert Solomon, the Bank of Algeria purchased $150 million in gold from the United States, 'presumably at French instigation'.[24] New archival evidence seems to challenge this assertion. According to the unpublished transcripts of the General Council of the Banque de France, French authorities were not involved. The minutes explain what happened. The Bank of Algeria held French francs with French commercial banks. These francs were convertible to any currency of choice. The Bank of Algeria heard of international instability in the wake of the sterling devaluation and decided to convert these French francs into dollars in order to buy gold.[25] The Banque de France noted that the Algerian institution could also have bought gold directly in the Paris market, but gold at the Fed window was cheaper.[26] In these secret minutes, the governor of the Banque de France told the General Council that it was 'surprising and annoying that people could suspect the Bank of France of wanting to behave in an ill-intentioned manner'.[27] Given France's past behaviour at the US gold window, the rumours were hardly surprising. However, the evidence from the transcripts of the General Council shows that France had nothing to do with the attack on the US gold reserve.

Another opportunity France had to undermine the Gold Pool occurred in the summer of 1967. At this point, France decided not to contribute more to the Pool. There was an increase to the resources of Gold Pool from $370 to $420 million. The Banque de France told other central banks that it would no longer participate in the allocation of the losses. Soon the Pool's deficit was going to surpass the maximum amount fixed in May 1967 at

---

[24] Robert Solomon, *The International Monetary System, 1945–1976: An Insider's View* (New York: Harper & Row, 1977), 115 (quoted in Eichengreen, *Global Imbalances*, 57).

[25] 'Procès-verbaux du Conseil Général [General Council minutes]', 50, 14 December 1967, Paris, Archive of the Bank of France, 783–4.

[26] Ibid.

[27] The original French reads: 'il est surprenant et un peu pénible que l'on ait pu, à propos de cette opération, suspecter le comportement et les intentions de la Banque de France', 'Procès-verbaux du Conseil Général [General Council minutes]', 50, 14 December 1967, Paris, Archive of the Bank of France, 783–4.

$370 million.[28] France, however, kept its initial contribution in the syndicate. This meant that it would only lose up to the share it had invested until September 1966. As France had only a 9 per cent share in the Pool, its participation before this limit increase was only $33.3 million. This sum would cover less than one day's Gold Pool activity at the height of the crisis. At this point, France was not instrumental to the success of the Pool. However, the news that it was leaving the Gold Pool could have had harmful consequences. France did not make public that it was leaving the gold syndicate.

Why did a country that publicly attacked the international monetary system in February 1965 decide not to do so in the summer of 1967? A confidential note from the international directorate of the Banque de France on 8 June 1967 helps explain.[29] It sets out the reasons why France stopped participating in the Pool without formally leaving it. At that time, the syndicate's losses were not seen as a major concern. Losses were moderate in comparison to the previous surpluses. According to this note, the main reason for leaving the syndicate was that it would 'no longer support without limit a monetary system that works in a way that we consider unsatisfactory'.[30] Yet the note recommended not leaving the Pool formally and publicly. France should instead suspend participation if the limit of resources was increased again. Leaving the Gold Pool 'would not have been a surprise' to other participants 'given the usual reserved attitude' of France in relation to the Pool.[31] But it would have been too strong an attack against political cooperation with its Western allies. Immediately following this recommendation, the Banque de France suspended its participation in the Pool. It was announced to other members at the thirty-first meeting of the gold experts held on 11 June.

Although it had not formally left the Pool by the end of November 1967, it became clear to other members that France would never contribute to it again. The Gold Pool was suffering from large losses following the sterling devaluation. In November 1967, three days after the devaluation, the French leaked to the press that they had left the Gold Pool. This move is analysed in further detail in the next section, discussing the run on gold. But despite this leak, they maintained their initial share in the scheme.

---

[28] 'Historique sommaire du Gold Pool. Confidentiel [Gold Pool chronology], document completed between June 1962 and October 1967, Paris, Archives of the Bank of France, 1489200803/60.

[29] 'Convient-il pour la France de quitter le Pool de l'Or ? [Should France leave the Gold Pool?]', internal memorandum by M. Théron, 8 June 1967, Paris, Archives of the Bank of France, 146720050173.

[30] Ibid.     [31] Ibid.

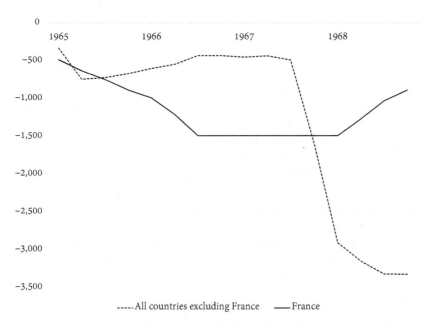

Figure 10.3. Cumulative gold purchases at the Fed gold window for France vs all other countries
*Source*: Data as in Figure 10.2 with categories merged.

Contrary to the accepted view, France's part in the fall of the Gold Pool was not instrumental. The most convincing argument comes from the gold window. For 1967 and 1968, when the Gold Pool fell apart, France *contributed* $600 million to US gold reserves. The Gold Pool over the same period drained $1,714 million from US reserves. Figure 10.3 summarises the main point. The data is reorganised from Figure 10.2. In late 1967, when the Gold Pool came under attack, France no longer purchased gold from the Fed. It even started contributing gold, thereby supporting the system. This does not mean that France would not have wanted the international monetary system to collapse. France wanted to replace it with an alternative, ideally with the French playing a more significant role. But France did not take the lead in the fall of the gold syndicate, as shown by new data. The syndicate collapsed because of market pressure.

## THE RUN-UP TO THE DEVALUATION

After looking at the role of France and sterling separately, the impact of different factors on the fall of the Gold Pool are analysed jointly. This analysis is run with monthly data to include a broader set of macroeconomic variables. The goal is to explain the behaviour of the Gold Pool. The explained variable is the monthly operations by the Bank of England for the Gold Pool on the gold market. Negative values represent gold sales to defend the price of gold. Positive values represent gold purchases to replenish the Pool's reserves. Three competing explanatory variables are tested: US domestic macroeconomic factors; French gold conversion of dollars into gold; and the sterling exchange rate.

US macroeconomic factors likely to affect the credibility of the dollar are proxied by the US inflation rate, the growth rate of US gold reserves and the change in the US government deficit. The government deficit is available at a quarterly frequency only. The series is interpolated with a quadratic trend.[32] At a monthly frequency, the change in US gold reserves is the best proxy for the state of the US balance of payments. Both US series come from the St Louis Federal Reserve database (FRED).[33] The pressure of the French central bank on US gold stocks is proxied by the growth rate of French gold reserves. The sterling exchange rate turmoil is proxied by the three-month dollar–sterling forward exchange rate from Accominotti et al.[34]

Since Gold Pool interventions directly and contemporaneously affected the growth rate of French and US reserves, these explanatory variables are used with a lag in the estimations. To isolate the effects of the sterling devaluation of November 1967, estimations are run on two samples. One sample (November 1961–October 1967) does not include the devaluation; the other (November 1961–March 1968) does. The raw data of Gold Pool interventions are used in the estimations since they are not seasonal. The series is stationary and it does not have a unit root. The results are reported in Table 10.1.

French operations seem to have had no impact on Gold Pool interventions as the coefficients are not significant. France did not operate in the London gold market as agreed under the Gold Pool rules. However, France could hoard or sell gold in Paris or Zurich. It could also make its mark on the system with its operation at the Fed gold window. These operations are the ones that previous literature thought were having an impact on the stability of the system. This means that when the French were hoarding or

---

[32] The US government deficit is the 'net operating surplus', seasonally adjusted, available from FRED (series FGOSNTQ027S). It is divided by GDP and interpolated using a quadratic interpolation to obtain a monthly series.

[33] Reference FGOSNTQ027S for the government deficit and M1476CUSM144NNBR for the US gold stocks.

[34] Accominotti et al., 'Currency Regimes and the Carry Trade'.

Table 10.1. *Determinants of Gold Pool interventions (monthly data)*

| | Dependent variable: Gold Pool interventions | | |
|---|---|---|---|
| | (1) November 1961–October 1967 | (2) November 1961–March 1968 | (3) November 1961–March 1968 |
| Growth rate of French gold (–1) | –0.11 | –1.86 | 2.90 |
| | (0.57) | (3.56) | (4.21) |
| Growth rate of US monetary gold (–1) | 4.58** | –44.86*** | 23.24** |
| | (2.29) | (12.00) | (10.84) |
| US inflation rate (–1) | –19.21*** | –40.05 | |
| | (6.42) | (39.27) | |
| Sterling forward rate (–1) | 355.01*** | 833.93*** | |
| | (129.60) | (111.19) | |
| US Federal deficit (–1) | –13.74** | –70.72** | |
| | (5.36) | (32.77) | |
| Constant | –968.44*** | –2250.18*** | |
| | (361.35) | (309.38) | |
| Adjusted R-square | 0.30 | 0.51 | 0.01 |
| No. of observations | 72 | 77 | 77 |

*Source*: See text. *** signifies statistical significance at the 1% level of significance; ** signifies statistical significance at the 5% level of significance; * signifies statistical significance at the 10% level of significance.

selling gold, the London gold market did not come under pressure. This does not mean that French operations did not matter during some periods. But they cannot be viewed as a major factor explaining the regular operations of the Gold Pool to stabilise the London price of gold. This is even true when not accounting for sterling, as in Table 10.1, regression (3).

The sterling forward rate has a strong and significant effect on Gold Pool operations. The effect is much stronger after the devaluation but is also important before (compare regressions 1 and 2 in Table 10.1). This is in line with earlier findings here. Before the devaluation, the sterling forward rate had an impact on the gold price.

US factors also played a significant role. This is in line with traditional explanations for the fall of the Bretton Woods system.[35] When inflation, government deficit or US gold losses increased, the Gold Pool deficit increased as the Gold Pool was forced to sell more gold. This effect of the US deficits was five times stronger when the period November

---

[35] Bordo and Eichengreen, 'Bretton Woods and the Great Inflation'.

1967–March 1968 is included in the sample. Alongside the sterling devaluation, US domestic policy played a role. This is especially true for the failed stabilisation plan of January 1968. This plan was also key for explaining the US decision to close the Gold Pool in early 1968.[36]

Gold Pool interventions were significantly determined by both US domestic economic conditions and the pressure on sterling, provided by its forward exchange rate. This was the case before the sterling devaluation. The effects became stronger after the devaluation.[37] The devaluation was a trigger. It led to unprecedented interventions. But the main factors influencing Gold Pool interventions were in place long before that.

## THE RUN ON GOLD

What were the different pressures on the gold market? Here I build a clearer timeline of the events putting the gold market under pressure after the devaluation. New data on Gold Pool intervention allow a clearer picture of the crisis to emerge. The timing of Gold Pool losses perfectly matches the 1967 devaluation. The run on gold started after the devaluation. According to the dealers' reports at the Bank of England, gold sales increased the week after the devaluation. They were $15 million on Tuesday, $59 million on Wednesday, $93 million on Thursday and $127 million on Friday. The Friday sales represent more than thirty-eight times the average sale of $3.31 million for the period before the crisis (November 1961 to November 1967). This is thirty-five standard deviations from the average for the period. The sales immediately after the weekend of the sterling devaluation stand out as exceptional. This is represented by what Figure 10.4 shows.

The week after the devaluation, the press reported that the French had left the Gold Pool.[38] De Gaulle saw the devaluation as an opportunity to attack the dollar at its weakest point. His attacks increased pressure on the

---

[36] On the stabilisation plan of January 1968, see Robert Solomon, *The International Monetary System, 1945–1981* (New York: Harper & Row, 1982), 117; Gavin, *Gold, Dollars, and Power*, 177–80.

[37] Between 1965 and March 1968, the cumulative deficit of the Gold Pool was $3,692 million (half of this was covered by the United States); during the same period, the US monetary gold stock diminished by roughly a quarter from $15,258 to $11,009 million. US Gold Pool losses account for 44 per cent of US gold stock diminution ($1,846 out of a $4,162 million drop). US monetary gold data are from FRED. Gold Pool losses are from BISA_7.18 (14) LAR27 Summary of Gold Pool operations, 28 June 1968. Eichengreen, *Global Imbalances*, 54, offers similar figures.

[38] Ibid., 57.

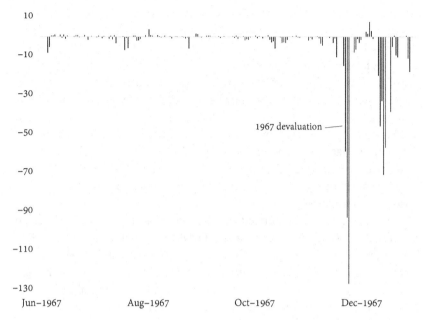

Figure 10.4. Daily Bank of England intervention in the gold market
*Source*: Bank of England dealers' reports (C8).

gold price. Yet de Gaulle was not the only one talking the gold price down. He was also greatly helped by statements by the US Treasury Secretary. He announced that the US dollar was 'in the front-line' on 22 November.[39] The 1967 devaluation triggered a run on gold. The run was then exacerbated by French attacks and US officials trying to deny the imminent devaluation of the dollar.

Before the devaluation, the press was already portraying the dollar as a potential target in the event of a sterling devaluation. On 17 November, two days before the devaluation, the *Wall Street Journal* wrote that 'speculation is rife about the future of the British pound. Will it be devalued and, if so, when?'[40] The journal argued: 'Devaluation would persuade many people that the U.S. dollar was under serious pressure, and in nervous world money marts [markets] the thought can father the fact.'[41] The *Wall Street Journal* thought that a sterling devaluation would probably trigger a run on the dollar. This could take the form of a run to the exit in a

[39] 'France Hits at Dollar through Gold', *Guardian*, 22 November 1967, 1.
[40] 'Devaluation Delusions', *Wall Street Journal*, 17 November 1967, 18.    [41] Ibid.

self-fulfilling crisis.[42] All this was before any leak from France. This helps the counter-factual that without any French leak, pressure would have probably built anyway. Investors had already been warned that a sterling crisis could trigger a dollar crisis. It encouraged them to be the first to move from the dollar to gold before the crisis occurred.

Even so, the French leak certainly helped. The next working day after the devaluation (Monday, 21 November), the Bank closed the London gold market along with most other London markets. The fallout from the devaluation was not felt until Tuesday, 22 November. At this point, the Gold Pool losses were substantial but still sustainable. On Wednesday, 23 November, the run accelerated. Things got worse on every day of the post-devaluation week.

News about France having left the Gold Pool earlier in June 1967 leaked on Monday, 21 November, in Paris. Markets were still closed in London. The information was relayed in the international press the following day. It is unclear when international investors got wind of the news of the French exit from the Pool. They either heard it on the Monday ahead of the reopening of the market or on the day the market reopened, when the international press picked it up. On the Tuesday, as the market reopened, a British newspaper broke the news. The *Guardian* reported that the French Ministry of Finance reacted with a 'tight-lipped "no comment"'.[43] The details collected from a journalist working for *Le Monde* 'point[ed] to a deliberate leak, apparently aimed at undermining confidence in the ability of the United States to guarantee the price of gold at $35 an ounce'.[44] France played a role in the momentum of the run on gold as the *Washington Post* pointed out a day later: 'The run was partially blamed on France's belated disclosure earlier this week that she pulled out of the nine-nation gold pool, which seeks to stabilize international transactions, last May.'[45] As the *Washington Post* stated, although France had the power to spread gossip, the country did not have dollar reserves big enough to inflict any direct damage on the United States. The *Washington Post's* assessment was that 'the de Gaulle government has insufficient dollar

---

[42] The rationality behind a self-fulfilling crisis was later theorised by economists, starting with Maurice Obstfeld, 'Rational and Self-Fulfilling Balance-of-Payments Crises', *American Economic Review* 76, 1 (1986), 72–81.

[43] 'Effort to Undermine Confidence in US', *Guardian*, 22 November 1967, 1.    [44] Ibid.

[45] The *Washington Post* was misinformed. France left in June not May. 'Heavy European Gold Trade Follows Pound Devaluation: Threat Is Unclear', *Washington Post*, 23 November 1967, L8.

reserves to make substantial purchases of U.S. gold'.[46] As seen, France had no firepower. It had stopped converting dollars into gold at the end of 1966. De Gaulle's attack on the dollar was no more than talk.

Not without irony, US officials were still arguing (publicly, at least) that France did not orchestrate an attack on gold. The *Guardian* reported that US officials 'dismissed the idea that the dollar was under attack and that France was leading the charge. "It just isn't the case," a Treasury official said'.[47] The US official continued: 'I put every credence in an official French Government statement. The French statement speaks for itself.'

If France played a role, the US management of the crisis did not help. One particular comment generated anxiety in the market. It was echoed in most newspapers over several days. It was a comment by Treasury Secretary Fowler. Fowler mentioned that the dollar was 'in the front line'. The *New York Times* quoted a 'non-French investment banker' saying that 'Mr. Fowler's words have been widely circulated in Europe as a sign of Administration anxiety'.[48] The *Washington Post* reporter attending Fowler's press conference also noted the context of the comment. He observed that 'Fowler conceded in answer to a question at the crowded press conference that the dollar could come under attack'.[49] The press did not miss an opportunity to compare US President Lyndon B. Johnson with UK Prime Minister Harold Wilson. The *Washington Post* wrote: 'Perhaps the best reason to feel edgy about the dollar is that President Johnson seems to be making the same irrevocable promises that we will "never" devalue that Prime Minister Wilson was making about the pound until the moment he took the plunge.'[50] Dramatic statements by politicians in times of monetary turmoil often spur more speculation rather than helping stem it.

Later, when the dust had settled, another alleged French attack failed to make a mark on markets. *The Times*, a week and a half after the devaluation, titled an article 'France May Decide to Leave Gold Pool Altogether'.[51] According to this article, France was considering removing its original contribution to the Gold Pool. Remember that it only had stopped additional contributions. But *The Times* argued that France's

---

[46] Ibid., L8.    [47] 'US Dollar "Not Under Attack"', *Guardian*, 24 November 1967, 1.

[48] Clyde H. Farnsworth, 'Swiss Act to Cool Gold Speculation', *New York Times*, 25 November 1967, 57.

[49] Hobart Rowen, 'Fowler Optimistic on Surtax Revival', *Washington Post*, 22 November 1967, A1.

[50] Hobart Rowen, 'U.S. Economic "Cool" Will Be Aid to Britain: Economic Impact', *Washington Post*, 26 November 1967, F1.

[51] 'France May Decide to Leave Gold Pool Altogether', *The Times*, 29 November 1967.

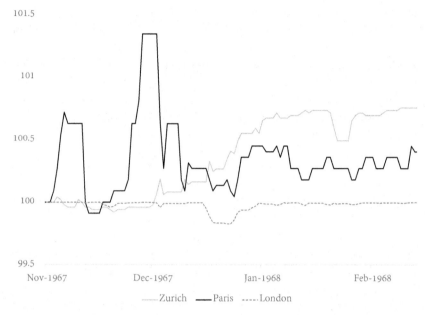

Figure 10.5. Gold prices in London, Paris and Zurich, indexed before the devaluation
*Source*: Paris: 'Cours pratiqués sur le marché libre de l'or', Paris, Archives of the Banque de France, 1377200101/21–25; Zurich: 'Goldkurse', Zurich, Archives of the Swiss National Bank, 9.6/9121; and London: Dealers' reports, London, Archive of the Bank of England, C8.

participation was 'negligible' (around 2.4 per cent at this point).[52] The newspaper attributed this 'new, if empty, threat' to France's 'exclusion from last Sunday's Frankfurt meeting of the other seven central banks'.[53] The meeting issued a 'statement of solidarity behind the dollar' which *The Times* thought would be enough to stop 'last week's gold rush'.[54]

By 29 November, the pressure on the London gold market had eased. Gold Pool operations were back to pre-crisis levels. But this lull in the run on gold would soon end. To understand the effect of the crisis on the London gold price, it is useful to compare it to two other gold markets: Paris and Zurich. Figure 10.5 sets out the three series. These daily series have been collected from the archives of three central banks. The prices are indexed before the devaluation (17 November = 100) to allow comparison.

---

[52] France's share in the Pool was $33.3 million (9 per cent of $370 million when France stopped contributing to additional tranches). $33.3 million represents 2.4 per cent out of the gold syndicate, which at this stage had reached $1,370 million.

[53] 'France May Decide to Leave Gold Pool Altogether', *The Times*, 29 November 1967.

[54] Ibid. This argument is also proposed by Schenk, *The Decline of Sterling*, 182.

The London price at the end of 1967 was bounded at its upper limit (close to \$35.20). It stays relatively stable thanks to Gold Pool operations. Was there contagion between the three markets after the devaluation? The London market was under tight control of the Gold Pool. But this is not true of the two other markets.

What emerges from Figure 10.5 is the progressive rise of the 'free' gold prices in Paris and Zurich. The selling pressure on the dollar in the London gold market had spilled over into the Paris market. The Banque de France was now forced to intervene. The *Guardian* reported that purchases by foreigners in Paris increased: 'American sources say that purchasers include United States citizens in France, who, for some days past, have been trading dollars for gold – illegally, according to their own law.'[55] The article also mentions 'English people who have no access to their own market'. The heavy foreign purchases probably explain in part the spike in the gold price in Paris shown in Figure 10.5.

France had opened the Paris market to foreigners in January 1967. The country hoped to increase the role of Paris as an international financial centre (Chapter 5). This is why France was defending the Paris gold price on the one hand while attacking the London gold price on the other. The *New York Times* understood this: 'The Bank of France was again meeting some of the demand from its reserves. It does this not because it is against a higher price for gold, but because it is anxious to keep gold prices in Paris in line with the far more important London market, with which it competes as an international gold trading center.'[56]

Similar reports emerged about the Zurich market being under pressure after the crisis. Swiss banks acted together under the guidance of the Swiss National Bank 'to try to cool off speculation by suspending credit purchases of gold for future delivery'.[57] Switzerland, in that regard, had a more cooperative attitude to the international system.

---

[55] Nesta Robert, 'Paris Gold Deals Multiply in Pressure on Dollar', *Guardian*, 24 November 1967, 15.
[56] Farnsworth, 'Swiss Act to Cool Gold Speculation', 57.     [57] Ibid.

11

# The Consequences of the Devaluation

## *Ongoing Crisis and Window Dressing at the Bank of England*

The previous chapter showed the consequences of the 1967 devaluation for the fall of the Gold Pool. But what were the consequences of the devaluation in Britain? It was intended to give the government breathing space to implement domestic policies and ease international pressure on sterling, but the 1967 devaluation did not ease Britain's position internationally. Worse still, it led to more instability.

For the British government after the devaluation, it was all about saving face. Wilson had promised that the devaluation was all that was needed even if it quickly appeared that more deflationary measures would be needed.[1] This devaluation, unpopular as it was, *needed* to have some positive effects. And if the positive effects were not apparent in a recovery in reserves, the Bank of England had to be creative in its presentation of the data. On the international front, cooperation started to be questioned. There was a shift towards the United States taking a more self-serving approach. The stability of the international monetary system was no longer a core US policy. And this was well before the Nixon shock of 1971. The Nixon administration was inaugurated in January 1969 and it quickly demonstrated that the United States was no longer willing to cooperate freely in international monetary matters.

## NOT A REAL SOLUTION

The 1967 devaluation meant to resolve the British balance of payments problems and move the economy towards growth and stability. Yet the opposite happened. On the London foreign exchange market, the situation

[1] Johnson, 'The Sterling Crisis of 1967', 10.

166

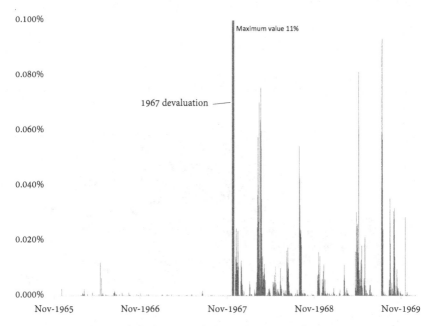

Figure 11.1. Dollar–sterling three-month forward ten-day volatility
*Source*: Volatility: author's calculation; forward data: Accominotti et al., 'Currency Regimes and the Carry Trade'. Values for the 1967 devaluation are out of the scale of the graph, they reach 11 per cent at peak.

notably worsened. Spreads widened as foreign exchange dealers became increasingly nervous. Volatility expanded significantly. After eighteen years of stable exchange rates, the pound was devalued by almost 14.3 per cent overnight. In the mind of dealers, this could lead to a further devaluation.

After the devaluation, the market became more unstable. It was more pessimistic about the monetary authorities' ability to maintain the exchange rate at the new \$2.40/sterling parity. The 1967 devaluation was more than a simple change in parity. It heightened instability and further decreased sterling's role in the international monetary system. The 1967 devaluation failed to improve the stability of the pound. Here I look at volatility, bid–ask spreads and forward exchange rates before and after the devaluation. This helps understand the impact of the devaluation.

Figure 11.1 illustrates the ten-day volatility of the three-month sterling–dollar forward rate. As shown previously, the forward is a better reflection of market forces. The figure demonstrates that after the devaluation,

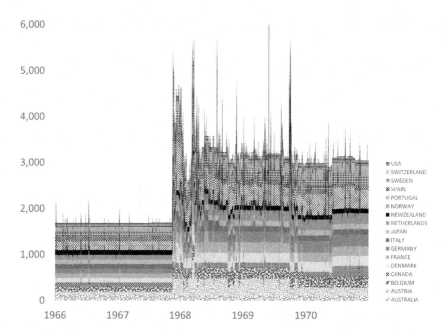

Figure 11.2. Sterling–dollar bid–ask spread index (whole year 1966 = 100), 1966–69
*Source*: Spread: author's calculation: forward data: Accominotti et al., 'Currency Regimes and the Carry Trade'.

volatility was much higher. The ten-day volatility increased on average by more than 126-fold when comparing 1964–66 with 1967–71.[2] This is a substantial increase. It shows that the devaluation made market dealers more nervous.

Figure 11.2 depicts the sterling three-month forward bid–ask spreads indexed to 100 for the beginning of the period in 1966. The spread is the difference between the buying and selling price. Here it is normalised to the average for 1966 for each currency to allow for comparison. This is just as in Chapter 3. The spreads inform us about the behaviour of the market-makers: commercial banks. These professionals made a profit from the difference between the buying and selling price. When market conditions worsened, they had to protect their profit by increasing the spread. Spread widening was consistent with the higher volatility presented in Figure 11.1. Both figures show increased uncertainty for dealers.

---

[2] The average ten-day volatility is 0.00022 per cent for the four years preceding the devaluation and 0.028 per cent for the four years after the devaluation, a 126 times bigger coefficient.

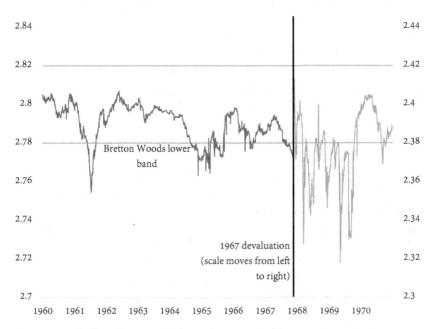

Figure 11.3. Sterling three-month forward rate
*Source*: Accominotti et al., 'Currency Regimes and the Carry Trade'.
*Note*: The scale switches after the 1967 devaluation to allow for continuous reading.

Figures 11.2 and 11.3 show that, in general, the sterling rate became more volatile and dealers became more risk-averse. This does not indicate the relative strength of sterling versus the dollar. The goal of the devaluation was to have a more stable and credible currency, yet at a lower nominal level. How did the devaluation perform in this regard?

Figure 11.3 represents the price of the three-month forward rate compared to the official Bretton Woods band. To allow for comparison before and after the devaluation, the scale is adjusted. On the adjusted scale, both the lower and upper bands before and after the devaluation match: 2.78 matches with 2.38 and 2.82 with 2.42.

Following Bordo, MacDonald and Oliver, the forward rate can be used as a proxy for the credibility of exchange rate bands.[3] Bordo et al. apply this technique between 1964 and 1967. Here I compare the pre- and post-devaluation period. Figure 11.3 shows that the 1967 devaluation was unsuccessful in restoring the credibility of sterling. After the devaluation, the forward rate was almost constantly breaking through the lower band of

---

[3] Bordo, MacDonald and Oliver, 'Sterling in Crisis, 1964–1967'.

the Bretton Woods system. This appears on the right-hand side of the figure. Before the devaluation, the breaks were less frequent. Breaks were linked to sterling crises, such as the 1961 crisis and the crisis in the wake of the 1964 general election. After the devaluation, the forward rate showed that sterling was not credible most of the time. Its falls below the lower band were much more marked.

## DISCLOSURE OF RESERVES

The devaluation failed to restore confidence in the system. How did the Bank deal with this? In a fixed exchange rate system, the exchange rate is credible only if the central bank behind a currency has the means to defend it. The Bank of England needed dollars or gold to be able to buy sterling when the exchange rate was dropping. The level of reserves in itself also has a signalling value for the strength of the currency. The higher the reserves, the more credible a currency appears to investors. During most of its history, the Bank managed to keep its balance sheet obscure enough to make it impossible for investors to understand its true reserve position.[4] This changed in the late 1950s.

The Bank of England was caught between two trends. There was a demand for more transparency following the publication of the 1959 Radcliffe Report. The report was an inquiry into the Bank's activities. This meant communicating reserves and being vulnerable in case of a reserve drop. At the same time, the Bank witnessed increased international financial flows following convertibility in 1958. This put even more strain on its reserves. The Bank had to satisfy both sets of pressure: more pressure on its reserves, and the need to be more transparent. It started communicating more while manipulating the data it published.

The government pushed the Bank to give an impression of stability and the institution used window dressing to do that. Here I show how window dressing functioned thanks to new data from the EEA account. The Bank worked with the Fed to prevent contradictory information from being shared by both institutions. New archival evidence attests to how the two central banks cooperated to conceal evidence of window dressing.

---

[4] This focus on opacity has been recognised by the current chief economist, Andrew Haldane, in a recent speech: 'For most of their history, opacity has been deeply ingrained in central banks' psyche. And for much the greater part of its history, the Bank of England was at the forefront of that opacity agenda.' Andrew G. Haldane, 'A Little More Conversation, A Little Less Action', 31 March 2017, www.bankofengland.co.uk/speech/2017/a-little-more-conversation-a-little-less-action.

Window dressing is the manipulation of accounting data before their official publication to make them appear better than they are. It has been a widespread practice among commercial banks throughout history. Roger Hinderliter and Hugh Rockoff show that *ante-bellum* banks in the United States used window dressing to manage their reserves.[5] Banks under the Bank of England's jurisdiction also practised window dressing. They moved balances among each other on set weekdays before publishing their reserves.

Reserve publication was a difficult exercise for central bankers during the Bretton Woods period. In a fixed exchange system, reserve information can create a run on the currency. This has been modelled in a second-generation currency crisis model, as first laid out by Maurice Obstfeld.[6] In these models, self-fulfilling dynamics make a run on a stable currency rational for investors as soon as other investors start selling. For this reason, the reserves announcements were well prepared. Credibility was key in currency management. If the central bank was credible enough, it could improve the stability of its currency by exaggerating its reserve position.

The reserves of the Bank were literately *made up*. An example of this is an internal memorandum from the Bank which read: 'It will be necessary shortly to decide what figure we are to show for the reserve loss for July.'[7] The wording establishes how the Bank saw reserve publication. It was a guessing game, somewhere between reality and what the Bank thought the market believed.

Disclosure of the reserve position was a communication exercise. High effort went into drafting these communications. An internal memorandum reads: 'The draft Press Notice is given in two alternative forms. The first alternative is designed to avoid having the fall mentioned at the beginning of the sentence and, therefore, the first thing that meets the eye from the ticker tape. The second alternative is in the conventional form.'[8] The ticker tape transmitted stock price information over telegraph lines. As the text was progressively printed on a thin paper ribbon, the first words mattered.

---

[5] Roger H. Hinderliter and Hugh Rockoff, 'The Management of Reserves by Ante-Bellum Banks in Eastern Financial Centers', *Explorations in Economic History* 11, 1 (1 September 1974), 52.

[6] Obstfeld, 'Rational and Self-Fulfilling Balance-of-Payments Crises'.

[7] Top secret memorandum, Denis Rickett to Hubback with copy to Parsons and four others, 24 July 1961, London, Archives of the Bank of England, C46/6.

[8] 'The reserves announcement for May 1966', R. L. Workman to Hubback with copy to Roy Bridge, 25 May 1966, London, Archives of the Bank of England, C43/49.

These words could lead to panic selling by traders. The Bank therefore put care into the order of the words in its communication. This problem illustrates how the publication of the reserve position was important to the Bank.

The Bank of England communicated its reserves in press releases before publishing them in the *Quarterly Bulletin*. The *Quarterly Bulletin* was first published in December 1960. The Bank launched the *Bulletin* because of recommendations in the Radcliffe Report. The Bank had anticipated these recommendations. It started internal discussions about a quarterly publication as early as 1958.[9] William Allen analysed the shift in attitude and transcribed the questions to Governor Cobbold in July 1957.[10] During his testimony before the Radcliffe committee, Cobbold was not keen to divulge too much information. He argued that 'it is of some doubt whether it would really clarify the issues for the public if the Bank were continually [issuing] statements with a different slant from similar statements made by Government to the public'.[11] Cobbold did not see any need for the Bank to communicate its reserves position. The Radcliffe Report, with its 2,294 questions, asked the Bank to change this, as Allen noted.[12]

The Fed was ahead in terms of transparency. It had published the *Federal Reserve Bulletin* since 1914, forty-six years before the Bank started doing the same.[13] The Fed viewed transparency by the Bank of England with amusement. In 1956, the Fed displayed some irony in stating that the Bank of England took 'a certain pride in pointing out that hardly anything can be inferred by outsiders from their balance sheet'.[14] In a memorandum by the Foreign Research Division in 1958, the Fed commented that the governor of the Bank of England 'for the first time' publicly considered more transparency. The Fed further commented, 'it seems clear that the Bank of England is being pushed – by much public criticism – into giving out more information'.[15]

---

[9] Richard Windram and John Footman, 'The History of the *Quarterly Bulletin*', *Quarterly Bulletin*, Q4 (2010), 258–66.

[10] Allen, *Monetary Policy and Financial Repression in Britain*, 205–13.

[11] [Radcliffe] Committee on the Working of the Monetary System, Question 753, Minutes of Evidence, HMSO, 1960, quoted in ibid., 208.

[12] Ibid., 209.    [13] Ibid., 210.

[14] Memorandum from Kriz to Sproul, 'Criticisms of the Bank of England Research and Public Information Policies by W. F. Crick of the Midland Bank', 30 March 1956, FRBNY archives, box 617015.

[15] Clarke to Exter, More information from the Bank of England, 25 February 1958, FRBNY archives, box 617015.

The Bank had to share more information, and so it did. Starting in 1960, reserve positions were announced to the press. They were then published in the appendix of the *Quarterly Bulletin*. At first, the Bank only reported a generic reserve figure. Later it started breaking it down into convertible currencies and gold. In an article in May 1963, *The Financial Times* welcomed this additional transparency. The article also stressed that other countries had been reporting more detailed reserve figures for some time.[16]

In a note about the meeting of the Court of Directors in October 1964, the governor mentioned that reserve publication would be 'accompanied by a statement that central bank assistance had been arranged, but that the extent of the assistance used would not be disclosed'.[17] It meant that the Bank would disclose that swaps with the Federal Reserve were used to increase reserves. But not the amount drawn on the swaps. This was the Bank's get-out-of-jail-free card. It could still keep how much it owed the Federal Reserve secret.

In the same meeting, the governor informed the court that he had written to the Chancellor of the Exchequer and to the Prime Minister. The governor was 'urging that the leader of the Opposition should be made acquainted with the true position in the hope that he would help to discourage irresponsible comment during the election campaign'.[18] But Downing Street did not think this was a good idea. The Prime Minister and the Chancellor reminded the governor that disclosure was their decision, not his. The EEA account belonged to the Treasury, not the Bank. And the government was managing the exchange rate. In this sense, it seems that window dressing was a political decision, and not one made by the Bank of England alone. Yet the Bank fully agreed with the decision to implement window dressing.

Swaps became the main tool for window dressing. As seen in Chapter 8, they were the Bank's favourite source of credit. They were readily available, cheap and discreet. Capie argues that swaps were 'essentially window-dressing arrangements and allowed a false picture of the reserves to be presented'.[19] From their inception, these devices were meant to help cover temporary losses to avoid speculative attacks on the currency. Over time, these temporary measures were made more permanent. Swaps became central to foreign exchange management.

---

[16] 'Raising of the Veil over U.K. Reserves Is Timely', *The Financial Times*, 1 May 1963.
[17] Separate note on court meeting, 8 October 1964, London, Archives of the Bank of England, G14/133.
[18] Ibid.　　[19] Capie, *The Bank of England*, 166.

But was it misleading investors and the public? Swaps raised ethical concerns on both sides of the Atlantic. In a November 1968 memorandum, the Bank presented two options for reserves publication. One was 'consistent with previous practice'.[20] It would withhold swaps from the public. The other option had 'been drafted on the assumption that we now decide to come "clean"'. This emphasises that the Bank believed that concealing reserves was not a 'clean' business. The Bank was recommending more disclosure in the reserve publication. The Bank argued that once the reserve situation had normalised, they would have to 'reveal the whole truth'. And then 'it would be embarrassing if there were then two versions of the "truth"'.[21] The frequent use of quotation marks in this memorandum shows the embarrassing position the Bank was in. It did not want to communicate reserves without the government's agreement. Yet officials at the Bank knew that they could be blamed for window dressing in the future.

## WINDOW DRESSING

The Bank of England was window dressing its reserves by publishing only the asset side of the balance sheet of the EEA. It was not disclosing any outstanding loans or swaps. Standard accounting practices require disclosing both the assets and the liabilities. Bordo et al. were the first to highlight the scale of the Bank of England's window dressing.[22]

Capie later published more data on window dressing between 1964 and 1967 from a report by Richard Kahn.[23] Capie demonstrated that the net reserve position of the Bank of England after December 1967 was negative. The Bank owed more reserves to foreign central banks than it possessed. Capie's figures are reproduced in Figure 11.4. The figure shows that net reserves continued to decrease after the November 1967 devaluation. Capie's data stop in 1968 and do not include the daily reserve figures of the EEA. EEA data give a more precise view of the mechanism behind window dressing and its very short-term nature.

The Bank of England reported its net position to the Treasury in monthly letters from 1962 to 1972.[24] These letters gave the net oversold

---

[20] EEA Accounts, memorandum from C. J. Wiies to Mr Copeman, 28 November 1968, London, archives of the Bank of England, 6A83/3.

[21] Ibid.     [22] Bordo, MacDonald and Oliver, 'Sterling in Crisis, 1964–1967', 448.

[23] Capie, *The Bank of England.*

[24] Foreign currencies forward exchanges monthly letters to the Treasury, various dates, London, Archives of the Bank of England, 6A152/1.

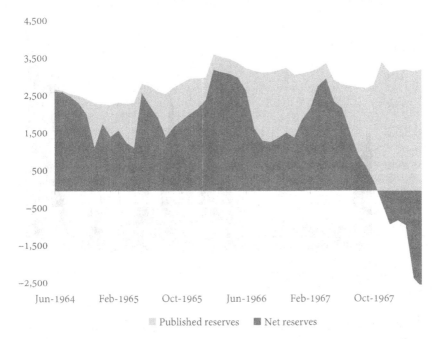

4,500

3,500

2,500

1,500

500

−500

−1,500

−2,500

Jun-1964    Feb-1965    Oct-1965    Jun-1966    Feb-1967    Oct-1967

▨ Published reserves    ■ Net reserves

Figure 11.4. Bank of England published vs net reserves
*Source*: Capie, *The Bank of England*, 231–2.

forward position. They also gave the amounts of window dressing. The term window dressing is avoided until 1965. It was too blunt. The more euphemistic term 'Net short-term aid from central banks' was used.[25] From 1965 onwards, the Bank of England explicitly uses the term 'window dressing'. The cat was out of the bag. The Bank no longer felt the need to use a euphemism when it came to terminology. In May 1968, window dressing reached its peak at $5,000 million.[26] At this stage, the Bank of England was borrowing up to $5 billion to conceal the fact that it had lost reserves. It amounted to 11 per cent of the country's gross domestic product.

Next, I use previously unpublished daily accounts of the EEA to show how the Bank used swaps to window-dress its reserve position at the end of each month. The EEA ledgers have not been used in previous literature. They contain daily data on EEA gold, dollar and other currency holdings. These accounts were not published or disclosed at the time. This means they were not window-dressed or manipulated. Rather, they were used for

[25] Ibid.    [26] Ibid.

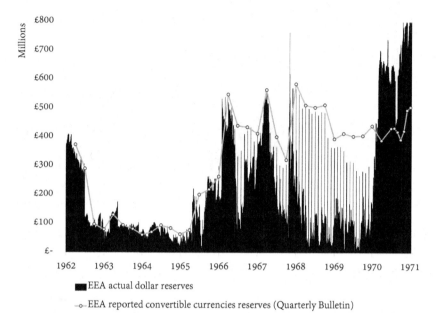

Figure 11.5. Published EEA convertible currency reserves vs actual dollar reserves held at the EEA
*Source*: EEA ledgers and *Quarterly Bulletin*.

internal and accounting purposes. Previous research has established that the Bank did use window dressing, but here I outline its short-term nature (typically a few days). This is important as it shows that swaps were not used for medium-term reserve management. They were used for investor manipulation. The goal was to convince currency buyers that the Bank was healthier than it really was.

Figure 11.5 illustrates how window dressing worked. The solid line reports the convertible reserves as published in the *Quarterly Bulletin*. This is the information that was available to market participants. The stacked columns show the actual daily dollar reserves.[27] Spikes appear at monthly intervals. They are the window dressing, and indicate the short-term borrowing. This borrowing was used to ensure the reserves level was high enough for the days when the reports were prepared.

The Bank borrowed dollars shortly before the actual reporting day. It drew on swap lines. Swap drawings could be as short as overnight. Table 11.1 illustrates how window dressing worked, using data from the

[27] Note that dollars represented 98 per cent of the convertible currencies at the time.

Table 11.1. *Daily entry in the EEA ledger showing how window dressing worked*

| Date | Reserves on the EEA account (£) | Reserve publication day | Change in reserves |
|---|---|---|---|
| Monday, 27 May 1968 | 29,953,509 | | |
| Tuesday, 28 May 1968 | 28,679,676 | | |
| Wednesday, 29 May 1968 | 31,362,587 | | |
| Thursday, 30 May 1968 | 31,426,358 | | |
| Friday, 31 May 1968 | 499,552,966 | Reserve publication day | +468,126,608 |
| Monday, 3 June 1968 | 499,552,966 | | |
| Tuesday, 4 June 1968 | 25,928,909 | | −473,624,057 |
| Wednesday, 5 June 1968 | 20,733,531 | | |
| Thursday, 6 June 1968 | 22,340,350 | | |
| Friday, 7 June 1968 | 22,878,336 | | |

EEA ledgers. On Friday, 31 May 1968, the Bank borrowed over £450 million. This represented an increase in reserves of 171 per cent. The swap operation was then reversed the next working day, and on Tuesday the reserves level was back to where it was before reporting.

The details of these operations emphasise how swap networks were not long-term instruments. They were short-term instruments to manipulate published figures. Another way of hiding the extent of reserves losses was by not publishing the open forward position.[28] Intervention on the forward market intensified in the late 1960s. The Bank of England was increasingly exposed to a large forward position. This exposure was not published either.

## SECRETS AMONG FRIENDS

Window dressing was an internal practice. Yet, being the main supplier of funds, the Fed was informed of the use of its funds. More than that, the Fed actively took part in concealing information from the public. This turned into a debate in the Federal Reserve system. The debate was between Coombs, who was inclined to do anything to save the pound in the short run, and some members of the FOMC, who raised ethical concerns. There was direct collaboration between the Bank and the Fed on window dressing, and window dressing worked because of the close cooperation between the two central banks.

[28] Bordo, MacDonald and Oliver, 'Sterling in Crisis, 1964–1967', 448.

Before publishing its *Quarterly Bulletin*, the Bank of England consulted the Fed on the precise wording of the reserve publication. This was important because the Fed would also communicate periodically on the swap position with the Bank of England. The public statements by the two institutions needed to mesh. Bridge from the Bank called David Bodner from the Fed in October 1966 to discuss strategy. Bodner reported Bridge's reasoning to his hierarchy: 'In order to come out in approximately the same position as in the end of September, that is, a slight reserve increase and no net recourse to central bank assistance, Bridge said he would require approximately $500 million.'[29] At this point Bridge wanted to publish reserves that increased slightly. But this had no relationship with the actual evolution of the Bank's reserves. It was only a perception that Bridge wanted to create in the market. The goal was either a stable or slightly increasing reserve position. Looking at the line in Figure 11.5 shows this tendency. Despite the true reserves being in decline, 'imagined' reserves were stable or increasing. There were some exceptions when the market expected heavy reserve losses and the Bank's imaginary reserves also dropped slightly.

Collaboration between the Fed and the Bank went much further. Before publishing the minutes of the FOMC, the Fed sent the excerpts of the minutes to the Bank of England. The Bank was to delete anything mentioning window dressing. In December 1971, before publishing the minutes of the FOMC for 1966, Coombs wrote:

You will recall that when you visited us in December 1969, we invited you to look over selected excerpts from the 1966 FOMC minutes involving certain delicate points that we thought you might wish to have deleted from the published version. We have subsequently deleted all of the passages which you found troublesome. Recently, we have made a final review of the minutes and have turned up one other passage that I am not certain you had an opportunity to go over. I am enclosing a copy of the excerpt, with possible deletions bracketed in red ink.[30]

Coombs suggested deleting passages in which some FOMC members criticised window dressing. Mitchell of the FOMC did not like window dressing. He suggested that the Bank of England would get better results 'if they reported their reserve position accurately than if they attempted to conceal their true reserve position'.[31] MacLaury, another FOMC member,

---

[29] UK position at the end of October, Bodner to Hayes, 25 October 1966, New York, Archives of the Federal Reserve Bank, 617031.

[30] Letter from Coombs to Hallet, 1 December 1971, New York, Archive of the Federal Reserve, box 107320.

[31] Ibid., 10.

was of a different opinion. He stressed that there was a risk of 'setting off a cycle of speculation against sterling' if the Bank published a loss of $200 million.[32] The amount was 'large for a single month', in comparison with what was published the previous month. Tension arose between the FOMC, which did not want to support unethical practices, and the New York Fed, which was dealing on the front line of international markets. Coombs held positions at both institutions. He was the link that attempted to convey to the FOMC the reasoning behind this short-term assistance.

The Bank of England understood the FOMC's reticence. A memorandum read that overnight swaps could not be used for window dressing as 'the F.O.M.C. regard that as unethical if not immoral'.[33] As the logical consequence of this stance, the note continues, 'this means that any drawing under the swap ought to be left outstanding at least for 32 days'.[34] The Bank would essentially increase the length of its swaps to make it less obvious that it was manipulation. The only technical difference was that the Bank of England had to pay interest for the period. Interest for a month would be more than for an overnight swap, for which the cost would be negligible. But the fact remained that the Bank used this short-term loan to avoid disclosing the real level of its reserves.

---

[32] Ibid., 9.
[33] Reserves report, end of April, unsigned memorandum on reserve publication, 26 April 1966, London, Archive of the Bank of England, C43/49.
[34] Ibid.

# 12

# Britain, Nixon and the End of Bretton Woods

In August 1971, Richard Nixon decided to 'to suspend temporarily the convertibility of the dollar into gold or other reserve assets'.[1] The international monetary system, which had intermittently relied on gold since 1821, would cut all ties with the yellow metal. Two main factors were at play in the final years of the Bretton Woods system. Inflation in the United States was increasing. This undermined the credibility of the dollar. Also, there was a decrease in international monetary cooperation. The shift to the Nixon administration, according to Coombs, meant that international financial policy 'became increasingly dominated by political considerations, much like French policy under de Gaulle'.[2] Nixon was the American equivalent of de Gaulle in trying to derail the international monetary system. Until that point many international monetary decisions were made after discussions in Basel. Nixon's in 1968 returned power to Washington.

This marked the end of the pound's influence within the international monetary system. Until then, despite its diminished importance, the pound still played a surprisingly significant role. The progressive dissolution of the Bretton Woods system with its two key reserve currencies (the dollar and sterling) meant the end of the pound's international role. The system would now be based on the dollar alone. The end of the fixed exchange rate system and market liberalisations during the 1970s and 1980s would remove the pound's significance as an international force. Further, the stability of the international monetary system would no longer rely on decisions made in Westminster.

---

[1] Richard Nixon, *Richard Nixon: Speeches, Writings, Documents*, ed. Rick Perlstein (Princeton, NJ: Princeton University Press, 2008), 219.

[2] Coombs, *The Arena of International Finance*.

Cooperation suffered from the run on gold that followed the 1967 devaluation. Unlike the interwar years, sterling devaluation did not lead to competitive devaluations. But just as the 1931 devaluation marked the beginning of the end for the gold standard, 1967 marked the beginning of the end for the Bretton Woods system. International monetary cooperation would suffer. The *New York Times* had summarised this shift a week after the 1967 devaluation. The paper read: 'The gold rush that has developed since sterling's devaluation represents a dangerous new challenge to the dollar and the existing monetary system that is based on cooperation between the United States and other industrial powers.'[3] The devaluation had unleashed the temptation for more nationalistic behaviour. These forces would lead to the end of the Bretton Woods monetary system. The system had always been based on cooperation.

An interwar-like beggar-thy-neighbour devaluation spree was only narrowly avoided. Just a few days before Britain devalued, France refused to commit *not* to devalue in response to sterling. The *New York Times* revealed that 'France took this ambiguous stand at the fateful moment 10 days ago [15 November] when experts of the Group of Ten discussed the possibility of the British pound' being devalued.[4] A sterling devaluation followed by a French devaluation might have triggered devaluations around the world. This could have created a currency war similar to that in the interwar years. And that was exactly what the Bretton Woods institutions were built to avoid.

## THE NIXON SHIFT

Nixon's election altered the landscape of international monetary cooperation. European monetary relations with the United States now became political. Technical cooperation was replaced by political blame. Central bankers and institutions set up in Basel continued to function. But Nixon shifted control over US monetary policy from the New York Fed to Washington and the US Treasury. Cooperation shifted from secret loans among friends to public speeches blaming Europe. Coombs noted the change: 'As the Nixon administration took office in January 1969, the Federal Reserve Bank of New York was abruptly cut off from

---

[3] 'The Defense of the Dollar', *New York Times*, 26 November 1967, E12.
[4] 'France Refused Pledge on Franc: Sources Confirm Her Stand on Eve of the Pound Cut. Paris Didn't Pledge Firm Franc on Eve of London's Devaluation', *New York Times*, 25 November 1967, 57.

Washington discussions of foreign financial policy.'[5] This was contentious, as decisions on cooperation were made at the central bank level, with limited government involvement. The Fed's discretionary power in Basel was now limited.

The incoming Nixon administration had a negative impact on international monetary cooperation. Using archival materials from the New York Fed, I document in detail how the new administration contributed to the breakdown in cooperation. If the Bank of England took roughly from 1945 to 1964 to warm up to the idea of cooperation with the Fed, 1969 marked a breakdown in cooperation – this time coming from the US side. Full and open cooperation between the Fed and the Bank of England lasted from 1964, when the Bank was finally ready to cooperate, to 1969. Then the Fed was slowly cut out of international monetary questions in favour of the Treasury under Nixon's tight control. The literature has shown that the Bretton Woods period was a time of monetary cooperation.[6] But cooperation took time to build up. And quickly collapsed.

The New York Fed recognised this shift in its 1971 annual report. The Fed described how Nixon closing the gold window (known as the Nixon shock) changed everything. The report reads: '[T]he operation of the International Monetary Fund (IMF) was almost completely immobilized, and the entire fabric of international monetary cooperation was badly strained.'[7] From that point on, routine operations were complicated. The new currency regime led to mistrust on both sides of the Atlantic. The tone of the dialogue between central banks changed.

A first example of this can be found in 1969. The Fed had just heard that the Bank of England had repaid $75 million to Germany 'at the insistence of the Germans'.[8] This was a problem for the Federal Reserve. It wanted to be the most senior creditor and be repaid first. In response, the president of the Fed, Alfred Hayes, called Karl Blessing, the Bundesbank president, to 'urge that the Germans allow the Federal Reserve priority in British debt repayments'.[9] Something similar occurred in 1970. The US Treasury and the Fed again were worried about being repaid after other central banks.

---

[5] Coombs, *The Arena of International Finance*, 204.
[6] This narrative is present throughout the literature. But maybe the most emblematic account is Toniolo and Clement, *Central Bank Cooperation*, 2005.
[7] Federal Reserve Bank of New York, annual report 1971, 3 March 1972, 32–3.
[8] British repayment of debt to Germany, David E. Bodner to files, 23 October 1969, New York, Archives of the Federal Reserve, box 107320.
[9] Ibid.

When asked to repay the Fed first, Hallet of the Bank of England replied that 'evidently there had been some misunderstanding between him and Coombs' on the schedule.[10] This meant that 'the Bank of England would not be able, without great embarrassment, to change the scheduled repayments'.[11] In response, Crowley of the Fed consulted the Treasury about extending the Bank's swap line with the Fed. He was told to 'hold up renewal of the facility, pending a determination as to priorities and schedules for repayment of debt'.[12] The Treasury was adding conditionality to swap lending. In Chapter 8, we saw how swaps were approved informally by telephone. They were available to the Bank within twenty-four hours or less. This changed with the new administration.

Another example comes from 1971 when the Bank needed to extend another credit agreement. Governor O'Brien called the Fed to express his concerns, because 'he had heard some comment from this country [the United States] to the effect that we hope to reduce American commitment and persuade the French to join in the credit'.[13] The rumours were that the Bank would have to ask France for credit. This was not only annoying but also quite humiliating for the Bank of England. O'Brien stressed that 'the French could be troublesome' and that 'he would consider it most unfortunate if the discussion of the [credit] renewal were to become anything more than a rather routine exercise'.[14] The Bank's views were communicated to Paul Volcker, Under Secretary for International Monetary Affairs at the Treasury. This episode, although benign in nature, illustrates the new atmosphere. Previously, such matters were routine. They could be resolved quickly and informally. Now, however, even if the Fed had 'general sympathy with the views expressed' by O'Brien, they could not do more than forward the information to Washington. The centre of power had shifted from New York and the Fed to Washington and the Treasury.

## THE NIXON SHOCK

The Nixon shock was the result of Nixon wanting to make a mark. He was unconcerned about the impact of US policies on the international

---

[10] Telephone conversation with Messrs Robeson and Hallett of the Bank of England, Robert J. Crowley to files, 18 March 1970, New York, Archives of the Federal Reserve, box 107320, p. 1.

[11] Ibid.    [12] Ibid., 2.

[13] Conversation with Governor O'Brien, memorandum sent to Alfred Hayes, 4 March 1971, New York, Archives of the Federal Reserve, box 107320.

[14] Ibid.

monetary system. The decision to close the gold window was made at Camp David (US presidents' country home in Maryland). It all happened over the weekend of 13–15 August. Nixon told the participants that there should be 'no telephone calls out of Camp David'.[15] Volcker had warned the president that 'it was too risky to wait before removing the threat of a run on America's remaining gold reserves, that a tidal wave of gold redemptions could come as early as Monday'.[16] The decision had to come before any run on the dollar.

The week before Nixon announced the closing of the gold window, the Bank of England managed to buy more dollars than usual. It accumulated $598.5 million on the market, a significant amount.[17] Before Nixon's declaration, the London market was under stress, with heavy dollar selling. The Bank was on the other side of these sales. It was an opportunity to replenish its dollar reserves. Meanwhile, the United States was planning its unofficial exit from the Bretton Woods system. Nixon later wrote:

The strongest opposition came from Arthur Burns, Chairman of the Federal Reserve Board. He wanted us to wait. Even if all the arguments were right, he said, he still felt that there was no rush. He warned that I would take the blame if the dollar were [sic] devalued. '*Pravda* would write that this was a sign of the collapse of capitalism,' he said. On the economic side he worried that the negative results would be unpredictable: the stock market could go down; the risk to world trade would be greater if the trade basis changed; and there might be retaliation by other countries.[18]

Burns' opposition did little to stop Nixon. Connally said the 'country was completely exposed to the world, and when Burns referred to the "goodwill" of allies, Connally interrupted: "We'll go broke getting their goodwill"'.[19] In the end, the debate concluded with a decision in favour of closing the gold window.

On Sunday night, Nixon addressed the nation. He announced a series of measures to stimulate the economy. Along with the closing of the gold window, he introduced a temporary 10 per cent surcharge on all dutiable imports. The belief was that other countries would feel compelled to revalue their currencies, as Irwin argued.[20] Finally, to curb inflation he announced ninety days of price and wage controls. The Nixon shock was

---

[15] Conrad Black, *Richard M. Nixon: A Life in Full* (New York: Public Affairs, 2007), 741.
[16] Ibid., 741.    [17] Dealers' reports, 1971, London, Archive of the Bank of England, C8.
[18] Richard Nixon, *RN: The Memoirs of Richard Nixon* (New York: Simon & Schuster, 2013).
[19] Black, *Richard M. Nixon*, 741.
[20] Douglas A. Irwin, 'The Nixon Shock after Forty Years: The Import Surcharge Revisited', *World Trade Review* 12, 1 (January 2013), 29.

the most important part of the announcement and had the most durable effects. As Thomas Zeiler puts it: '[B]etween 1929 and 2008 there occurred another crisis that signalled a profound shift in the country and the world, and in the psyches of ordinary people. It began on August 15, 1971. On that date, Richard Nixon took the first steps towards ending the gold standard.'[21]

Ironically, Nixon used the frequency of financial crises as an argument to close the gold window: 'In the past 7 years, there has been an average of one international monetary crisis every year. Now, who gains from these crises? Not the working man; not the investor; not the real producers of wealth. The gainers are the international money speculators. Because they thrive on crises, they help to create them.'[22] With hindsight, this is interesting as the literature shows that the Bretton Woods period was a time with the fewest financial crises of any type.[23] Certainly, closing the gold window did not help reduce the number of crises. Facts aside, it remains that Nixon had excellent skill to explain complex questions to the public.

Kissinger later admitted that Nixon knew that his decision would be long-lasting and could guarantee his legacy: '[H]e saw himself as revolutionizing international economics as he had already transformed international diplomacy. He reveled in the publicity coup he had achieved. As he often did he asked me innumerable times to recite foreign reactions, which were mixed at best; he was delighted by the domestic approval.'[24]

According to Nixon, closing the gold window 'turned out to be the best thing that came out of the whole economic program'.[25] The way Kissinger describes it is telling:

This was to have many, largely unforeseen, consequences as the years went on. The immediate significance of the new program was its effect abroad; it was seen by many as a declaration of economic war on the other industrial democracies, and a retreat by the United States from its previous commitment to an open international economic system.[26]

Nixon's focus was domestic. He cared little for the rest of the world. According to Ronald McKinnon, the 'dollar devaluation violated the

---

[21] Thomas W. Zeiler, 'Requiem for the Common Man: Class, the Nixon Economic Shock, and the Perils of Globalization', *Diplomatic History* 37, 1 (1 January 2013), 2.

[22] Nixon, *Richard Nixon*, 217.

[23] Michael Bordo et al., 'Is the Crisis Problem Growing More Severe?', *Economic Policy* 16, 32 (April 2001), 51.

[24] Henry Kissinger, *White House Years*, reprint ed. (New York: Simon & Schuster, 2011), 1126.

[25] Nixon, *RN*.    [26] Kissinger, *White House Years*, 1126.

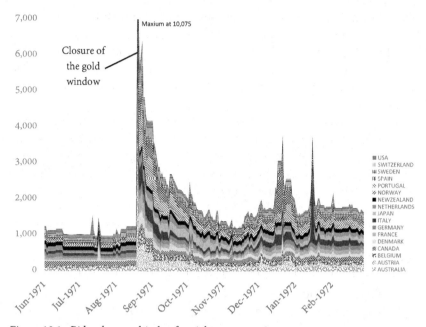

Figure 12.1.  Bid–ask spread index for eighteen countries
*Source*: Bid–ask data: Accominotti et al., 'Currency Regimes and the Carry Trade'; computation: the author.
*Note*: The data are indexed to avoid any single currency spread biasing the graph and showing the shock in a comparable way for all currency pairs. All spreads are indexed on the average of the whole of 1971–72 = 100.

unwritten rule (understandings) by which the fixed-rate dollar standard had successfully operated for the previous twenty years'.[27]

How much of a surprise was the decision to close the gold window? And how much had markets already factored in this 'shock' in prices? The London market gives an indication of the magnitude of the shock. Here again I rely on the bid–ask spreads. They are presented as an index (average for 1971–72 = 100). This allows a comparison of the magnitude of the shock on each currency individually in a single chart.

News of the gold window's closure came as a shock to market-makers in London. The spreads on foreign exchange quotes increased ten-fold after the announcement. Figure 12.1 illustrates this extraordinary shock. Even

[27] Ronald I. McKinnon, 'Bretton Woods, the Marshall Plan, and the Postwar Dollar Standard', in *A Retrospective on the Bretton Woods System: Lessons for International Monetary Reform*, ed. Michael D. Bordo and Barry Eichengreen (Chicago, IL: University of Chicago Press, 1993), 604.

for the whole of September, dealers were still offering five times higher spreads on average across the seventeen currencies in Figure 12.1. Dealers were most likely protecting themselves against uncertainty in the market following the initial shock.

## STABILISATION AT LAST

The end of Bretton Woods was a time of crisis and reinvention for the international monetary system. For sterling, things finally seemed to improve, for a while at least. It was a period of respite for sterling. There was less pressure on the foreign exchange market. Reserves seemed to be increasing somewhat. The Bank's dealers were less busy defending the pound and the currency exhibited less volatility. The Nixon shock brought an end to this quieter period. Even if sterling benefited from the Nixon shock, its positive effects on the dollar would be only temporary. The 1970s would again be a difficult time for sterling.

After being close to the lower band for most of the Bretton Woods period, the pound finally appreciated against the dollar from the late 1970 onwards. As Figure 12.2 illustrates, the three-month forward rate improved against the dollar following the Nixon shock. The sterling forward rate even broke the Bretton Woods upper band of $2.42 per sterling after July 1971.

Similar trends can be seen in ten-day volatility. Figure 12.3 highlights that the three-month forward market, the most volatile official sterling market, was stable from the end of 1969 to the summer of 1971. After the Nixon shock, the market again became volatile.

In terms of intervention, dealers were less busy defending the pound and only reported nine dollar sales in 1971. In that year, only 3 per cent of the trading days were spent defending sterling. In 1967 as a comparison, dealers spent short of 30 per cent of the trading days defending sterling. In 1970, their job was even easier as market conditions allowed them to buy dollars and not worry about sterling on 91 per cent of trading days.

The reserve position improved in 1970, as the figures from the EEA show in Figure 12.4. But the United Kingdom's reserve position was still not good. Gold reserves were diminishing starting in 1970. Dollars on the EEA account mainly came from foreign credits and the gold reserves were low. On average during the Bretton Woods period, EEA gold reserves stood at £458 million.[28] At around £200 million during 1969–70, they were substantially below this average and the situation was far from ideal.

---

[28] This is calculated from 31 March 1947 to 10 February 1971 based on all the available daily data.

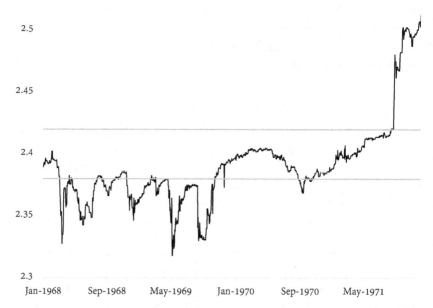

Figure 12.2. Three-month sterling–dollar forward exchange rate
*Source*: Accominotti et al., 'Currency Regimes and the Carry Trade'.

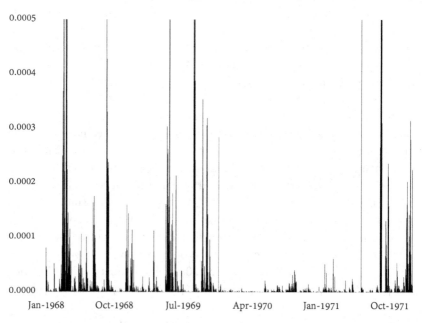

Figure 12.3. Three-month sterling–dollar forward exchange rate, ten-day local volatility
*Source*: Accominotti et al., 'Currency Regimes and the Carry Trade'. Note: The scale is cut at
0.0005 for better readability.

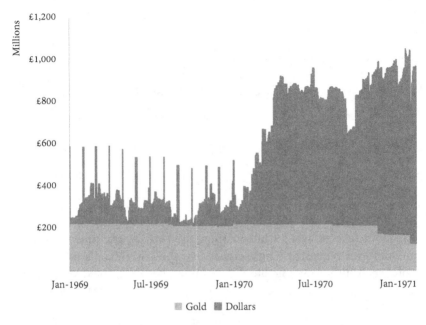

Figure 12.4. EEA dollar and gold reserves
*Source*: EEA ledgers.

Another trend is that the Bank no longer used swaps to hide reserve losses after 1969. The periodic spikes that appeared in 1968 ceased in 1970. There are still increases around the month-end at some points, but they are not as marked and last longer than at the height of window dressing.

This calmer period would not last. New crises would arise, requiring more loans from the international community. Additionally, the international monetary system would go through several new frameworks, such as the Smithsonian agreement of December 1971, followed by the snake in the tunnel in April 1972 before Britain officially floated its currency on 23 June 1972. As Kissinger put it, 'The Bretton Woods agreement, which had regulated international monetary arrangements since 1944, was being made irrelevant' by Nixon's speech.[29] This marked the end of over a century and a half of gold-based systems and the beginning of a new era in the international monetary system.

[29] Kissinger, *White House Years*, 1126.

13

# The 1976 IMF Crisis

The 1976 IMF crisis was a severe currency crisis which led the United Kingdom to borrow \$3.9 billion from the IMF, at the time the largest amount ever requested. Capie argues that the crisis 'stands out as a low point in British economic life'.[1] It has often been presented as a humiliation, with the British government having to bow to the IMF's conditions to receive this loan.[2]

The focus here will not be on this political crisis and the dealings with the IMF. Rather, I will focus on discussing the causes of this significant crisis. How did it start? Was it triggered by British policymakers themselves, as some have argued? Or was it accidentally triggered by them, after trying to manage exchange rates down, as they had rarely done in the past?

In this chapter I use intervention data and new archival evidence to get a picture of the Bank of England operations during the crisis. I focus on the Bank of England, and not on the political drama unfolding following the initial currency crisis. On the political crisis, many authors have done a brilliant job describing the issue, with four full monographs on the subject.[3]

Despite this large body of literature, there are still unanswered questions. The most important being whether the Bank started the crisis at least somewhat voluntarily. I argue that the crisis was not 'natural', so to speak, and triggered by the Bank of England at the request of the Chancellor.

---

[1] Capie, *The Bank of England*, 742.   [2] James, *Making a Modern Central Bank*, 32.
[3] Kathleen Burk and Alec Cairncross, *Good Bye Great Britain – The 1976 IMF Crisis* (New Haven, CT: Yale University Press, 1992); Mark Harmon, *The British Labour Government and the 1976 IMF Crisis* (London: Palgrave MacMillan, 1997); Douglas Wass, *Decline to Fall: The Making of British Macro-Economic Policy and the 1976 IMF Crisis* (Oxford: Oxford University Press, 2008); Richard Roberts, *When Britain Went Bust: The 1976 IMF Crisis* (London: OMFIF Press, 2016).

Other accounts have shown this based on archival material. Here I use quantitative evidence to show that the dollar purchase on the first day of the crisis was different from any dollar purchase in the past. Statistically speaking, it is unlikely that this crisis was just an accident. The Bank of England wanted to devalue the pound. If the initial devaluation was a policy success, the Bank rapidly lost control of the market and sterling fell further than was desired.

During this crisis, the Treasury frequently instructed the Bank on exchange rate management goals. Instructions were sometimes unclear or contradictory. Needham even goes to say that the Bank was 'kept on a tight leash by the Treasury in its currency market operations'.[4] This was not the case in other crises. In 1967, for example, the instructions were clear and never changing: the Bank was simply asked to do its best to prevent the pound from dropping in value. As we have seen in previous pages, the Bank had discretion to do so. Here, because the pound was now floating and no longer fixed, things changed. The Chancellor and the Treasury were more involved in managing the pound on a day-to-day basis.

Another contribution of this chapter is to show that the Central Bank of Nigeria had nothing to do with the 1976 IMF crisis. In many (but not all) previous accounts, it was argued that the Nigerian sterling balances were at the root of the crisis. This was indeed a rumour circulating in newspapers at the time. But evidence from the Bank's archives shows that these were nothing more than rumours.

## WAS THE IMF CRISIS 'NATURAL' OR 'MANMADE'?

Sterling devaluations described in the previous pages of this book were always either officially announced or happened without the intervention of the Bank of England, which was fighting depreciation. Here the story is a bit different. At the start, there was a view at the Treasury that sterling was overvalued. The Bank broadly agreed with this view. A public devaluation was not an option, as it would upset public sterling balance holders.[5] As was the case before, a devaluation would also not protect sterling from future devaluations. If there was a devaluation, it would have to look like a natural market depreciation. The Bank nudged sterling into depreciation.

---

[4] Duncan Needham, *UK Monetary Policy from Devaluation to Thatcher, 1967–82*, Palgrave Studies in the History of Finance (New York: Palgrave MacMillan, 2014), 97.
[5] Ibid., 94. The term devaluation is somewhat inadequate as sterling was officially floating.

But that little push scared markets, unused to such a dismissive attitude from the Bank regarding its currency. This triggered a proper currency crisis. And before long, the Bank was trying to reverse a fall it had itself initiated.

Part of the literature on the topic seems to think the manoeuvre was an accident, even though a depreciation was wanted.[6] Or that it could not have been on instruction from the Treasury, as the Chancellor and the Prime Minister were against it.[7] Most accounts seem to agree that the Treasury and Bank thought the pound was overvalued, but also that the event on 4 March was an accident. The Permanent Secretary of the Treasury, Douglas Wass, met with the Governor of the Bank on 1 March. Wass explained that the Treasury had decided on a depreciation of sterling.[8]

Burk and Cairncross argue that one of the reasons the fall in the pound could not have been initiated by the Bank was that Wilson had been against it.[9] The fall, they argue, was not 'knowingly initiated' by either the Treasury or the Bank.[10] Wilson was planning to retire and did not need a currency crisis. But as Needham points out, Chancellor Denis Healey was hiding exchange operations from Wilson and the Cabinet. And the Bank did indeed initiate the fall, as we will see. Needham writes that 'Healey also appears to have been playing a dangerous game with his cabinet colleagues, assuring the Prime Minister that the pound would be held at $2'.[11] $2 was a symbolic threshold that was broken shortly after the Bank covertly devalued the pound.

Callaghan, the incoming resident of 10 Downing Street, was also not aware of the exchange rate operations at the Bank. He later thought that it was orchestrated:

The Chancellor and the Bank of England apparently agreed during February 1976 that the exchange rate of sterling, which was then about two dollars to the pound, was unrealistically high and the Bank set out to edge it down, but the manoeuvre got out of hand when foreign exchange dealers realised what was afoot, sterling fell faster and further than was intended, and the Bank of England was forced to spend substantial reserves to hold the exchange rate up.[12]

[6] Wass, *Decline to Fall*, 179.      [7] Burk and Cairncross, *Good Bye Great Britain*, 28.
[8] James, *Making a Modern Central Bank*, 32.
[9] Burk and Cairncross, *Good Bye Great Britain*, 28.
[10] Ibid., 29. Note that they did not have access to the archives when they wrote their account.
[11] Needham, *UK Monetary Policy from Devaluation to Thatcher*, 96.
[12] Callaghan, *Time and Chance*, 414.

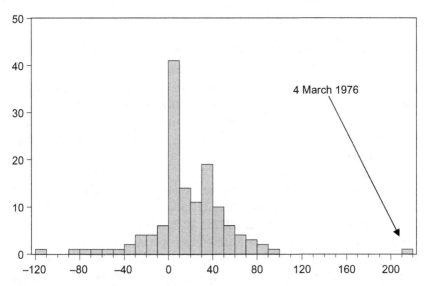

Figure 13.1. Number of interventions by amount, September 1975–September 1976
*Source*: Dealers' reports (C8).

While Callaghan is right that the manoeuvre eventually got out of hand, it is not clear when. The Bank surely did not want to trigger the IMF crisis, but, I will argue, it did want to trigger a sharp fall on 4 March.

Needham argues that the idea from the Treasury and the Chancellor was that the Bank would cream off the market. The practice, which was often used, involved 'selling sterling on a rising market to replenish the reserves'.[13] This would prevent sterling from appreciating too much. On this occasion, however, the creaming off was much stronger than usual. The devaluation was therefore manufactured by the Bank of England, and not an accident.

The Bank had constantly been accumulating reserves since September 1975, building up to $2,253 million by the day of the crisis. But what is really striking is the size of the purchase on 4 March. The Bank bought, on one day, just about 10 per cent of what it had taken six months to accumulate. The purchase of dollar on 4 March was fifteen times bigger than the average purchase over the previous six months. Figure 13.1 shows the distribution of the Bank's operations for one year up to September 1975. Only one operation was a purchase of more than $100 million.

---

[13] Needham, *UK Monetary Policy from Devaluation to Thatcher*, 94.

The distribution shows that the operations of 4 March stand out by several orders of magnitude.

Another way to understand the exceptional nature of that fateful day is to compare it to all the operations the Bank did after the Second World War. Comparing intervention data over time can be problematic. Inflation plays a role. Because of inflation, interventions are generally larger in nominal terms as time passes. But for transparency, I compare 4 March with two samples. One sample includes potentially 'larger', later operations. And the other includes only potentially 'smaller', earlier operations. Looking at all the interventions from 1952 to 1992, 3 March is 3.5 standard deviations from the mean. It is the ninety-ninth largest purchase out of 9,586 intervention operations. These include purchases and sales. When looking at the same figures from 1952 to 1976, it is the twelfth largest dollar purchase from a total of 4,678 intervention operations. As many of these operations occurred in 1971 around the fall of Bretton Woods, reducing the sample to 1972 to 1976 makes it the second largest dollar purchase over that four-year period.

These numbers show that the operation was exceptional in nature. The purchase was unlikely to have been an accident by the dealers. They wanted sterling to depreciate on that given day. This is corroborated by the archival evidence presented by Needham that we will dive into later on.[14]

### UNFOUNDED RUMOURS

The literature has argued that the fall of sterling on 4 March was due in part to sales from the Central Bank of Nigeria. Looking more closely at archival evidence, this is untrue. Nigeria was an OPEC member, and official sterling balance holder. It could at any point ask the Bank to convert sterling balances into dollars. But in early March 1976, it did not.

The idea possibly started with Burk and Cairncross. They quoted *The Economist*, which wrote that the market participants 'feared that the Bank was either selling pounds under instructions from an overseas central bank, such as Nigeria, or that it was carrying out deliberate government

---

[14] Ibid.; Duncan Needham, '"Goodbye, Great Britain"? The Press, the Treasury, and the 1976 IMF Crisis', in *The Media and Financial Crises: Comparative and Historical Perspectives*, ed. Steve Schifferes and Richard Roberts (London: Routledge, 2014), 289–304.

policy to make sterling cheaper'.[15] But Burk and Cairncross do not take a stance on the article in *The Economist* and just present it as is. Most of the later literature up to the present seems to have gone with this interpretation, with only a few exceptions.[16]

The narrative goes that the Nigerian Central Bank had sold sterling to the Bank of England. To rebuild reserves which had gone to Nigeria, the Bank of England had purchased dollars on the market. According to the narrative, this was in 'accordance with normal practice'.[17] But this makes little sense. The Bank constantly tried to build reserves when market conditions allowed. It did not link its purchases to previous operations for third-party central banks. Reserves could always be rebuilt later, while a currency crisis could never be undone with a few operations. The two things had different time horizons. The focus was always on exchange rate management first, reserve building second.

Let us illustrate this with an extreme example. Imagine that one day before Black Wednesday, the Bank had sold dollars for sterling to the Nigerian central bank. On Black Wednesday, the Bank's main concern would not be to rebuild its reserves according to the previous day's sale, it would have been to defend the pound. This is to say, reserve management considerations came second to exchange rate considerations. Yes, the Bank wanted to hold as much reserves as possible, but never at the cost of losing control of the exchange rate. Reserves are just a tool to defend the currency, not the other way around. Needham goes further. He argues that this would go against an implicit pledge by dealers: 'This was interpreted by currency dealers as the Bank selling sterling on a falling market, something it was pledged never to do.'[18] Here I show that the Bank wanted to devalue the currency.

The evidence that there were no sales from Nigeria is clear in the archives. First there is no record in the dealers' report of a sale of dollars for sterling on 4 March 1976.[19] But there are on other days. For example,

---

[15] Burk and Cairncross, *Good Bye Great Britain*, 30, quoting an article in the *Economist* of 13 March 1973.

[16] For the story in one form or another, see Wass, *Decline to Fall*, 178; James, *Making a Modern Central Bank*, 33; Roberts, *When Britain Went Bust*; William Keegan, *Nine Crises: Fifty Years of Covering the British Economy – From Devaluation to Brexit* (London: Biteback Publishing, 2019), 114; Atkin, *The Foreign Exchange Market of London*, 126.

[17] Wass, *Decline to Fall*, 178.

[18] Needham, *UK Monetary Policy from Devaluation to Thatcher*, 96.

[19] This in itself is not enough. The reports compiled by the Books and Statements section of the Gold and Foreign Exchange Office might give additional information.

on 13 September 1977, the dealers' report reads 'Nigeria –20'. This means that the Bank sold $20 million against sterling from the Central Bank of Nigeria. Such operations are common with holders of sterling balances. Just a day following the start of the 1976 IMF crisis, one such operation happened. The Bank sold $5 million against sterling from the Reserve Bank of New Zealand. This was again recorded in the reports as 'New Zealand –5'.[20]

The other piece of evidence comes from a special report by the Bank's dealers. The report aimed to take stock of the ongoing crisis. It was written a few days after the crisis started. It reads:

On Friday 5th, after heavy selling during the morning the pound fell below the psychological barrier of $2 in the early afternoon and weakened further in an acutely nervous market when the cuts in m.l.r. [minimum lending rate] was announced amid growing – *but unfounded* – rumours that Nigerian selling had started the fall.[21]

Other authors have already argued that Nigerian sales played no role, but the reference seems to have stuck in the literature. In 1997, Hamon quoted a Cabinet meeting where the Chancellor said that: 'The Bank had *not* intervened to bring the rate down and it wasn't true that Nigeria was selling sterling.'[22] This we now know is untrue. The Bank did intervene. The Chancellor, however, conceded that the 'Treasury had allowed for a fall of this size and there was nothing to worry about'.[23] The Chancellor would have denied intentional intervention in any case. It is likely that he wanted the Bank to devalue the pound, but he did not want the Cabinet to know his intention. This is in line with what Needham argues.[24] In the meeting, the Chancellor also affirmed that the Nigerian rumours were unfounded. As shown, on this last point he probably told the truth. The market slide was not a result of Nigerian sales.

Capie also bases his narrative on the dealer reports and notices that there were no sales from Nigeria. He argues it was only a 'City theory' following a 'political skirmish with Britain'.[25] It was true though that the Nigerian Central Bank reduced its position from £1.8 billion in early

---

[20] While this sale put more pressure on sterling, it clearly was too small to have any significant effect on the price.

[21] Archives of the Bank of England, Foreign Exchange and Gold Markets (15th December 1975–16th March 1976), 17 March 1976, reference C8 (emphasis added).

[22] Harmon, *The British Labour Government*, 134. Harmon takes the quote from Barbara Castle, *The Castle Diaries 1974–76* (London: Weidenfeld & Nicolson, 1980), 683–4.

[23] Ibid.      [24] Needham, *UK Monetary Policy from Devaluation to Thatcher*, 96.

[25] Capie, *The Bank of England*, 743.

1975 to £800 million around the time of the crisis.[26] These operations happened over a longer time span. They are not the direct cause of the March 1976 crisis. Other sterling holders were also liquidating their sterling holdings. Nigeria was not specific in that regard. But no holder did it on 4 March, when our crisis was triggered.

## RATE CUT AND FURTHER FALL

The following day, 5 March, the Bank lowered the Minimum Lending Rate (MLR). The rate cut made the pound drop below the symbolic threshold of $2 (Figure 13.2). The cut in itself probably did not surprise the market. Interest rates were on a downward trend. What surprised markets was that it happened the day after a large reserve purchase. This certainly helped the pound drop. It was an endorsement of the fall in the exchange rate.

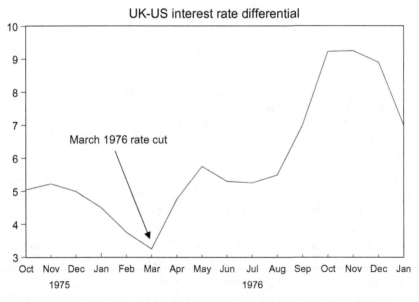

Figure 13.2. Prime lending rate differential of main UK and US banks. Lower differentials were likely to put more pressure on sterling (average monthly rates, for the 15th of each month).
*Source*: Refinitiv, references UKBANKR and USBANKR.

[26] Ibid., 743.

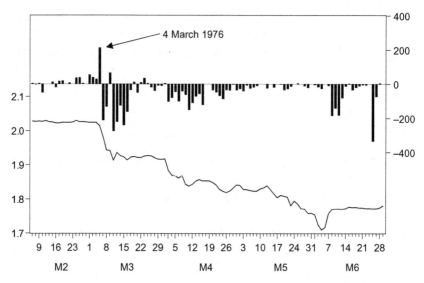

Figure 13.3. Intervention and exchange rate
*Sources*: Dealers' reports for the intervention figure and Accominotti et al., 'Currency Regimes', for the exchange rate.

The dealers were fighting a sterling depreciation following the rate cut. They reported:

Yesterday's pressure on sterling resumed the instant markets opened this morning. Largescale selling, which built up across a broad front throughout the morning, swept sterling past $2.00 by lunchtime despite sizeable official support, and left the pound at 31.5% effective depreciation [since 1971] at the close, a drop of 1.2% on the day.[27]

Instead of encouraging the rate to fall further, the Bank started selling considerable amounts of its reserves to keep the pound from dropping too fast. They needed to look as if they were stopping the fall. Not doing so could have made things worse. Figure 13.3 shows that right after their aggressive operation to make the pound drop (the positive vertical bar pointed with an arrow), the Bank intervened to keep it from dropping. See the negative values in intervention figures following 4 March. The goal was to avoid suspicion. Needham quotes the notes from a meeting between the Bank and the Chancellor. Healey said that his 'instinct was not to intervene further' to make the pound drop as 'the essence of a slide was to conceal

[27] Archives of the Bank of England, Dealers' report, 5 March 1976, reference C8.

the authorities' hand as long as possible'.[28] This policy is visible in Figure 13.3. The Bank spent large amounts of resources to stop the pound from falling over the next few days. It spent $1.35 billion in two weeks, which represented 20 per cent of its reserves.

The next Monday (8 March), pressure was still high. Sterling dropped by a further 5 per cent in the first hours of trading. It was 'the biggest drop since the float of sterling in June 1972'.[29] The dealers wrote: 'Sterling suffered its largest ever fall in a single day.'[30] They continued: 'The severest pressure occurred in the first three hours, when widespread selling – though with no evidence of any single large sellers – propelled sterling down through 32.4% [decrease since 1971] when the morning effective rate was published ... to an extreme of 33.8%.' Intervention to defend the pound did little to help. The Bank's dealers wrote: '[B]ut as the dealers [on the currency market] came to appreciate that the authorities were prepared for stronger resistance at lower levels, sterling bottomed out at 1.9287.' Finally the Bank was gaining some control over the monster it had itself unleashed. 'Market regained a degree of poise' they wrote on Tuesday, 9 March,[31] but the respite was short-lived, and on Wednesday they reported that 'the calm proved deceptive'.[32] The Bank spent the rest of the year trying to make the currency appreciate again. From 4 March until November, the Bank of England spent a net total of $5.5 billion on the foreign exchange market.

A few days later on 10 March, Second Permanent Secretary of the Treasury D. J. Mitchell wrote to the Chancellor. The sterling slide the Bank had manufactured was still secret. The letter reads: 'while some suspect that the recent lurch was a deliberate act, no one can prove it ... we have just had a new demonstration of how much an unplanned burst of pressure can achieve'.[33] Burk and Cairncross cite articles in *The Sunday Times* by Fay and Young. The articles had hinted at the possibility of a

---

[28] Needham, *UK Monetary Policy from Devaluation to Thatcher*, 96 quoting a note of 5 March: 'Note of a meeting held at the Chancellor of the Exchequer's office', archives of the Bank of England, reference C43/779.

[29] Roberts, *When Britain Went Bust*, ebook section 785, quoting an article an article from *The Times* on 9 March 1976, 'Bank Takes Action to Support Pound after Fall of 5 Cents'.

[30] Archives of the Bank of England, Dealers' report, 8 March 1976, reference C8. Also the next two quotes.

[31] Archives of the Bank of England, Dealers' report, 9 March 1976, reference C8.

[32] Archives of the Bank of England, Dealers' report, 10 March 1976, reference C8.

[33] Needham, *UK Monetary Policy from Devaluation to Thatcher*, 96, quoting D. J. Mitchell, 'Exchange Rate Policy', 10 March 1976, Archives of the Bank of England, reference C43/779.

Bank manipulation. Another article in *The Economist* (quoted earlier) hesitated between voluntary devaluation and Nigerian sales as a cause of the drop.[34] But no one knew for sure. The Treasury was celebrating this victory while the Bank was more concerned. There was a rapid fall in the currency.

## THE CAT IS OUT OF THE BAG

From 4 March onward, for the rest of the year, the Bank was busy defending the pound. The depreciation had worked too well. The Bank spent two-thirds of trading days trying to make the pound appreciate again. During only a third of the days was the Bank trying to make sterling depreciate or accumulating reserves (Figure 13.4).[35] Looking at this more formally, I run a Bai–Perron break test on the Bank's foreign exchange

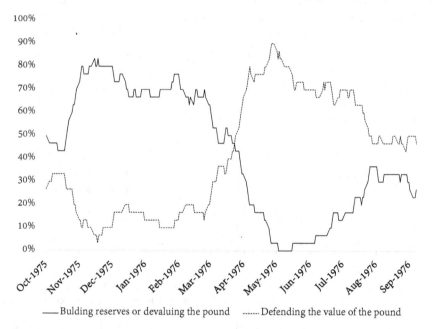

Figure 13.4. Percentage of days in a month with Bank of England sale and purchase operations (thirty-day rolling average)

---

[34] Burk and Cairncross, *Good Bye Great Britain*, 30, quoting an article in the *Economist* of 13 March 1973.

[35] In view of the context it was probably attempts at reserve replenishing rather than depreciation.

Table 13.1. *Bai–Perron break test on Bank of England foreign exchange operations in 1976*

| Dates according to Bai–Perron break test | Daily average dollar operations |
| --- | --- |
| 1 January–4 March | 24 million reserves accumulation |
| 5 March–28 April | 67 million reserves sales |
| 29 April–1 November | 22 million reserves sales |
| 2 November–31 December | 18 million reserves accumulation |

*Note*: the test breaks down the data into up to five periods to best fit the data.
*Source*: Dealers' reports (C8).

interventions for the year 1976. This is a way to obtain a periodisation of the data in an objective fashion. The break test works without human decision and is based on the average values of each period. The results in Table 13.1 highlight a period 'before 4 March'. This pre-crisis period shows average daily interventions of around $24 million purchases to try to depreciate sterling. The pound was still on the rise. And then there is a period 'after 4 March'. This second period shows interventions to try to appreciate the currency at around $67 million per day.[36] The Bank went from being able to buy reserves, to being forced to sell reserves. The intervention pattern is completely reversed after the event of 4 March.

Another way to understand what happened to the Bank is to analyse its behaviour on the market. Figure 13.4 shows dollar sales (meant to support sterling) and dollar purchases (meant to either devalue sterling or simply build up reserves). The crossing point in the graph was reached in March 1976, after the Bank's undercover devaluation. From this point on, the Bank spent more days defending the currency than trying to devalue it. And this was in large part its own doing. Its 4 March operation had reversed the sterling bull run, or at least it reversed the trend more quickly than without its action.

After 4 March, the Bank completely lost control of the market. The $232 million purchase led sterling to fall. But the $1.3 billion then spent in the following eight days to potentially reverse the trend had little or no effect (see Figure 13.3). Part of it was the fact that the devaluation operation

---

[36] The break periods over the year are as follows (with the average amount of intervention in bracket): 1/01/1976–3/04/1976 (average of 24), 3/05/1976–4/28/1976 (average –67), 4/29/1976–11/01/1976 (average –22) and 11/02/1976–12/31/1976 (average 18). Standard setting with trimming at 0.15, maximum number of breaks at 5 and threshold significance level at 0.05.

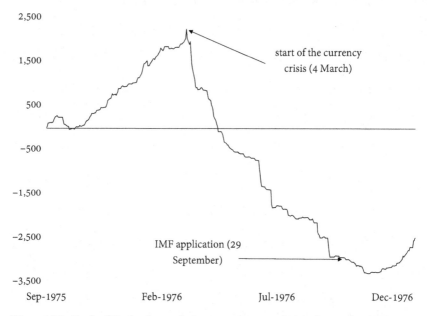

Figure 13.5. Bank of England cumulative reserve accumulation, September 1975–
December 1976. September 1975 is used as a benchmark at the value of 0.
*Source*: Dealers' reports (C8), author's calculation of a cumulative sum of intervention figures.

surprised the market. But also a central bank is more credible when
spending domestic currency (which it has in infinite supply) than spending
precious limited foreign exchange reserves.

On 23 April, the currency again was under pressure and interest rates
had to be increased. The MLR was raised by 1.5 points to 10.5 per cent. It is
likely that this had a positive impact on intervention, as the Bai–Perron
breaks in Table 13.1 show. Interventions after the end of April 1976 were
on average lower than before that date. Monetary authorities had managed
to somewhat reassure markets that they no longer wanted sterling to fall.
The table also shows that the IMF loan finally managed to reverse the
reserve loss tendency. On average, after the IMF loan request in September
1976, the Bank was again able to build up reserves.

On 21 May, the Bank again had to raise the MLR rate to 11.5 per cent.
Figure 13.5 shows that from the secret devaluation on 4 March, the Bank
started to constantly bleed reserves. The small devaluation initiated by the
Bank of England transformed into a full-blown currency crisis. This does
not account for a counterfactual. What would have happened had the
Bank not tried to devalue sterling discreetly on 4 March? The timing

shows that 4 March marked a complete reversal of trends. It led the Bank to constantly lose reserves, eventually having to turn to the IMF. In fact, at the peak of the crisis, on 1 November 1976, the Bank had lost $5,539 million to defend sterling on the market. This reserve loss of $5.5 billion more than helps explain the need for the $3.9 billion financing that the IMF loan provided.

14

# Britain's Last Currency Crisis

The 1992 ERM crisis was the last currency crisis in the history of the pound under fixed exchange rates.[1] It marked the end of British intervention on the foreign exchange market. After 1992, the Bank started to target inflation instead of exchange rates. It was a case of market forces overpowering state intervention. Global foreign exchange markets had just become too big and the Bank of England could not follow.[2] The size of global foreign exchange transactions (all currencies included) had reached $880 billion a day.[3] That is thirty-nine times as much as the United Kingdom spent on Black Wednesday. In 1952 the Bank of England was still able to overpower the market, as shown in Chapter 3. This was no longer the case in 1992.

The crisis showed the limits of fixed exchange rates. Without clear commitment to restrictive domestic monetary policy, an exchange rate peg could not work. The British government was willing to join the ERM, but not keen enough to make the country suffer through higher mortgage rates and potential unemployment because of higher interest rates. Speculators became aware of these shortcomings. They started to bet

---

[1] Some of the text in this chapter draws on a joint paper with Barry Eichengreen: Eichengreen and Naef, 'Imported or Home Grown?'

[2] Advanced economies' central banks still intervening today usually only do it to depreciate their currency. And this often leads to the accumulation of massive foreign exchange reserves, see for example Alain Naef, 'The Investment Portfolio of the Swiss National Bank and Its Carbon Footprint', *Applied Economics Letters* (10 December 2020), 1–6, https://doi.org/10.1080/13504851.2020.1854436.

[3] Tobias Straumann, *Fixed Ideas of Money: Small States and Exchange Rate Regimes in Twentieth-Century Europe*, 1st ed. (New York: Cambridge University Press, 2010), 312, quoting BIS, Annual Report, 1993, 196.

against the Bank of England. At the same time, pressure was mounting on other European countries.

The United Kingdom joined the ERM to try to subdue inflation, not as a Europhile project. Thatcher saw it as a 'spine' to structure inflation in the United Kingdom.[4] Just like the gold standard in its time, the ERM would be an external force to manage British inflation. But the commitment of Britain faded once it was faced with an increase in interest rates. Higher rates would have threatened mortgage owners with higher mortgage costs. This went against one of the main electoral promises of the Conservative party.[5] Britain's economy was also in recession. The government hesitated to hike rates on the morning of Black Wednesday, even after the pound had already broken the ERM peg overnight.[6] Markets took this hesitation and ran. This left no chance to the Bank of England, which had to sell over $22 billion in reserves in a few hours.[7] The crisis then spread to France, which just survived it, thanks to a less hesitant government, heavy foreign exchange interventions and more support from Germany.

In this chapter, I present new evidence of Bank of England operations during the crisis.[8] The British press made a request under the Freedom of Information Act, trying to understand more about the losses of the Bank of England. But not all information was disclosed. Thanks to the new disclosure policy of the Bank of England, moving from thirty to twenty years, the full archives are now available.

## A EUROPEAN CRISIS

The 1992 ERM crisis is one of the most severe currency crises of the pound in the twentieth century. While it is a key event in British monetary

---

[4] James, *Making a Modern Central Bank*, 268–9.

[5] Wolf Hassdorf, 'Contested Credibility: The Use of Symbolic Power in British Exchange-Rate Politics', in *Power in World Politics*, ed. Felix Berenskoetter and Michael J. Williams, 1st ed. (London: Routledge, 2007), 141–61.

[6] 'Sterling had traded below its ERM floor overnight', Archives of the Bank of England, Dealers' report, 16 September 1992, reference C8.

[7] It is important to note that while the United Kingdom spent $22 billion in reserves, the net loss for the United Kingdom was only around $4.91 billion, see James, *Making a Modern Central Bank*, 306.

[8] Some of the data presented here is also used in the following two papers Eichengreen and Naef, 'Imported or Home Grown?'; Alain Naef, 'Blowing against the Wind? A Narrative Approach to Central Bank Foreign Exchange Intervention', Working Paper (European Historical Economics Society (EHES), June 2020), https://econpapers.repec.org/paper/heswpaper/0188.htm.

history, it has its roots in the European context. It all starts with the Maastricht Treaty. The treaty presented a roadmap for European integration, based on economic convergence criteria. It was negotiated in December 1991 and then took two years to be ratified by all members. The ratification process was painful and led to many currency crises for member countries, including Britain.

The ERM crisis started around 2 June 1992, when Denmark rejected the Maastricht Treaty in a referendum.[9] The outcome had not been forecast by opinion polls. It cast into doubt the transition to the Single Currency.

While the Danish crisis was important, pressure on European exchange rates had already started before the Danish referendum.[10] Still, the referendum reminded investors that the future monetary union was not guaranteed. This led to pressure on the exchange rates of most European currencies. The referendum caused the Italian lira to fall to its lower limit and forced the Bank of Italy to intervene. Italy's weaknesses were macroeconomic in nature, something that the Maastricht Treaty's convergence criteria were tailored to address. Pressure on the Portuguese escudo and Irish punt also appeared around the time of the Danish referendum.

In contrast, the pound was overvalued coming into the summer of 1992. Yet it does not appear to have experienced significant exchange-market pressure at this point. This would remain the case until shortly before the crisis, as we will see.

Next, the Irish punt came under pressure. Ireland was the next place where a referendum was scheduled. There were fears that if the Irish voted no, the punt would come untethered from the ERM.[11] On 18 June, more than two-thirds of Irish voters backed the treaty.

While both the Danish and Irish currencies survived their respective referenda (this despite the Danish no), Italy seemed to systematically be a collateral victim. This stands out when looking at Bank of Italy interventions, interest rates and exchange rates.[12] Italy was also in a constitutional

---

[9] Denmark was one of two countries, along with Ireland, required to hold a referendum on the Maastricht Treaty. France also held a referendum, although it had the option of treaty ratification by parliamentary vote, which would have required a three-fifths majority in both the Assembly and Senate.

[10] Eichengreen and Naef, 'Imported or Home Grown?', place the start of the crisis earlier in 1992.

[11] There were also worries about the systematic implications: the *Financial Times* wrote that if 'the Irish follow the Danes and vote "no", there would seem little alternative to scrapping the treaty'. 'One in Four Irish Voters Undecided about Maastricht', *Financial Times*, 18 June 1992, 1.

[12] This is measured in Eichengreen and Naef, 'Imported or Home Grown?'

crisis, with a new government to be formed on 19 June. And things started to get worse in the following month. In August 1992, pressure on the lira, but also on the peseta and escudo, mounted further. On 3–4 September, Germany stepped in with its largest intervention of the crisis, spending over $4 billion to support the lira. The Bank of Italy increased its interest rate by 1.75 percentage points, the largest increase in eleven years.

While this European drama was unfolding, the pound still seemed somewhat shielded against pressure. In the dealers' room at the Bank of England, the mood was still optimistic. Only thirteen days before the biggest currency crisis in the history of the pound, the dealers noted that 'sentiment is a good deal more positive than earlier in the week'.[13] The positive outlook of the dealers shows that they were not expecting such a large shock.

## AN UNEXPECTED AND BRUTAL SHOCK

While the ERM crisis affected many European countries, the shock in the United Kingdom was several orders of magnitude greater than that of other countries. The British crisis was unparalleled because of its sudden nature. As hinted at the beginning of this book, the Bank of England spent in a few hours what two other European countries took a year to accumulate.[14] The Bank spent $22 billion on Black Wednesday to defend sterling before the government decided to throw in the towel.

To understand the exceptional nature of the crisis, I rely on an Exchange Market Pressure index for all European countries. Here the index uses daily intervention data from the Bank of England archives, interest rates from various central banks and spot exchange rates.[15] The EMP index is constructed following Aizenman and Binici and the formula is as follows:[16]

---

[13] Archives of the Bank of England, Dealers' report, 4 September 1992, reference C8.

[14] That is Bulgaria with a GDP of $10.18 billion and Croatia with a GDP of $12.16 billion, a total of $22.34 billion or roughly the interventions of Black Wednesday.

[15] The data is from previous work with Barry Eichengreen but the country data presented here has not been shown elsewhere: Eichengreen and Naef, 'Imported or Home Grown?'

[16] Joshua Aizenman and Mahir Binici, 'Exchange Market Pressure in OECD and Emerging Economies: Domestic vs. External Factors and Capital Flows in the Old and New Normal', *Journal of International Money and Finance*, The New Normal in the Post-Crisis Era, 66 (1 September 2016), 65–87, https://doi.org/10.1016/j.jimonfin.2015.12.008. This is also what we did in Eichengreen and Naef, 'Imported or Home Grown?'

$$EMP = \frac{\Delta e_t - \mu_e}{\sigma_e} - \frac{\nabla r_t - \mu_r}{\sigma_r} - \frac{int - \mu_{int}}{\sigma_{int}}$$

where $\Delta e_t$ is the change in a country's exchange rate; $\Delta r_t$ the differential between the interest rate in a given country and that in Germany; *int* is a daily measure of intervention; $\pi$ and $\sigma$ are the means and standard deviations of the variables in question. The dataset for this index spans 1986–95.

The uniqueness of the British crisis in the European context is apparent in Figure 14.1. It plots the EMP index for twelve European countries (note that Germany is not shown as it is the core country in this approach). Among the approximately 3,200 trading days shown in Figure 14.1, Black Wednesday is the day with the most pressure on any exchange rate. The day lies 35 standard deviations away from the average day on the market.[17] Intervention amounts unimaginable to any central banker at the time and a double interest rate hike on the same day (more on this double hike later) explain this exorbitant pressure index figure.

While tensions among European currencies were somewhat palpable in the wake of the Danish referendum, they were not yet completely out in the open. Things changed in Bath. The town held the Economic and Financial Affairs Council (ECOFIN) meeting on 4–5 September. During

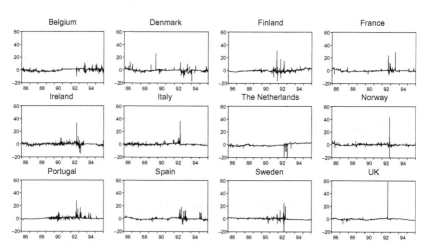

Figure 14.1. The Exchange Market Pressure indices for twelve ERM countries.
Data and methodology from Eichengreen and Naef, 'Imported or Home Grown?'

[17] The other peak in Figure 14.1 is on 20 November 1992, when the Norges Bank was forced to abandon its Ecu peg

this meeting, Chancellor Norman Lamont harangued the Bundesbank president Helmut Schlesinger for further reductions in German rates. The most Schlesinger was prepared to concede was that there was no immediate need for German rates to increase.[18] Lamont, in his post-meeting press briefing, characterised the German position as a firm promise not to raise rates. This assertion reassured investors about ERM currencies, such as the lira. But it also marked a period of tension between Lamont and Schlesinger. This would later become damaging for the pound and is at the heart of the British crisis.

Despite the events in Bath, it was still smooth sailing on Threadneedle Street. According to the dealers, the Monday after the Bath meeting, the week opened 'on a quiet note'.[19] The Bundesbank's 'commitment on interest rates [not to raise rates] at the weekend meeting in Bath was seen as constructive for the dollar'.[20] It is not certain if the dealers were aware that the German 'commitment' had more to do with the British Chancellor than with the true position of the Bundesbank. The *Financial Times*, in retrospect, had a reading closer to reality. Its front page read, 'Doubts emerge over effectiveness of efforts by EC to stabilize financial markets'.[21] The newspaper noticed that Schlesinger 'declined to give explicit support to the statement issued by Mr Norman Lamont' that ERM currencies would not have to align.

On 8 September, European central bank governors met at the BIS in Basel in their monthly meeting. Banque de France governor Jacques de Larosière suggested that the European central bankers 'strongly reaffirm[ed]' the commitments made after the Bath meeting.[22] The Bundesbank president said not to mention the Bath statement. He argued that 'the Deutsche Bundesbank had not been a party to the agreement to which it referred, nor could it be'. Schlesinger did not want to commit Germany to not raising rates in the future. This would have limited the Bundesbank's independence. He saw the solution in a realignment, a solution which he advocated indirectly to German media (more on this later). On the fringe

---

[18] Harold James, *Making the European Monetary Union* (Cambridge, MA: Belknap Press, 2012), 352.

[19] Archives of the Bank of England, Dealers' report, 7 September 1992, reference C8.

[20] Ibid.

[21] 'Doubts Emerge over Effectiveness of Efforts by EC to Stabilize Financial Markets', *Financial Times*, 7 September 1992, 1

[22] Minutes of the 269th meeting of the Committee of Governors of the Central Banks of the Member States of the European Economic Community, held in Basel on Tuesday, 8 September 1992 at 9.30 am.

of the meeting in Basel, Schlesinger also met with George Soros. The meeting convinced Soros that the lira and the pound would fall soon.[23]

Meanwhile, the crisis kept on going elsewhere in Europe. Finland abandoned its unilateral markka peg the following day, 8 September. And once more, Italy was collateral damage. Germany, the Netherlands and Belgium all intervened to prevent the lira from breaking through its bilateral fluctuation bands. Sweden then followed with pressure on its currency in the midst of a banking crisis. On Friday, 11 September, the lira felt unprecedented levels of pressure. On Saturday, the German Finance Ministry and the Bundesbank agreed that the German central bank would refrain from further intervention on behalf of the lira, invoking its authority under the Emminger letter.[24] The Bundesbank immediately conveyed the news to a shocked Bank of Italy governor, Carlo Ciampi.[25]

Despite all this pressure on other European currencies, the United Kingdom still seemed to be in a safe place. On 8 September, the Bank of England dealers thought that things were under control. They wrote: 'Sterling was uncomfortable but not under great pressure.'[26] Even discounting for the usual British phlegm, this statement seemed a genuine expression of confidence. The following day, despite being 'rather soft', the dealers still saw 'no real pressure on sterling'.[27] On Thursday, 10 September, dealers still witnessed some 'good two way demand all day' for sterling.[28] And on the Friday, the last week of over 150 years of sterling fixed exchange rates, the dealers still thought that all was well. They reported that sterling 'was helped by Mr Major's speech'.[29] But they did note that 'demand was deterred by realignment fears'. Was this British composure by dealers before a catastrophic currency crisis just a living

---

[23] Sebastian Mallaby, *More Money than God: Hedge Funds and the Making of a New Elite*, Illustrated ed. (New York: Penguin Books, 2011), 156–7; James, *Making a Modern Central Bank*, 294.

[24] The Emminger letter is discussed in Barry Eichengreen and Charles Wyplosz, 'The Unstable EMS', *Brookings Papers on Economic Activity* 1 (1993), 51–143, https://doi.org/10.2307/2534603. See more in William Keegan, David Marsh and Richard Roberts, *Six Days in September: Black Wednesday, Brexit and the Making of Europe* (London: OMFIF Press, 2017), 103. See also Otmar Emminger, *The D-Mark in the Conflict between Internal and External Equilibrium, 1948–75* (International Finance Section, Department of Economics, Princeton University, 1977).

[25] James, *Making the European Monetary Union*, 356.

[26] Archives of the Bank of England, Dealers' report, 8 September 1992, reference C8.

[27] Archives of the Bank of England, Dealers' report, 9 September 1992, reference C8.

[28] Archives of the Bank of England, Dealers' report, 10 September 1992, reference C8.

[29] Archives of the Bank of England, Dealers' report, 11 September 1992, reference C8.

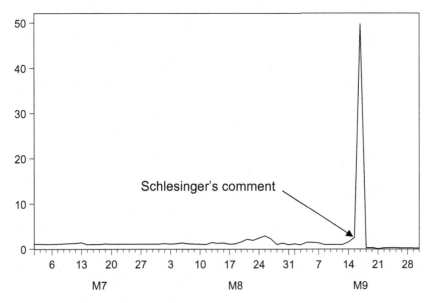

Figure 14.2. The British EMP index

expression of the adage 'keep calm and carry on', or is there more to it? When looking at this problem with numbers, the dealers had no reason to worry.

Figure 14.2 is an explanation of the dealers' calm in the form of a graph. It shows values for the EMP pressure index presented for the United Kingdom in the three months leading to Black Wednesday. Up to Friday 11 September (or three working days before the crisis), there was no pressure on sterling, as measured by the EMP. If the internal reports at the Bank showed nothing but relative calm, it is because sterling was calm. And this is even more marked when compared with other countries that also faced currency crises around the same time as the United Kingdom. Looking at Figure 14.3, one could predict that Italy, Portugal and Spain were under a lot of pressure and likely to experience a currency crisis. The same cannot be said for the United Kingdom. The British EMP index is higher than usual but stable. It explodes on Black Wednesday, the worst day for any European currency over that seven-year period.

The weekend before the week of Black Wednesday, things got tougher for Italy. On Sunday, European policymakers announced a 3.5 per cent devaluation of the lira and 3.5 per cent revaluation of other ERM currencies. This was a cosmetic way of devaluing the lira by 7 per cent. Normally, currency realignment decisions would consist of a Saturday meeting of the

## Britain's Last Currency Crisis

| | Average | FRANCE | IRELAND | ITALY | PORTUGAL | SPAIN | UK |
|---|---|---|---|---|---|---|---|
| August 20, 1992 | 1.1 | 0.9 | 0.2 | 1.0 | 1.9 | 0.7 | 2.1 |
| August 21, 1992 | 2.0 | 0.6 | 0.7 | 0.9 | 8.0 | -0.3 | 1.9 |
| August 24, 1992 | 2.6 | 1.3 | 1.0 | 1.5 | 8.8 | 0.8 | 2.4 |
| August 25, 1992 | 2.9 | 0.7 | 2.5 | 5.6 | 2.6 | 3.3 | 2.9 |
| August 26, 1992 | 2.5 | 0.7 | -1.0 | 5.1 | 6.4 | 1.3 | 2.2 |
| August 27, 1992 | 2.9 | 0.8 | 1.2 | 3.8 | 3.1 | 7.9 | 1.0 |
| August 28, 1992 | 2.7 | 0.7 | 4.1 | 6.5 | 1.8 | 2.0 | 1.3 |
| August 31, 1992 | 1.1 | 0.7 | 1.2 | 1.0 | 1.8 | 1.2 | 1.0 |
| September 1, 1992 | 1.6 | 0.7 | 1.2 | 1.0 | 4.5 | 1.2 | 1.1 |
| September 2, 1992 | 1.5 | 0.7 | 3.2 | 1.0 | 2.2 | 1.2 | 0.9 |
| September 3, 1992 | 1.7 | 0.8 | 1.2 | 3.5 | 2.4 | 0.7 | 1.4 |
| September 4, 1992 | 3.0 | 0.9 | 1.2 | 9.4 | 4.4 | 0.9 | 1.4 |
| September 7, 1992 | 1.1 | 0.8 | 1.9 | 0.3 | 1.8 | 0.7 | 1.3 |
| September 8, 1992 | 2.6 | 0.8 | 2.8 | 0.8 | 7.9 | 2.1 | 0.9 |
| September 9, 1992 | 1.0 | 0.8 | 1.2 | 0.3 | 1.8 | 0.7 | 0.9 |
| September 10, 1992 | 4.8 | 0.7 | 1.3 | 10.7 | 8.4 | 6.5 | 0.9 |
| September 11, 1992 | 3.3 | 0.8 | 1.3 | 13.2 | 2.9 | 0.7 | 0.9 |
| September 14, 1992 | 0.7 | 1.6 | 0.7 | -2.1 | 1.8 | 0.8 | 1.5 |
| September 15, 1992 | 5.5 | 0.6 | 1.1 | 8.3 | 8.7 | 11.7 | 2.5 |
| September 16, 1992 | 18.6 | 0.4 | 2.3 | 30.6 | 22.9 | 5.6 | 49.7 |
| Black Wednesday | | | | Black Wednesday | | | |
| September 17, 1992 | 7.9 | 10.1 | 28.0 | -0.6 | 8.5 | 1.1 | 0.2 |
| September 18, 1992 | 2.3 | 10.8 | -3.3 | -0.6 | 5.0 | 1.6 | 0.3 |
| September 21, 1992 | 1.1 | 3.3 | 0.9 | -0.5 | 0.7 | 1.9 | 0.1 |
| September 22, 1992 | 5.1 | 14.2 | 5.0 | -0.6 | 0.8 | 10.8 | 0.2 |
| September 23, 1992 | 2.6 | 7.6 | 6.7 | -0.5 | 1.2 | 0.0 | 0.3 |
| September 24, 1992 | 0.9 | 0.5 | 4.0 | -0.5 | 1.5 | -0.1 | 0.3 |

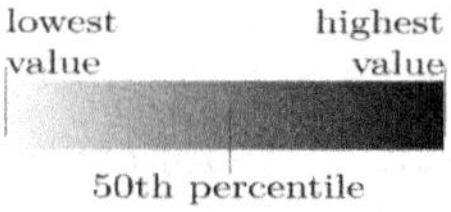

lowest value · highest value

50th percentile

Figure 14.3. The EMP index around Black Wednesday for selected European countries

EU Monetary Committee. Their decision could then be ratified by the ECOFIN committee on Sunday. And early on Monday, Ministers would announce a new parity grid, including all currencies in the ERM. On this occasion, the procedure was not followed. There was a risk that a meeting of the Committee would lead to discussions about a potential change of the parity of the French franc. So there was no meeting of the Monetary Committee. But the Italian devaluation was announced. Eyes turned to the United Kingdom and other weaker ERM countries.

In a show of good faith, the Bundesbank cut interest rates. It cut the discount rate by 50 basis points and the Lombard rate by 25. Markets considered the package inadequate for the small size of the German interest rate cut and the fact that no other countries accompanied Italy in realigning. At the same time, the *Financial Times* headline read 'Bundesbank Bows to External Pressure'.[30] This likely created anxiety among Bundesbank officials. Their nightmare was to appear committed

[30] 'Bundesbank Bows to External Pressure', *Financial Times*, 14 September 1992.

to anything else but low inflation. The *Financial Times* wrote that it was 'the biggest concession made in the history' of the Bundesbank. It was 'admitting the limitations of its independence'. It is understandable that faced with such criticism, senior Bundesbank officials wanted to change the view of the press. The press also became aware that Chancellor Helmut Kohl had paid the Bundesbank a secret visit the Friday before the rate cut. The day after the German rate cut announcement, the press really focused on Schlesinger as a person. He was asked about his resignation. The *Financial Times* ran an article titled 'Schlesinger Puts on a Brave Face'.[31] The article read: 'If Mr Helmut Schlesinger felt any embarrassment yesterday, he hid it well'. The paper also referred to Mr Issing doing 'his best not to look like someone forced to eat his words'. This press conference was clearly a humiliating exercise for the Bundesbank management. The press singled them out personally. This set the stage for retaliation.

## BLACK WEDNESDAY

Black Wednesday was an unexpected crisis. But what explains the magnitude of the shock? The Monday after the Italian devaluation (day minus two), the pressure mounted in the United Kingdom. Yet it was still in line with the previous weeks. The EMP index reached 1.5 on the Monday, a value in line with the average of the previous twenty days (see Figure 14.3). On Tuesday, the day before the crisis, the index jumped to 2.5, indicative of pressure, but still less than a few days earlier on 25 August. The day before Black Wednesday, still nothing indicated the crisis to follow.

On Monday 14 (day minus two), dealers started to get worried. 'The market eyed it [sterling] as the next devaluation candidate', they wrote.[32] On the Tuesday (day minus one), they noted that 'investors began to position themselves ahead of the French referendum'.[33] The French referendum on the Maastricht Treaty was looming on 20 September. Opinion polls suggested that the outcome would be razor thin.[34] Pressure on currency markets in Europe was palpable ahead of the French deadline. At the same time, Downing Street confirmed to the press that the

---

[31] 'Schlesinger Puts on a Brave Face', *Financial Times*, 15 September 1992.

[32] Archives of the Bank of England, Dealers' report, 14 September 1992, reference C8.

[33] Archives of the Bank of England, Dealers' report, 15 September 1992, reference C8.

[34] Michael S. Lewis-Beck and Daniel S. Morey, 'The French "Petit Oui": The Maastricht Treaty and the French Voting Agenda', *Journal of Interdisciplinary History* 38, 1 (23 May 2007), 65–87, https://doi.org/10.1162/jinh.2007.38.1.65.

probability of an ERM realignment was 'zero'.[35] These types of announce-ments have in the past been indicative of risks of crises. Sterling also went through a fall of 1.16 per cent during that day, and the Bank intervened with $788 million to support the pound. Italy, Portugal, Spain and Sweden also intervened heavily on foreign exchange markets to support their currencies.

And then the irreversible happened on Tuesday, 15 September, after the London market closed. Schlesinger told reporters from the *Handelsblatt* and the *Wall Street Journal* that a more comprehensive realignment would have been more effective and that further exchange market pressure could not be ruled out. The remarks were published the following day but had already hit markets overnight. Schlesinger's comments planted doubts in the minds of investors. It was now unclear whether the Bundesbank was prepared to engage in unlimited interventions to prevent the Deutschmark from breaching its bilateral limits against other currencies.

Sterling had already broken the ERM floor before the market opening in London on Black Wednesday (16 September).[36] In overnight trading, either at the end of the day in New York or during trading in Asia, the market showed doubts about maintaining sterling's peg. The *Handelsblatt* had sent a summary of its story to the news agencies before publication. So, by 8 pm on Tuesday the story was 'humming on the wires'.[37] As soon as the Bank saw it, it contacted the Bundesbank and was told that the story was 'unauthorised'.[38] The Bundesbank had stories checked by its press department before authorising them. Authorised or not, the story had hit the markets.

There is some dispute about the intent and impact of the Schlesinger interview.[39] Some have argued that Schlesinger may have been unaware

---

[35] 'German Rate Cut May Stave Off UK Increase', *Financial Times*, 15 September 1992, 1.

[36] Archives of the Bank of England, Dealers' report, 16 September 1992, reference C8.

[37] 'Inflexibility Meets Naievety', *Financial Times*, 17 September 1992, 25.

[38] Schlesinger later wrote that the reporter from the *Handelsblatt* 'released an unauthorised text to the news agencies' and he 'could not deny what I had actually said'. Quote from Philip Stephens, *Politics and the Pound: The Tories, the Economy and Europe*, 3rd ed. (London: Trans-Atlantic Pubns, 1997), 248, found in Keegan, Marsh and Roberts, *Six Days in September*, 113.

[39] For different views on the question, read the preface by Schlesinger himself in Keegan, Marsh and Roberts, *Six Days in September*; James, *Making the European Monetary Union*; James, *Making a Modern Central Bank*. Press articles at the time include Quentin Peel and Andrew Fisher, 'Inflexibility Meets Naivety', *Financial Times*, 17 September 1992, 25; and Craig Whitney, 'Bundesbank Chief Is at Eye of Currency Storm', *New York Times*, 8 October 1992, D1.

that he would be quoted. Or he may have been responding to Lamont's earlier provocation. Other commentators downplay the remarks. They argue that the remarks were disclosing nothing that investors did not already know. The subsequent crisis came from macroeconomic and financial imbalances, not from the statements of the Bundesbank president.

Evidence presented in Figure 14.2 is consistent with the view that a shock of an unexpected nature took markets by surprise after Schlesinger's statements. This happened somewhere between London market close and the overnight trading. The timing matches with the release of the interview. While sterling had been in the news for weeks, pressure on the currency was still moderate as measured by the EMP index. On the first two days following the Italian realignment, sterling and the French franc were under limited pressure (Figure 14.3). The pressure exploded with the news of Schlesinger's interview. If another event did cause the crisis within this narrow time frame of a few hours, it did not leave any written trace. It was most likely the interview.

This was not Schlesinger's first time. Harold James reports conversations in June 1992 when the British Government told the Bank about Schlesinger's 'deeply unhelpful' comments in the *Herald Tribune*.[40] The Bank did bring the issue to Schlesinger in July 1992 in Basel. But Schlesinger denied it and said that 'he had never made any reference about devaluing any of the EMS currencies', the minutes read.[41] Later in the same meeting, Robin Leigh-Pemberton, governor of the Bank, stressed that the German attitude was not helpful: '[T]he situation was made more difficult when the media reported on statements which appeared to have been made by the Deutsche Bundesbank concerning a realignment of the ERM currencies.'[42] The minutes do not record any reply by Schlesinger to Leigh-Pemberton's accusations.

There seemed to be a pattern on Schlesinger's side of sharing his opinion with German and foreign media, more or less directly. Later he would deny it in official arenas. James notes that the Bank 'began to suspect that the Bundesbank was playing a double game'.[43] After Black Wednesday, Chancellor Lamont blamed the Bundesbank. Lamont detailed 'at least five

---

[40] James, *Making a Modern Central Bank*, 290.
[41] Minutes of the 268th meeting of the Committee of Governors of the Central Banks of the Member States of the European Economic Community, held in Basel on Tuesday, 14 July 1992 at 9.30 am.
[42] Ibid.    [43] James, *Making a Modern Central Bank*, 290.

occasions on which senior Bundesbank board members or bank sources had used language that had undermined the pound'.[44] The Bundesbank was an easy target for the undermined British government on the evening of defeat. But the fact remained that the Bundesbank obtained its realignment by playing the press against the pound. And this was probably not a decision for the Bundesbank to make alone.

Schlesinger himself has apologised for his remarks in a recent book on the topic. He wrote: 'I regret to this day – without being able to assess the effect – that a general remark by myself, not focused especially on the pound, should have played a role in aggravating sterling's position.'[45] Schlesinger then goes on to say that Soros had 'already geared himself to the pound's depreciation'. Yet Schlesinger forgot that he had talked to the hedge fund manager a few days earlier, likely shaping his view on the question.[46]

Regardless of the intention of the remarks, the damage was done. During Black Wednesday, William Allen was in charge of foreign exchange intervention operations. He wrote a detailed summary of the event a few days later.[47] The following paragraphs draw on this narrative from 1992 and the dealers' reports.

The Bank of England most often intervened in secret, without communicating its intervention. On Black Wednesday, the Bank ran 'several rounds of overt intervention' which had 'momentary success', according to the dealers.[48] Allen reported that the Bank bought '£325mn publicly between 8–8.30 AM' and then 'a further £300mn publicly shortly afterwards'. By 9 am, the Bank had spent over £1 billion (around $1.8 billion), or 8 per cent of what it was about to spend during the course of the day.

On that day, the government announced two interest rate hikes (one at 11 am and another at 2:15 pm), an exceptional event in British monetary history. The timing of the first announcement played an important role in the chaos that followed. Normally, the Bank announced rate hikes at 9:45 am. On 16 September, the announcement was delayed until 11:00, indicative of internal debate. The government feared going against mortgage owners, having made housing access a core political promise. First there was an interest rate increase to 12 per cent, but it 'failed to stem'

---

[44] 'Britain Blames the Bundesbank', *Financial Times*, 17 September 1992, 1.

[45] Keegan, Marsh and Roberts, *Six Days in September*, v.

[46] On the meeting with Soros, see Mallaby, *More Money than God*, 156–7; James, *Making a Modern Central Bank*, 294.

[47] Allen's remark dates from 20 September 1992, or four days after the event, and bears the note 'written from memory'.

[48] Archives of the Bank of England, Dealers' report, 16 September 1992, reference C8.

interventions.[49] The second hike, to 15 per cent, 'reduced the scale of intervention' but did not manage to lift sterling from the ERM floor.

Communication at the governor level seemed to be difficult between the Bank and the Bundesbank.[50] Keegan et al. report that Leigh-Pemberton tried to reach Schlesinger during the day, but he was unavailable. At the operational level, cooperation was still functioning. Allen noted that 'Bundesbank and the Bank of France were extremely helpful' to buy '£100 million and £50 million respectively'.[51] These operations funded by the Bank of England were done without 'making clear to the press that they were dealing for our [the BoE's] account'.[52] The French and German central banks were making it look like genuine operations, a sign of faith in the pound. Allen also noted that the Bank had advised the government to leave the ERM. But the advice was not followed during the day.

Throughout concerted interventions among European Community central banks, the Bundesbank 'insisted on sticking to the rules obliging central banks to intervene'.[53] This behaviour led to heavy losses for the United Kingdom. The whole day, European Community governments were in contact to try to find a solution. The United Kingdom wanted a temporary suspension of the ERM to avoid a devaluation, which a few days earlier in Italy had done little to solve problems. This was an issue for the French. They needed to stick to the ERM before the vote on the Maastricht Treaty a few days later.

Keegan et al. report that John Mayor was taking his time to decide and kept to his scheduled agenda to give an impression of normality.[54] However, on the market it was anything but a normal day. At 4 pm the Bank announced to other central banks that Britain was temporarily leaving the ERM. At 7:30 pm Lamont officially announced to the public that Britain was throwing in the towel. And the second rate hike was rescinded as it was supposed to take effect the following day.

James quotes a letter to Schlesinger after the crisis, where Leigh-Pemberton wrote: 'As you will be aware, the Bundesbank bought sterling only for our own account, and we were given the very clear signal that you were not willing to do so for your own account.'[55] The Bundesbank could have supported sterling with its own reserves. To the credit of the

---

[49] Ibid.   [50] Keegan, Marsh and Roberts, *Six Days in September*, 120.
[51] Allen's note, 20 September 1992.   [52] Ibid.
[53] James, *Making a Modern Central Bank*, 302.
[54] Keegan, Marsh and Roberts, *Six Days in September*, 119.
[55] James, *Making a Modern Central Bank*, 304.

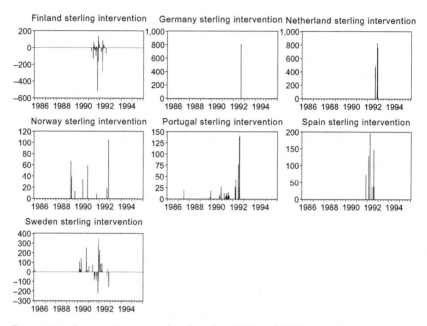

Figure 14.4. Interventions in sterling by other ERM and ERM-pegged countries. Positive numbers mean support for the pound, negative numbers usually mean support for the domestic currency against the pound.

Bundesbank, it did disguise its support as Germany's own account operations (even if operations were financed by Britain).[56] This point is also clear when looking at Figure 14.4, showing sterling intervention by ERM countries. The Bundesbank only supported sterling once for £809 million on Black Wednesday. It never supported the pound outside of its ERM obligations, only intervening at the margins as was required.

## WHAT IF?

Black Wednesday was the result of Schlesinger's attacks and British hesitancy to raise rates in time, in the context of the French referendum moving European priorities far from Britain. While the pound was already under pressure, it was not the most exposed currency, as Figure 14.3 makes clear. The pressure on the pound might have receded after the French yes to Maastricht. This would have cleared the way for a completely different path for Britain in the ERM.

---

[56] Allen's note, 20 September 1992.

While counterfactuals are always imperfect, can we measure the pressure on the British exchange rate, absent Schlesinger's remarks? The model proposed here is based on a few assumptions, which might not be perfect, but provide an idea. Pressure on the pound was dependent on several variables: First, I use the differential with German monetary policy. Higher German rates likely led to more pressure on the pound. Second, I use the Deutschmark–dollar exchange rate with the assumption that a stronger Deutschmark led to more pressure.[57] And finally, I use the pressure in other ERM countries. The link with other countries might not be causal. More pressure in France probably does not cause more pressure in the United Kingdom, but they are correlated. So I assume that if Italy, Portugal, France and Spain were under more pressure, it would be likely that the United Kingdom was as well.[58]

I forecast the pressure on sterling after 15 September, absent Schlesinger's comments. I run the model as a Vector Autoregression (VAR). I delete existing data for the British EMP (but only that variable) after 15 September 1992. The model then forecasts the data for the British EMP. It uses the observations of all the variables presented above during the year 1992. I only use the model to forecast twelve days after Schlesinger's remarks, as forecasts tend to lose explanatory power over time. The model is as follows:

$$EMP_{UK} = \text{FX}_{USD-GER} + \nabla r_t + EMP_{FR} + EMP_{IT} + EMP_{PT} + EMP_{SP} + \varepsilon$$

where $EMP_{UK}$ is the EMP index for the United Kingdom which we want to forecast, $Fx_{USD-GER}$ is the dollar–Deutschmark rate, $\nabla r_t$ the difference between the British and German rate and finally $EMP_n$ is the EMP indices for country $n$, namely France, Italy, Portugal and Spain respectively. The forecast is shown in Figure 14.5.

The counterfactual in Figure 14.5 shows (again with the caution linked to such exercises) that without Schlesinger's remarks, the United Kingdom would still have been under substantial pressure after Black Wednesday, but nowhere near as much. This is visible in Figure 14.5 when comparing the dashed with the full line after 17 September. Once the United Kingdom left the ERM, it was under much less pressure as the country stopped intervening (remember interventions are one of our three EMP variables). Caution is needed with this counterfactual. Yet it seems to show that

---

[57] On the role of the dollar, see the main argument in Eichengreen and Naef, 'Imported or Home Grown?'

[58] Including Nordic countries in this list could be problematic as they went to crises linked to their banking systems, in part independent from EMS-related events.

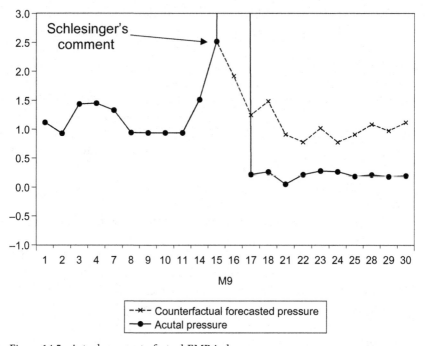

Figure 14.5. Actual vs counterfactual EMP index

*Note*: The actual index reaches a value of just 50 but this is not shown on this graph to improve readability (for the full picture, see Figure 14.3).

nothing outside the Bundesbank president's remarks would have led the United Kingdom to leave the ERM at that point.


MORE LUCK ACROSS THE CHANNEL

As the crisis transmitted from the United Kingdom to France following Black Wednesday (Figure 14.3), the reactions of the two countries were diametrically different. Both France and the United Kingdom sold over $20 billion to the market in September 1992. France managed to recoup all its losses within a month, making a profit. The United Kingdom, on the other hand, lost almost everything on one day. The Bank could not compensate its interventions without great exchange rate losses. These were estimated as just short of $5 billion.[59] The British crisis also became the focus of national criticism (or possibly fascination). The French intervention

---

[59] James, *Making a Modern Central Bank*, 306.

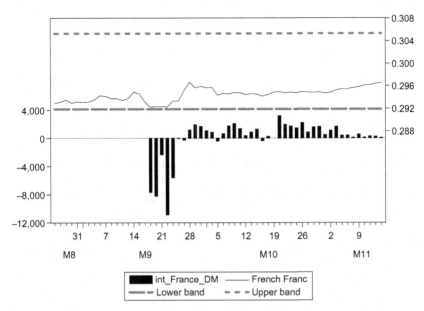

Figure 14.6. Banque de France intervention and franc/DM exchange rate (millions of $US left-hand scale, francs per DM right-hand scale). The upper and lower band are the ERM limits of the exchange rate.

record, however, has barely been mentioned in scholarly accounts or otherwise. The French data are presented here in detail for the first time. They also come from the publicly available archives of the Bank of England. They were collected in a process called the concertation.[60]

The central position of France played a role in its more successful path within the ERM. But also its commitment to the peg and Europe was much stronger than the United Kingdom's.[61] Figure 14.6 shows both French interventions on the foreign exchange market to support the franc and the franc–Deutschmark exchange rate. Between 17 and 25 September, the Banque de France spent $35 billion, according to the concertation data. This is 50 per cent more than the United Kingdom spent. But after 25 September, a few days after the Maastricht 'oui', the wind changed

---

[60] The concertation was a process of intervention information exchange between central banks in advanced economies. This exchange was a way for central banks to monitor use of their currency by other members. It may have also discouraged offsetting interventions and avoided introducing volatility into the market.

[61] On the fact that the United Kingdom felt it was treated unfairly in comparison with France, see James, *Making a Modern Central Bank*, 304.

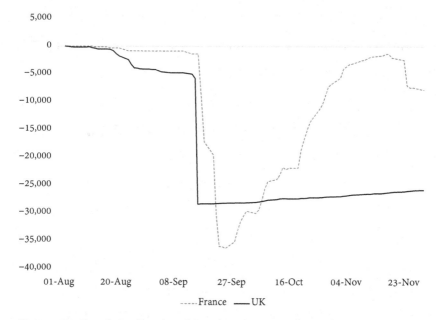

Figure 14.7. Cumulative French and British interventions (in USD)

direction. Over the next twenty-three trading days, the Banque de France bought back $35 billion of reserves.[62]

Figure 14.7 shows the parallel trajectories of intervention between France and the United Kingdom. The size of French losses is similar to British ones. Around Black Wednesday, France experienced a V-shaped reserve loss and recovery. The United Kingdom experienced a definitive reserve loss with no recovery. The French equivalent of Black Wednesday does not have a name, as it was quickly forgotten. Black Wednesday, on the other hand, shaped the future of the United Kingdom.

Around the Maastricht referendum crisis, the Banque de France bought French francs with DM for a value of FF –71.7 billion. Over the next three weeks, the Banque bought back the same amount of DM, paying only FF70.6 billion (Figures 14.6 and 14.7). The Banque de France made a profit of over FF1 billion in the operations.[63] The Banque de France bought

---

[62] The exact numbers almost perfectly match up, with losses of $35,036 million and $35,029 million recouped.

[63] The exact numbers adjusted at each day's closing price are FF71,686.3 million and FF70,583.1 million. Note that this calculation might be wrong if the transaction happened at another price than the closing price, which is likely.

cheap French francs against DM and managed to resell these francs at a higher price over the next few weeks. It is striking to contrast the $214.7 million (= FF1 billion) French gain with the $5 billion British loss. An older strand of literature on foreign exchange intervention links central bank profit with successful interventions.[64] This is a great case in point.

These differences in performance were not only due to poorly managed interest rate announcements on the British side. They also reflect the position of both countries in the ERM. Germans needed the French to be in the ERM while the same cannot be said for Britain. And the French government really wanted to join the European monetary project. The British government only joined it as an effective way to manage inflation.

The consequences of Black Wednesday remained important for the United Kingdom. It stopped foreign exchange interventions after the event, bar a few instances for international cooperation. It marked a new era of inflation targeting by the Bank. The episode was also one among many showing British independence from the European institutions, forecasting a future of more distance between British and European interests.

---

[64] See Milton Friedman and Marilyn Friedman, *Essays in Positive Economics* (Chicago, IL: University of Chicago Press, 1953), for the original idea, and a more modern take on the idea in Francesco Chiacchio, Gregory Claeys and Francesco Papadia, 'Should We Care about Central Bank Profits?', Research Report (Bruegel Policy Contribution, 2018), www .econstor.eu/handle/10419/208020. See also Christopher Neely, 'Technical Analysis and the Profitability of U.S. Foreign Exchange Intervention', *Review* 80 (July 1998), 3–17; Friedman and Friedman, *Essays in Positive Economics*.

# Conclusion

The 1992 ERM crisis was the pound's last currency crisis. Or at least the last one where the Bank managed sterling. The market had won. The Bank no longer dared to fight against speculators, and international finance became too large to control. The Bank switched to inflation targeting and put foreign exchange intervention aside. There were some minor episodes of interventions, notably in 2011 to support the yen. An earthquake and tsunami in Japan had pushed the yen down and the G7 conducted a concerted intervention. Apart from this, intervention had lost its place in the normal arsenal of the Bank.

Strictly speaking, 1992 was not sterling's last currency crisis. Brexit and the ensuing uncertainty triggered a series of crises. The long process from the referendum, to triggering Article 50, to finally leaving the EU all came with its fair share of shocks to the currency. But the difference with the episodes studied in this book is that the Bank was a bystander. The pound was now facing its troubles wholly unassisted by Bank of England dealers.

The end of the intervention era meant less stress for policymakers at the Bank. There were no more late-night calls to decide how much to spend to defend sterling in Tokyo or New York. Free float meant less embarrassment for Bank officials and policymakers. They no longer had to publicly admit defeat after an unexpected devaluation. By focusing only on inflation, the Bank became more independent. It could now set its own policy, focusing on inflation and not exchange rate management, which still today is the prerogative of the government.

But is intervention still a relevant policy tool today? The academic literature since the 1990s has progressively moved in that direction.[1]

---

[1] Emmanuel Farhi and Matteo Maggiori, 'A Model of the International Monetary System', Working Paper (National Bureau of Economic Research, May 2016), https://doi.org/10.3386/w22295.

Some of foreign exchange intervention's most virulent critics have toned down their views. Even the IMF, once opposed to foreign exchange intervention, has taken a more conciliatory view in its revised policy framework.[2] Intervention, the IMF argues, should not be used to generate competitive advantages. But it could be used to help steer monetary policy. This change was in part a reaction to the 2008 Financial Crisis, when traditional monetary policy lost some edge.

Foreign exchange intervention is now a legitimate policy tool. Britain's experience over half a century offers some policy lessons. First, intervention usually does not work when it is not aligned with economic fundamentals. That is, intervention alone is rarely going to protect a country from what international finance thinks of its economy. Interest rates are usually a much more powerful tool to adjust international capital flows. They show real commitment to a policy while intervention alone does not.

Another lesson is that secrecy might not be the best solution. Transparency with market actors helps better guide exchange rates. Intervening on currency markets without communicating about it might be inefficient. The 1976 IMF crisis of the pound is a case in point. The Bank of England tried to secretly devalue sterling. Market actors did not understand what the Bank of England was trying to communicate, triggering a currency crisis.

Finally, cooperation among central banks can be powerful enough to move markets, but there are limits. The Gold Pool is a good example. Most major Western central banks joining forces to support the gold price provided stability to the international monetary system. But even the best forms of international technical cooperation can be stopped by political will. This was the case for the election of Nixon, which broke down central bank cooperation with the Fed.

---

[2] Tobias Adrian, Gita Gopinath and Martin Mühleisen, 'Toward an Integrated Policy Framework for Open Economies', *IMF Policy Brief*, 2020, https://www.imf.org/en/Publications/Policy-Papers/Issues/2020/10/08/Toward-an-Integrated-Policy-Framework-49813.

# Data Availability

The data for all the figures presented in this book are available online for replication or use in further research. For any third party data, please contact the authors directly and quote the original data creators. The data is available on the following repositories:

- Harvard dataverse at https://doi.org/10.7910/DVN/NXRRBI
- SocArxiv at https://osf.io/mkwtz/ or https://doi.org/10.17605/OSF.IO/MKWTZ

# References

Accominotti, Olivier. 'The Sterling Trap: Foreign Reserves Management at the Bank of France, 1928–1936.' *European Review of Economic History* 13, no. 3 (2009): 349–76.

Accominotti, Olivier, and David Chambers. 'If You're So Smart: John Maynard Keynes and Currency Speculation in the Interwar Years.' *Journal of Economic History* 76, no. 2 (June 2016): 342–86. https://doi.org/10.1017/S0022050716000589.

Accominotti, Olivier, Jason Cen, David Chambers, and Ian Marsh. 'Currency Regimes and the Carry Trade.' *Journal of Financial and Quantitative Analysis* 54, no. 5 (October 2019): 2233–60. https://doi.org/10.1017/S002210901900019X

Adrian, Tobias, Gita Gopinath, and Martin Mühleisen. 'Toward an Integrated Policy Framework for Open Economies.' *IMF Policy Brief*, 2020. www.imf.org/en/Publications/Policy-Papers/Issues/2020/10/08/Toward-an-Integrated-Policy-Framework-49813.

Aizenman, Joshua, and Mahir Binici. 'Exchange Market Pressure in OECD and Emerging Economies: Domestic vs. External Factors and Capital Flows in the Old and New Normal.' *Journal of International Money and Finance*, Special Issue 'The New Normal in the Post-Crisis Era', 66 (September 2016): 65–87. https://doi.org/10.1016/j.jimonfin.2015.12.008.

Alexander, Sidney S. 'Effects of a Devaluation on a Trade Balance.' *Staff Papers (International Monetary Fund)* 2, no. 2 (1952): 263–78.

Allen, William A. *The Bank of England and the Government Debt: Operations in the Gilt-Edged Market, 1928–1972.* New York: Cambridge University Press, 2019.

'The British Attempt to Manage Long-Term Interest Rates in 1962–1964.' *Financial History Review* 23, no. 1 (April 2016): 47–70.

*Monetary Policy and Financial Repression in Britain, 1951–59.* New York: Palgrave Macmillan, 2014.

Altamura, Carlo Edoardo. *European Banks and the Rise of International Finance: The Post-Bretton Woods Era.* London: Routledge, 2016. https://doi.org/10.4324/9781315640426.

Alvarez, Sebastian. *Mexican Banks and Foreign Finance: From Internationalization to Financial Crisis, 1973–1982.* London: Palgrave Macmillan, 2019. https://doi.org/10.1007/978-3-030-15440-0.

Arnold, Anthony John. 'Business Returns from Gold Price Fixing and Bullion Trading on the Interwar London Market.' *Business History* 58, no. 2 (February 2016): 283–308. https://doi.org/10.1080/00076791.2015.1083012.

Atkin, John. *The Foreign Exchange Market of London: Development since 1900*. London: Routledge, 2004.

Avaro, Maylis. 'Essays in Monetary History.' IHEID PhD dissertation. Graduate Institute of International Studies, 3 March 2020.

'Zombie International Currency: The Pound Sterling 1945–1973.' IHEID Working Paper. Economics Section, Graduate Institute of International Studies, 3 March 2020. https://econpapers.repec.org/paper/giigiihei/heidwp03-2020.htm.

Bai, Jushan, and Pierre Perron. 'Critical Values for Multiple Structural Change Tests.' *Econometrics Journal* 6, no. 1 (June 2003): 72–8. https://doi.org/10.1111/1368-423X.00102.

'Estimating and Testing Linear Models with Multiple Structural Changes.' *Econometrica* 66, no. 1 (1998): 47–78. https://doi.org/10.2307/2998540.

Balaban, Ioan. 'International and Multinational Banking under Bretton Woods (1945–1971): The Experience of Italian Banks.' PhD dissertation, European University Institute, 2021. https://doi.org/10.2870/429226.

Bank for International Settlements. 'Triennial Central Bank Survey of Foreign Exchange and OTC Derivatives Markets in 2016.' *BIS Triennial Report*, 11 December 2016.

Bank of England. 'The Exchange Equalisation Account: Its Origins and Development.' *Bank of England Quarterly Bulletin*, December 1968, 377–90.

'The London Gold Market.' *Bank of England Quarterly Bulletin*, March 1964, 16–21.

'The U.K. Exchange Control: A Short History.' *Bank of England Quarterly Bulletin*, September 1967, 245–60.

Bew, John. *Clement Attlee: The Man Who Made Modern Britain*. New York: Oxford University Press, 2017.

Black, Conrad. *Richard M. Nixon: A Life in Full*. New York: Public Affairs, 2007.

Blackaby, Frank Thomas. *British Economic Policy 1960–74: Demand Management*. 2nd ed. Cambridge: Cambridge University Press, 1979.

Blagg, Michele. 'Gold Refining in London.' In *The Global Gold Market and the International Monetary System from the Late 19th Century to the Present: Actors, Networks, Power*, edited by Sandra Bott, 88–109. Houndmills: Palgrave Macmillan, 2013.

Blanchard, Olivier, Gustavo Adler, and Irineu de Carvalho Filho. 'Can Foreign Exchange Intervention Stem Exchange Rate Pressures from Global Capital Flow Shocks?' NBER Working Paper, July 2015. www.nber.org/papers/w21427.

Bordo, Michael D. 'The Bretton Woods International Monetary System: A Historical Overview.' In *A Retrospective on the Bretton Woods System: Lessons for International Monetary Reform*, edited by Michael D. Bordo and Barry Eichengreen, 3–109. Chicago, IL: University of Chicago Press, 1993.

'The Operation and Demise of the Bretton Woods System: 1958 to 1971.' Working Paper. National Bureau of Economic Research, February 2017. https://doi.org/10.3386/w23189.

Bordo, Michael D., and Barry J. Eichengreen. 'Bretton Woods and the Great Inflation.' In *The Great Inflation: The Rebirth of Modern Central Banking*, edited by Michael

D. Bordo and Athanasios Orphanides, Chapter 9. Chicago, IL: University of Chicago Press, 2013.

Bordo, Michael D., Barry Eichengreen, Daniela Klingebiel, and Maria Soledad Martinez-Peria. 'Is the Crisis Problem Growing More Severe?' *Economic Policy* 16, no. 32 (April 2001): 51.

Bordo, Michael D., Owen F. Humpage, and Anna J. Schwartz. *Strained Relations: US Foreign-Exchange Operations and Monetary Policy in the Twentieth Century.* Chicago, IL: University of Chicago Press, 2015.

Bordo, Michael D., Ronald MacDonald, and Michael J. Oliver. 'Sterling in Crisis, 1964–1967.' *European Review of Economic History* 13, no. 3 (December 2009): 437–59. https://doi.org/10.1017/S1361491609990128.

Bordo, Michael D., Eric Monnet, and Alain Naef. 'The Gold Pool (1961–1968) and the Fall of Bretton Woods: Lessons for Central Bank Cooperation.' National Bureau of Economic Research Working Paper, no. 24016 (2017).
'The Gold Pool (1961–1968) and the Fall of the Bretton Woods System: Lessons for Central Bank Cooperation.' *Journal of Economic History* 79 (2019): 1027–59. https://doi.org/10.1017/S0022050719000548.

Bordo, Michael D., Eugene N. White, and Dominique Simard. 'France and the Breakdown of the Bretton Woods International Monetary System.' In *International Monetary Systems in Historical Perspective*, edited by Jaime Reis, 153–81. New York: St. Martins Press, 1995. www.springer.com/gp/book/9780312125400.

Borio, Claudio, and Gianni Toniolo. 'One Hundred and Thirty Years of Central Bank Cooperation: A BIS Perspective.' In *One Hundred and Thirty Years of Central Bank Cooperation*, edited by Claudio Borio, Gianni Toniolo, and Piet Clement, 16–76. Cambridge: Cambridge University Press, 2008.

Bott, Sandra. 'South African Gold at the Heart of the Competition between the Zurich and London Gold Markets at a Time of Global Regulation, 1945-68.' In *The Global Gold Market and the International Monetary System from the Late 19th Century to the Present: Actors, Networks, Power*, edited by Sandra Bott, 109–39. Houndmills: Palgrave Macmillan, 2013.

Burk, Kathleen, and Alec Cairncross. *Good Bye Great Britain - The 1976 IMF Crisis.* New Haven, CT: Yale University Press, 1992.

Burnham, Peter. *Remaking the Postwar World Economy - Robot and British Policy in the 1950s.* London: Palgrave Macmillan, 2003.

Cairncross, Alec. *Years of Recovery: British Economic Policy 1945-51.* London: Methuen, 1985.

Cairncross, Alec, and Barry Eichengreen. *Sterling in Decline.* Oxford: Wiley-Blackwell, 1983.

Callaghan, James. *Time and Chance.* London: HarperCollins, 1987.

Capie, Forrest. *The Bank of England: 1950s to 1979.* Cambridge: Cambridge University Press, 2010.

Castle, Barbara. *The Castle Diaries 1974-76.* London: Weidenfeld & Nicolson, 1980.

Chiacchio, Francesco, Gregory Claeys, and Francesco Papadia. 'Should We Care about Central Bank Profits?' Research Report. Bruegel Policy Contribution, 2018. www .econstor.eu/handle/10419/208020.

Comstock, Alzada. 'The British Exchange Equalization Account.' *American Economic Review* 23, no. 4 (1933): 608–21.

Coombs, Charles A. *The Arena of International Finance*. New York: Wiley, 1976.

Despres, Emile, Charles Poor Kindleberger, and Walter S. Salant. *The Dollar and World Liquidity: A Minority View*. Washington, DC: Brookings Institution Press, 1966.

Edison, Hali J. *The Effectiveness of Central-Bank Intervention: A Survey of the Literature after 1982*. Vol. 18. Princeton, NJ: Princeton University Press, 1993.

Eichengreen, Barry. *Global Imbalances and the Lessons of Bretton Woods*. Cambridge, MA: MIT Press, 2007.

—— *Globalizing Capital: A History of the International Monetary System*. 2nd ed. Princeton, NJ: Princeton University Press, 2008.

—— 'Sterling's Past, Dollar's Future: Historical Perspectives on Reserve Currency Competition.' Working Paper. National Bureau of Economic Research, May 2005. www.nber.org/papers/w11336.

Eichengreen, Barry, and Bradford De Long. 'The Marshall Plan: History's Most Successful Structural Adjustment Program.' In *Postwar Economic Reconstruction and Lessons for the East Today*, edited by Rudiger Dornbusch, Wilhelm Nolling, and Richard Layard, 189–231. Cambridge, MA: MIT Press, 1993.

Eichengreen, Barry, and Poonam Gupta. 'Tapering Talk: The Impact of Expectations of Reduced Federal Reserve Security Purchases on Emerging Markets.' *Emerging Markets Review* 25 (December 2015): 1–15. https://doi.org/10.1016/j.ememar.2015.07.002.

Eichengreen, Barry, and Alain Naef. 'Imported or Home Grown? The 1992–3 EMS Crisis.' CEPR Working Paper, no. DP15340 (2020).

Eichengreen, Barry, Romain Lafarguette, and Arnaud Mehl. 'Cables, Sharks and Servers: Technology and the Geography of the Foreign Exchange Market.' Working Paper. National Bureau of Economic Research, January 2016. https://doi.org/10.3386/w21884.

Eichengreen, Barry, Andrew K. Rose, and Charles Wyplosz. 'Speculative Attacks on Pegged Exchange Rates: An Empirical Exploration with Special Reference to the European Monetary System.' In *The New Transatlantic Economy*, edited by Matthew Canzoneri, Paul Mason, and Vittorio Grilli, 191–229. Cambridge: Cambridge University Press, 1995.

Eichengreen, Barry, and Charles Wyplosz. 'The Unstable EMS.' *Brookings Papers on Economic Activity* 1993, no. 1 (1993): 51–143. https://doi.org/10.2307/2534603.

Einzig, Paul. *Leads and Lags, The Main Cause of Devaluation*. London: Macmillan, 1968.

—— *The History of Foreign Exchange*. 2nd ed. London: Palgrave Macmillan, 1970.

Emden, Paul H. 'The Brothers Goldsmid and the Financing of the Napoleonic Wars.' *Transactions (Jewish Historical Society of England)* 14 (1935): 225–46.

Emminger, Otmar. *The D-Mark in the Conflict between Internal and External Equilibrium, 1948–75*. Princeton, NJ: International Finance Section, Department of Economics, Princeton University, 1977.

*Exchange Control Act 1947*. London: HMSO, 1947.

Farhi, Emmanuel, and Matteo Maggiori. 'A Model of the International Monetary System.' Working Paper. National Bureau of Economic Research, May 2016. https://doi.org/10.3386/w22295.

Fforde, John. *The Bank of England and Public Policy, 1941–1958*. Cambridge: Cambridge University Press, 1992.

Fratzscher, Marcel, Oliver Gloede, Lukas Menkhoff, Lucio Sarno, and Tobias Stöhr. 'When Is Foreign Exchange Intervention Effective? Evidence from 33 Countries.' *American Economic Journal: Macroeconomics* 11, no. 1 (January 2019): 132–56. https://doi.org/10.1257/mac.20150317.

Friedman, Milton, and Marilyn Friedman. *Essays in Positive Economics*. Chicago, IL: University of Chicago Press, 1953.

Gavin, Francis J. *Gold, Dollars, and Power: The Politics of International Monetary Relations, 1958–1971*. Chapel Hill: University of North Carolina Press, 2007.

Goodwin, Ralph, John Glennon, David Mabon, and David Stauffer, eds. *Foreign Relations of the United States 1949*. Vol. IV: *Western Europe*. Washington, DC: United States Government Printing Office, 1975.

Green, Timothy. *The World of Gold*. 2nd ed. London: Rosendale Press, 1993.

Hall, Noel Frederick. *The Exchange Equalisation Account*. London: Macmillan, 1935.

Harmon, Mark. *The British Labour Government and the 1976 IMF Crisis*. London: Palgrave MacMillan, 1997.

Harris, Max. *Monetary War and Peace*. Cambridge: Cambridge University Press, 2021.

Harvey, Rachel. 'Market Status/Status Markets: The London Gold Fixing in the Bretton Woods Era.' In *The Global Gold Market and the International Monetary System from the Late 19th Century to the Present: Actors, Networks, Power*, edited by Sandra Bott, 181–99. Houndmills: Palgrave Macmillan, 2013.

Hassdorf, Wolf. 'Contested Credibility; the Use of Symbolic Power in British Exchange-Rate Politics.' In *Power in World Politics*, edited by Felix Berenskoetter and Michael J. Williams, 1st ed., 141–61. London: Routledge, 2007.

Hinderliter, Roger H., and Hugh Rockoff. 'The Management of Reserves by Ante-Bellum Banks in Eastern Financial Centers.' *Explorations in Economic History* 11, no. 1 (September 1974): 37–53. https://doi.org/10.1016/0014-4983(74)90017-5.

Howson, Susan. *British Monetary Policy, 1945–51*. Oxford: Clarendon Press, 1993.

'Money and Monetary Policy since 1945.' In *The Cambridge Economic History of Modern Britain: Volume 2*, edited by Roderick Floud and Paul Johnson, 2nd ed., 134–66. New York: Cambridge University Press, 2014.

*Sterling's Managed Float: The Operations of the Exchange Equalisation Account, 1932–39*. Princeton, NJ: International Finance Section, Department of Economics, Princeton University, 1980.

Humpage, Owen F. 'The United States as an Informed Foreign-Exchange Speculator.' *Journal of International Financial Markets, Institutions and Money* 10, no. 3 (December 2000): 287–302. https://doi.org/10.1016/S1042-4431(00)00031-7.

'U.S. Intervention: Assessing the Probability of Success.' *Journal of Money, Credit and Banking* 31, no. 4 (1999): 731–47. https://doi.org/10.2307/2601220.

Irwin, Douglas A. 'The Nixon Shock after Forty Years: The Import Surcharge Revisited.' *World Trade Review* 12, no. 1 (January 2013): 29–56. https://doi.org/10.1017/S1474745612000444.

Ito, Takatoshi, and Tomoyoshi Yabu. 'What Prompts Japan to Intervene in the Forex Market? A New Approach to a Reaction Function.' *Journal of International Money and Finance* 26, no. 2 (March 2007): 193–212. https://doi.org/10.1016/j.jimonfin.2006.12.001.

James, Harold. *International Monetary Cooperation since Bretton Woods*. Washington, DC: New York: Oxford University Press, 1996.

*Making a Modern Central Bank: The Bank of England 1979–2003*. Studies in Macroeconomic History. Cambridge: Cambridge University Press, 2020. https://doi.org/10.1017/9781108875189.

*Making the European Monetary Union*. Cambridge, MA: Belknap Press, 2012.

Johnson, Harry G. 'The Gold Rush of 1968 in Retrospect and Prospect.' *American Economic Review* 59, no. 2 (1969): 344–8.

'The Sterling Crisis of 1967 and the Gold Rush of 1968.' *Nebraska Journal of Economics and Business* 7, no. 2 (1968): 3–17.

Keegan, William. *Nine Crises: Fifty Years of Covering the British Economy – From Devaluation to Brexit*. London: Biteback Publishing, 2019.

Keegan, William, David Marsh, and Richard Roberts. *Six Days in September: Black Wednesday, Brexit and the Making of Europe*. London: OMFIF Press, 2017.

Kim, Seung Woo. 'The Euromarket and the Making of the Transnational Network of Finance 1959–1979.' PhD dissertation, University of Cambridge, 2018. https://doi.org/10.17863/CAM.23876.

Kindleberger, Charles P. *Europe and the Dollar*. London: MIT Press, 1968.

Kissinger, Henry. *White House Years*. Reprint ed. New York: Simon & Schuster, 2011.

Klug, Adam, and Gregor W. Smith. 'Suez and Sterling, 1956.' *Explorations in Economic History* 36, no. 3 (July 1999): 181–203. https://doi.org/10.1006/exeh.1999.0720.

LaFantasie, Glenn W., ed. *Foreign Relations of the United States, 1958–1960, Foreign Economic Policy, Volume IV – Office of the Historian*. Washington, DC: United States Government Printing Office, 1992.

Lewis-Beck, Michael S., and Daniel S. Morey. 'The French "Petit Oui": The Maastricht Treaty and the French Voting Agenda.' *Journal of Interdisciplinary History* 38, no. 1 (May 2007): 65–87. https://doi.org/10.1162/jinh.2007.38.1.65.

Lyons, Richard K. *The Microstructure Approach to Exchange Rates*. Cambridge, MA: MIT Press, 2006.

Mallaby, Sebastian. *More Money than God: Hedge Funds and the Making of a New Elite*. Illus. ed. New York: Penguin Books, 2011.

Mancini, Loriano, Angelo Ranaldo, and Jan Wrampelmeyer. 'Liquidity in the Foreign Exchange Market: Measurement, Commonality, and Risk Premiums.' *Journal of Finance* 68, no. 5 (2013): 1805–41.

McCauley, Robert N., and Catherine R. Schenk. 'Central Bank Swaps Then and Now: Swaps and Dollar Liquidity in the 1960s.' BIS Working Paper, 1 April 2020. www.bis.org/publ/work851.htm.

McKinnon, Ronald I. 'Bretton Woods, the Marshall Plan, and the Postwar Dollar Standard.' In *A Retrospective on the Bretton Woods System: Lessons for International Monetary Reform*, edited by Michael D. Bordo and Barry Eichengreen, 597–604. Chicago. IL: University of Chicago Press, 1993.

Meltzer, Allan H. *A History of the Federal Reserve, Volume 2, Book 1, 1951–1969*. 1st ed. Chicago, IL: University of Chicago Press, 2010.

'U.S. Policy in the Bretton Woods Era – Review – St. Louis Fed.' *Federal Reserve Bank of St. Louis Review*, no. 73 (May/June) (1991): 54–83.

Moessner, Richhild, and William A. Allen. 'Banking Crises and the International Monetary System in the Great Depression and Now.' *BIS Working Papers*, no. 333 (December 2010).

Monnet, Eric. *Controlling Credit: Central Banking and the Planned Economy in Postwar France, 1948–1973*. Studies in Macroeconomic History. Cambridge: Cambridge University Press, 2018. https://doi.org/10.1017/9781108227322.

'French Monetary Policy and the Bretton Woods System: Criticisms, Proposals and Conflicts.' In *Global Perspective on the Conference and the Post-War World Order*, edited by Gilles Scott-Smith and Simon Rofe, 73–89. London: Palgrave Macmillan, 2017.

'Une Coopération à La Française: La France, Le Dollar et Le Système de Bretton Woods, 1960–1965.' *Histoire@Politique. Politique, Culture, Société* 19 (2013): 83–100.

Naef, Alain. 'Blowing against the Wind? A Narrative Approach to Central Bank Foreign Exchange Intervention.' Working Paper. European Historical Economics Society (EHES), June 2020. https://econpapers.repec.org/paper/heswpa per/0188.htm.

'Central Bank Reserves during the Bretton Woods Period: New Data from France, the UK and Switzerland.' SocArXiv, 18 January 2021. https://doi.org/10.31235/osf .io/he7gx.

'Dirty Float or Clean Intervention? The Bank of England in the Foreign Exchange Market.' *European Review of Economic History* 25, no. 1 (February 2021): 180–201. https://doi.org/10.1093/ereh/heaa011.

*Sterling and the Stability of the International Monetary System, 1944–1971*. Cambridge: Cambridge University Press, 2019. https://doi.org/10.17863/CAM .32540.

'The Investment Portfolio of the Swiss National Bank and Its Carbon Footprint.' *Applied Economics Letters* (published online 10 December 2020): 1801–6. https:// doi.org/10.1080/13504851.2020.1854436.

Naef, Alain, and Jacob Weber. 'How Powerful Is Unannounced, Sterilized Foreign Exchange Intervention?' *SocArXiv*, 22 February 2021. https://doi.org/10.31235/ osf.io/bfehz.

Needham, Duncan. '"Goodbye, Great Britain"? The Press, the Treasury, and the 1976 IMF Crisis.' In *The Media and Financial Crises: Comparative and Historical Perspectives*, edited by Steve Schifferes and Richard Roberts, 289–304. London: Routledge, 2014.

*UK Monetary Policy from Devaluation to Thatcher, 1967–82*. Palgrave Studies in the History of Finance. New York: Palgrave MacMillan, 2014.

Neely, Christopher. 'An Analysis of Recent Studies of the Effect of Foreign Exchange Intervention.' Federal Reserve Bank of St. Louis Working Paper, 1 June 2005.

'Technical Analysis and the Profitability of U.S. Foreign Exchange Intervention.' *Review* (July 1998): 3–17.

Newton, Scott. 'The Two Sterling Crises of 1964 and the Decision Not to Devalue.' *Economic History Review* 62, no. 1 (2009): 73–98.

Nixon, Richard. *Richard Nixon: Speeches, Writings, Documents*. Edited by Rick Perlstein. Princeton, NJ: Princeton University Press, 2008.

*RN: The Memoirs of Richard Nixon*. New York: Simon & Schuster, 2013.

Nogues-Marco, Pilar. 'Competing Bimetallic Ratios: Amsterdam, London, and Bullion Arbitrage in Mid-Eighteenth Century.' *Journal of Economic History* 73, no. 2 (June 2013): 445–76. https://doi.org/10.1017/S0022050713000326.

North, Douglass C., and Barry R. Weingast. 'Constitutions and Commitment: The Evolution of Institutions Governing Public Choice in Seventeenth-Century England.' *Journal of Economic History* 49, no. 4 (December 1989): 803–32. https://doi.org/10.1017/S0022050700009451.

Obstfeld, Maurice. 'Rational and Self-Fulfilling Balance-of-Payments Crises.' *American Economic Review* 76, no. 1 (1986): 72–81.

Oliver, Michael J. 'The Two Sterling Crises of 1964: A Comment on Newton.' *Economic History Review* 65, no. 1 (February 2012): 314–21. https://doi.org/10.1111/j.1468-0289.2011.00598.x.

Reinhart, Carmen M., and Kenneth Rogoff. *This Time Is Different: Eight Centuries of Financial Folly.* Princeton, NJ: Princeton University Press, 2011.

Roberts, Richard. *When Britain Went Bust: The 1976 IMF Crisis.* London: OMFIF Press, 2016.

Roy, Raj. 'The Battle for Bretton Woods: America, Britain and the International Financial Crisis of October 1967-March 1968.' *Cold War History* 2, no. 2 (January 2002): 33–60. https://doi.org/10.1080/713999955.

Ryland, Thomas, Sally Hills, and Nicholas Dimsdale. 'The UK Recession in Context – What Do Three Centuries of Data Tell Us?', *Bank of England Quarterly Bulletin* 50, no. 4 (2010): 277–91.

Sarno, Lucio, and Mark P. Taylor. 'Official Intervention in the Foreign Exchange Market: Is It Effective and, If so, How Does It Work?' *Journal of Economic Literature* 39, no. 3 (2001): 839–68. https://doi.org/10.1257/jel.39.3.839.

Sayers, Richard Sidney. *The Bank of England, 1891–1944.* Cambridge: Cambridge University Press, 1976.

Schenk, Catherine. *Britain and the Sterling Area: From Devaluation to Convertibility in the 1950s.* London: Routledge, 1994.

*The Decline of Sterling: Managing the Retreat of an International Currency, 1945–1992.* Cambridge University Press, 2010.

Schwartz, Anna Jacobson. *From Obscurity to Notoriety: A Biography of the Exchange Stabilization Fund.* Cambridge, MA: National Bureau of Economic Research, 1996.

Solomon, Robert. *The International Monetary System, 1945–1976: An Insider's View.* New York: Harper & Row, 1977.

*The International Monetary System, 1945–1981.* New York: Harper & Row, 1982.

Spufford, Peter. 'From Antwerp and Amsterdam to London: The Decline of Financial Centres in Europe.' *De Economist* 154, no. 2 (June 2006): 143–75. https://doi.org/10.1007/s10645-006-9000-7.

Stephens, Philip. *Politics and the Pound: The Tories, the Economy and Europe.* 3rd ed. London: Trans-Atlantic Pubns, 1997.

Straumann, Tobias. *Fixed Ideas of Money: Small States and Exchange Rate Regimes in Twentieth-Century Europe.* 1st ed. New York: Cambridge University Press, 2010.

Svensson, Lars E. O. 'Assessing Target Zone Credibility: Mean Reversion and Devaluation Expectations in the ERM, 1979–1992.' *European Economic Review* 37, no. 4 (May 1993): 763–93. https://doi.org/10.1016/0014-2921(93)90087-Q.

Toniolo, Gianni, and Piet Clement. *Central Bank Cooperation at the Bank for International Settlements, 1930–1973.* Cambridge: Cambridge University Press, 2005, 2nd ed. 2007.

Ugolini, Stefano. 'The Bank of England as the World Gold Market Maker during the Classical Gold Standard Era, 1889–1910.' In *The Global Gold Market and the International Monetary System from the Late 19th Century to the Present: Actors, Networks, Power*, edited by Sandra Bott, 64–88. Houndmills: Palgrave Macmillan, 2013.

Van Hoang, Thi Hong. 'The Gold Market at the Paris Stock Exchange: A Risk-Return Analysis 1950–2003 / Der Goldmarkt an Der Pariser Börse: Eine Rendite-Risiko-Analyse 1950–2003.' *Historical Social Research / Historische Sozialforschung* 35, no. 3 (133) (2010): 389–411.

Waight, Leonard. *The History and Mechanism of the Exchange Equalisation Account*. Cambridge: Cambridge University Press, 1939.

Wass, Douglas. *Decline to Fall: The Making of British Macro-Economic Policy and the 1976 IMF Crisis*. Oxford: Oxford University Press, 2008.

Watson, Andrew M. 'Back to Gold-and Silver.' *Economic History Review* 20, no. 1 (1967): 1–34. https://doi.org/10.2307/2592033.

Wilson, Harold. *Labour Government, 1964–70: A Personal Record*. London: Michael Joseph, 1971.

Windram, Richard, and John Footman. 'The History of the Quarterly Bulletin', *Quarterly Bulletin* Q4 (2010): 258–66.

Wood, Geoffrey E., and Forrest Capie. 'Policy-Makers in Crisis: A Study of Two Devaluations.' In *Monetary and Exchange Rate Policy*, edited by Donald R. Hodgman and Geoffrey E. Wood, 166–93. Basingstoke: Palgrave Macmillan, 1987.

Yeager, Leland B. *International Monetary Relations: Theory, History and Policy*. 2nd ed. New York: Joanna Cotler Books, 1976.

Zeiler, Thomas W. 'Requiem for the Common Man: Class, the Nixon Economic Shock, and the Perils of Globalization.' *Diplomatic History* 37, no. 1 (January 2013): 1–23. https://doi.org/10.1093/dh/dhs009.

# Index

Printed in the United States
by Baker & Taylor Publisher Services